Darrell Tracy
211 W. Utica St.
Broken Arrow, Ok. 74011
918-455-2870

D0898171

Prescription
for
Preaching

Prescription for Preaching

Woodrow Michael Kroll

Baker Book House
Grand Rapids, Michigan

Copyright 1980 by
Baker Book House Company
ISBN: 0-8010-5409-5

Printed in the United States of America

All Scripture references from the King James Version
except as otherwise noted.

First printing, August 1980
Second printing, July 1984

This book
is dedicated to

Dr. Floyd Gardinor Ellis, Jr.

Preacher, Teacher, Friend
and a jewel in God's heaven

Preface

At the outset of this work it is legitimate to ask: "Why another book on preaching?" Why indeed? Charles W. Koller correctly observed: "The last word has not been spoken or written in the field of homiletics. The need for fresh studies continues, and the interest never wanes."

Prescription for Preaching is a fresh approach to homiletics. It is a self-contained course on the theory and practice of public speaking and homiletics. The book is designed to aid the reader, either at home or in the classroom, to become more effective, more concrete, more persuasive in preaching and teaching the Word of God. It contains time-tested principles of speech with a heretofore unknown, but equally time-tested, approach to homiletics.

The "Practical" approach to homiletics was devised by the late Dr. Gordon C. Davis, President of the Practical Bible Training School of Binghamton, New York, and revised by his two homiletical successors; first by Dr. John L. Benson, and then by myself. This approach is time consuming and thought consuming. It appears to be burdensome and laborious, and it is. It is designed to prevent "quickie" sermons, thoughtless in character and meaningless in outcome. It is useful to preachers who want to make their pulpit ministry as precious as fine gold. But in order for the approach to work, you have to work it. Use it. Labor through it. Reuse it until it becomes a part of the warp and woof of your homiletical being. Then it will no longer be a chore but an invaluable aid. It will not work if you abandon it before it becomes a part of you. So, don't give up. Use it.

Preaching is too important to be relegated to a secondary position in the ministry. If you are a young preacher and are anticipating a great ministry for the Lord, you will need to get the principles of preaching down cold. If, as an experienced preacher, you find your preaching anemic and ineffective, you need to reestablish workable principles of preaching. In either case, I trust this book will be of great assistance to you.

Prescription for Preaching will not make you a preacher: only the Lord God can do that. But perhaps it will make you a better preacher, and that's a goal worth striving for.

WOODROW MICHAEL KROLL

Foreword

Every great revival fire in history has been sparked and fanned by great preaching. If the world is to see another revival before the Lord returns, this revival will begin in the hearts of preachers.

When revival came in the days of King Josiah of Judah, all the essential elements of revival were present. II Kings 22–23 records: (1) a return to the house of the Lord (22:3–4); (2) a rediscovery of the Word of God (22:8–10); and (3) a renewal of commitment to the public proclamation of the Word (23:1–2). Preaching the Word is at the very heart of revival.

During the past decades there has been a sad decline in the quality of preaching exhibited in our churches. There are many reasons for this, but much of the problem can be traced to the noticeable lack of emphasis on the fundamentals of preaching. Colleges and seminaries have too long keyed on social or specialized ministries and neglected the centrality of preaching. We must recover those fundamentals and couple them with fire in the hearts of our young preachers.

Dr. Woodrow Michael Kroll has written this volume with both the fundamentals and the fire in mind. *Prescription for Preaching* is a practical "how to" guide to homiletics and preaching, but it is a "how to" with heart. Dr. Kroll is eminently qualified to have written this volume. He is not only an excellent teacher and administrator, but a great preacher as well. The methods of sermon preparation presented in this volume are tried and true and will be of benefit both to young preachers and to those of us who have been preaching for years.

It is absolutely vital that in the years ahead, should the Lord tarry, young men who feel the call to preach receive the optimum training. *Prescription for Preaching* will be in the forefront of that training.

Revival will come to America and the world. It must. Faithful and dynamic preaching of the Word from the hearts of faithful and dynamic preachers is the catalyst God uses in bringing revival. This volume will help prepare preachers to be such a catalyst, to be champions for Christ.

JERRY FALWELL, PASTOR

THOMAS ROAD BAPTIST CHURCH

Contents

1

Let's Put Preaching in Its Place

"The work of preaching is the highest and the greatest and the most glorious calling to which anyone can ever be called" *—D. Martyn Lloyd-Jones.*

"I am to speak today on the preacher's life and ministry in the pulpit. There is no sphere of labour more endowed with holy privilege and sacred promise, and there is no sphere where a man's impoverishment can be so painfully obtrusive. The pulpit may be the center of overwhelming power, and it may be the scene of tragic disaster" *—John Henry Jowett.*

What Is Preaching?

In his book, *God Speaks to Man*, J. I. Packer has included an introductory chapter called "The Lost Word" in which he draws a parallel between preaching in our day and that of the prophet Amos. Amos prophesied: "Behold, the days come, saith the Lord God, that I will send a famine in the land, not a famine of bread, nor a thirst for water, but of hearing the words of the Lord" (Amos 8:11). Dr. Packer says: "Show us the present state of much of Christendom. . . . Preaching is hazy; heads are muddled; hearts fret; doubts drain our strength; uncertainty paralyzes action. . . . Why is this?" Then Dr. Packer answers his own question saying: "For two generations our churches have suffered from a famine of hearing the words of the Lords."[1]

Perhaps the lack of "hearing the words of the Lord" and the resultant muddled minds and hazy preaching are caused by today's preachers who are unsure about the real nature of preaching. They simply do not understand what preaching is, or what it is supposed to be. For the young man entering the ministry this is tragic. If he does not have a clear understanding of the essential features of preaching, he will but add to the present confusion. It is necessary, then, to thoroughly understand what is meant by "preaching" before we can undertake a study of its methods and mechanics.

Definitions of preaching are as plentiful as preachers to give them. This does not mean they should be rejected; the student should simply consider those of the greater merit. Such definitions range from Kearns' simple statement that preaching is "Lifting up the cross that men may look and live" to the more encompassing "Preaching is the use of the Bible for sermons which are hermeneutically accurate, theologically oriented, psychologically directed, rhetorically structured, and orally communicated to the audience by a God-called minister led by the Holy Spirit."[2] Ian MacPherson defines preaching as "the transmission of a Person, through a person, to a company of persons, the Person so conveyed being the Person of Jesus Christ."[3] W. A. Criswell, pastor of the First Baptist Church of Dallas, Texas, indicates that "preaching is the truth of God mediated through a man's voice, life, heart, mind, in fact, his whole being."

Perhaps the classic definition of preaching is given by Phillips Brooks in 1877 Yale Lectures on Preaching. Brooks said: "Preaching is the communication of truth by man to men. It has in it two essential elements: truth and personality. Neither of those can it spare and still be preaching. The truest truth, the most authoritative statements of

---

[1]James I. Packer, *God Speaks to Man* (Philadelphia: The Westminister Press, 1965), p. 9.

[2]H. C. Brown, Jr., *A Quest for Reformation in Preaching* (Waco, TX: Word Books, 1968), pp. 28–29.

[3]Ian MacPherson, *The Burden of the Lord* (New York: Abingdon Press, 1955), p. 14.

God's will, communicated in any other way than through the personality of brother man to men is not preached truth.''[4]

Warren Wiersbe modifies Brooks' definition as follows: "Preaching is the communication (know homiletics) of divine truth (know the Word of God) through human personality (know yourself) to human personality (know your people).''[5]

From these definitions of preaching we can glean two truths. First, preaching must have some content; that is, it must have a message. Second, this message must be communicated to men through a God-called and God-ordained man.

What Preaching Is Not

In light of these words about what preaching is, perhaps it is of value to consider what preaching is not. Preaching is not the Gospel proclaimed through the printed page. Books, tracts, magazines, even the Bible itself—none of these is preaching. They may contain the truth, but this truth is not communicated through personality.

The proclamation of any non-Gospel message is also not preaching. Much of the so-called preaching heard today is not really preaching at all. Discussion of politics or pollution, current events or communism, may be interesting and in some cases profitable, but such discussion is not preaching. It does not contain divine truth. Preaching is not essaying, rhetoricizing, or moralizing. Although preaching uses the principles of homiletics and rhetoric, these are to be a means, not the end. They are but vehicles used to present biblical truth through the God-called personality.

Again, preaching is not simply extolling the virtues of the Christian life. The Golden Rule, the Ten Commandments, and the Psalms are all excellent in virtue and should both be preached and practiced. But if our preaching stops there, we have simply instructed our people to be good or do good. This is certainly good advice, but preaching should be more than good advice; it must be good news.

---

[4]Phillips Brooks. *Lectures on Preaching* (Grand Rapids: Baker Book House, 1969), p. 5.
[5]Preaching lectures delivered at Liberty Baptist College (Lynchburg, Virginia), September 10, 1977.

Finally, preaching is not teaching. Although his arguments have come under attack as of late, C. H. Dodd in his book, *The Apostolic Preaching and Its Developments,* has correctly observed: "The New Testament writers draw a clear distinction between preaching *(kerygma)* and teaching *(didache).* Teaching is, in a large majority of cases, ethical instruction. Preaching, on the other hand, is the public proclamation of Christianity to the non-Christian *(unsaved)* world. For the early church, then, to preach the Gospel was by no means the same thing as to deliver moral exhortation. It was by *kerygma,* says Paul, not by *didache,* that it pleased God to save men."[6]

To be sure, true preaching or *kerygma* will contain teaching or *didache.* This is inescapable. When Paul indicated in Ephesians 4:11 that Christ "gave some, apostles; and some, prophets; and some, evangelists; and some, pastors and teachers," he did not mean that a pastor would never lead a soul to Christ as the evangelist does. A proper sermon has elements of teaching, preaching, and evangelism. The verbs *keryssein,* to herald, and *didaschein,* to teach, are sometimes used interchangeably in the Gospels and in Acts. Dr. Robert Mounce writes of a "didactic kerygma" which is teaching, expounding in detail what has been proclaimed. "*Kerygma* is foundation and *didache* is superstructure; but no building is complete without both."[7] Thus, even though *kerygma* will contain *didache,* it must be held apart from pure *didache.* Overlapping is proper, but preaching is not just teaching.

Charles W. Koller comments:

"Preaching is that unique procedure by which God, through His chosen messenger, reaches down into the human family and brings persons face to face with Himself. Without such confrontation it is not true preaching. Since preaching originated in the mind of God, and is His own distinctive medium for reaching the hearts of men with a message that is calculated to save the soul, it is obviously His prerogative to set the standards. It follows that the only valid conception of preaching is the conception which God Himself has revealed in the Holy Scriptures."[8]

---

[6]C. H. Dodd, *The Apostolic Preaching and Its Developments* (New York: Harper and Brothers, 1950), p. 7.

[7]Robert Mounce, *The Essential Nature of New Testament Preaching* (Grand Rapids: Eerdmans Publishing Company, 1960), pp. 42–43.

[8]Charles W. Koller, *Expository Preaching Without Notes* (Grand Rapids: Baker Book House, 1962), p. 13.

In the words of John Henry Jowett:

> "First, we are to find our mission in the service of good news. That is
> our primary calling, to be tellers of good news, to be heralds of salva-
> tion. Here are the emphatic words: 'Preach!' and again, 'Preach!' 'Pro-
> claim!' 'As ye go, preach!' "[9]

What Are Some Objections to Preaching?

We have often heard the cry, "Preaching has had it. It's out of date,
outmoded, simply not an effective way of reaching today's generation." But is this true? Has preaching seen its better days? Was it
effective for Paul, Martin Luther, John Calvin, or D. L. Moody and
not for us? Are things really so different now?

These are questions we must answer before we can embark on a
study of preaching. In his book, *The Empty Pulpit*, Clyde Reid con-
tends that preaching is passé.[10] Many seminaries do not require their
seminarians to take even a single course in preaching any more. If
preaching is outmoded, then for the sake of the Gospel we must find
another form of communication. Ours is a day in which nothing is left
unchallenged. Preaching has now received the greatest challenge to its
validity. Can it meet and defeat that challenge?

Of all the objections raised against preaching, three seem to be the
most potent and prominent.[11] They are these: (1) *Can a religion which
developed its tradition in a mythological age still make its voice heard
in an age of scientific realism?* (2) *The ethos of modern life seems to be
too remote from the Gospel.* (3) *Preaching is out of harmony with a
democratic society.* Let us consider these objections individually.

1. *Can a religion which developed its tradition in a mythological
age still make its voice heard in an age of scientific realism?* The
answer must be in the affirmative. The fact that Christianity, and
especially the Old Testament, was developed in an age of so-called
mythology does not mean that it is permeated with myth. This is not a

---

[9]John Henry Jowett, *The Preacher: His Life and Work* (Grand Rapids: Baker Book
House, 1968), p. 33.

[10]Clyde Reid, *The Empty Pulpit* (New York: Harper and Row Publishers, 1967).

[11]Other objections are raised and answered by D. Martyn Lloyd-Jones in *Preaching
and Preachers* (Grand Rapids: Zondervan Publishing House, 1971), chapters 1-3.

treatise on the accuracy of the transmission of the Old Testament oral tradition. Nor is it designed to convince the reader of the trustworthiness of the Bible. Adequate works of this nature have been produced to convince the believing mind, and, apart from the enlightening of the Spirit of God, adequate works will never be produced to convince the unbelieving mind. However, through the sovereign protection of God, these accounts are accurate, inerrant, and to be believed.

Many have tried to prove the inaccuracies of Scripture, but all have failed. One example is the famed archaeologist Sir William Ramsay who, by his own admission, set out to prove that the account of the Book of Acts was not historical. After intensive investigation Ramsay wrote:

> I may fairly claim to have entered on this investigation without prejudice in favour of the conclusion which I shall now attempt to justify to the reader. On the contrary, I began with a mind unfavourable to it, for the ingenuity and apparent completeness of the Tübingen theory had at one time quite convinced me. It did not then lie in my line of life to investigate the subject minutely; but more recently I found myself brought in contact with the book of Acts as an authority for the topography, antiquities and society of Asia Minor. It was gradually borne in upon me that in various details the narrative showed marvellous truth. In fact, beginning with the fixed idea that the work was essentially a second century composition and never relying on its evidence as trustworthy for first century conditions, I gradually came to find it a useful ally in some obscure and difficult investigations.''[12]

Sir William Ramsay was prejudiced against the trustworthiness of Acts. His purpose was to prove that this biblical account of the first century was highly inaccurate. His scientific investigation proved otherwise, however, and he was honest enough to admit it. He came to accept Acts as inspired of God, an accurate account of the first century, and said of Luke that he was ''among the historians of the first rank.''

The question here is not whether or not the contents of the Bible are historical, but whether we *believe* they are historical. Each one comes to this question with certain presuppositions. Either we believe the Bible is historically accurate because it claims to be, or we believe it is historically inaccurate because one of the sciences believes it to be

---

[12]W. M. Ramsay, *St. Paul the Traveller and the Roman Citizen* (Grand Rapids: Baker Book House, 1962), pp. 7–8.

inaccurate. Thus, this objection to preaching boils down to the question, "Who is God?" Is Jehovah, the God of the Scriptures, really God or is man and his science god? Who will have the last word?

Again, this question has been discussed in great detail elsewhere and the interested reader must go elsewhere to be informed of the discussion. But the question still remains, "Can a religion which developed its tradition in a mythological age still make its voice heard in an age of scientific realism?"

Our realism will depend on whom we make God—Jehovah or science. Today many believe that science will have the final word, that our outdated religious beliefs will someday vanish under the scrutiny of scientific realism. Science, however, is always in a state of flux. Can you imagine the expressions on the faces of the fifteenth-century scientists when Columbus didn't sail off the "edge" of a flat world? Science had to change its mind and it is commendable that the men and women of science were honest enough to adapt to the given facts.

To update this illustration, scientists thought that when Neil Armstrong took that "one small step for man, one giant leap for mankind" on July 20, 1969, that he would encounter great clouds of dust and sink to his knees in moonpowder. That just didn't happen. Again science had to change. Scientific and technological changes move ahead so rapidly that large companies like IBM and ITT must entirely retrain their personnel every few years just to keep up.

Science frequently has to change its mind and, when it appears it is following a fallacious path, it must recant and reroute its efforts. What we do today in science may be just the opposite of what we did yesterday, and what we do tomorrow might be something different still. As man's finite mind gains more knowledge he frequently has to change his position to accommodate that knowledge.

How unlike the omniscient God of Scripture this is. He had no knowledge to gain. He is omniscient, all-knowing. Hence, He does not change. The psalmist says of God: "Of old hast thou laid the foundation of the earth: and the heavens are the work of thy hands. They shall perish, but thou shalt endure . . . thou art the same, and thy years shall have no end" (Ps. 102:25–27). God told the prophet Malachi: "I am the Lord, I change not. . ." (Mal. 3:6). The New Testament writer James indicates that, "every good gift and every perfect gift is from above, and cometh down from the Father of lights, with whom is no variableness, neither shadow of turning" (James 1:17).

Who will have the final say? Will it be science that never stabilizes or God who never varies? Will your god be one that when you put your trust in him you will always have to be prepared to recant and change your mind, or will He be one you can always count on? The prophet Elijah once cried: "If the Lord be God, follow him: but if Baal, then follow him" (I Kings 18:21). Each of us must come to a commitment that if the LORD is God, we must follow Him alone.

Preachers of the Gospel need something more stable to rely upon than science. People and their needs haven't changed, and regardless of when the message of Christ's atonement was first given, it is that same message which meets the needs of this unstable age of scientific realism.

2. *Does the ethos (characteristic) of modern life seem to be remote from the Gospel?* Again, as with the first objection to preaching, the answer is yes. The way man looks at life and the way God looks at life are poles apart. "For my thoughts are not your thoughts, neither are your ways my ways, saith the LORD" (Isa. 55:8).

Someone has listed ten axioms which are characteristic of American life. They are:

1. Truth is a basic underlying truth and there is no ultimate truth knowable, no absolute.
2. Look out for number one; if you don't, no one else will.
3. Human nature is fundamentally sound.
4. There is progress in history, but it may be destroyed by science if science isn't controlled.
5. There always have been wars and there always will be.
6. God is a projection of man's ideals.
7. A man's religion is his own business and no one should interfere.
8. Otherworldliness is dangerous; it distracts from today's problems.
9. Jesus was a good man; we need more like him, Abe Lincoln, for example.
10. Do a good turn when you can but don't be a sucker.

With these axioms in mind, it can be readily seen that the *ethos* of modern life does indeed seem to be remote from the Gospel. Modern man is anthropocentric, that is, he considers himself as the center of his life. His chief concern is himself. Look again at axioms number two, three, six, seven, and ten. The "big number one" is all that matters.

Man's own greed is his outstanding characteristic. Materialism has become a way of life. Our insatiable desire to have more has caused prices for goods and services to skyrocket out of sight. Inflation has hit an all-time high because of human greed.

One may contrast this with Jesus' words on the Mount: "Lay not up for yourselves treasures upon earth, where moth and rust doth corrupt, and where thieves break through and steal: but lay up for yourselves treasures in heaven, where neither moth nor rust doth corrupt, and where thieves do not break through nor steal: for where your treasure is, there will your heart be also.... But seek ye first the kingdom of God, and his righteousness; and all these things shall be added unto you" (Matt. 6:19-21,33).

Every aspect of modern life is remote from the Gospel. But isn't that exactly the point? If the characteristics of modern life were in close harmony with those of the Bible, there would be little need for the preaching of the good news. The fact that these characteristics are not in harmony with biblical principles is exactly the reason why the Gospel story is so necessary and preaching such a necessary avenue of proclaiming the good news. It is because modern life is so anthropocentric and greedy that preaching is so vital. Preaching exists because twentieth-century citizens are separated from God, and through all their mystical religions and inner peace movements they are getting no closer to Him.

The problem every preacher faces is bringing modern life into a relationship with God. Mankind has been separated from God by his own sin. This estrangement cannot profitably exist and thus Paul instructs us that "all things are of God, who hath reconciled us to himself by Jesus Christ, and hath given to us the ministry of reconciliation" (II Cor. 5:18). In other words, the purpose of our preaching is the reconciliation of estranged mankind to God. If the *ethos* of modern life were not as it is, and if man did not need to be reconciled to God as he does, then there would be little reason for preaching. The fact that modern man is yet unreconciled to God, as is evident by his life style, brings about the necessity of proclaiming the good news.

3. *Is preaching out of harmony with a democratic society?* This third objection to preaching is probably the most popular today. Someone has said that a sermon is the last place in the modern world where a fool can speak for 30 minutes without someone interrupting him. This may not be true today, for with the breakdown of respect in our society

hardly a sermon or speech can be fully delivered without some interruption. However, it has been said that the preacher alone chooses the Sunday text, decides exactly how long he will speak, decides the context of what is said, decides the method of presentation, and speaks with authority which is not directly given to him by the audience. It sounds like a pretty one-sided show. In a time when freedom is sought for freedom's sake, with little or no thought of accompanying responsibility, such a method of communication as preaching does seem a bit unfair.

Recently I was at a wedding reception and noticed a distinguished-looking man with a greying beard. He was obviously alone and did not appear to know anyone at the reception. I went over to him and introduced myself inviting him to sit at my table. He graciously accepted. This gentleman is a professor of Classics in the state university system of New York. He is considered an expert in his field. After some preliminary questioning he finally came to the question which he was eager to ask. "Do you really think that pulpit preaching is just? Is it fair that no one has opportunity to challenge what the preacher has to say?"

This is a typical criticism. Although a popular criticism today, it is by no means new. Years ago the British preacher George A. Buttrick was asked the same question, "Is preaching democratic?" His interesting reply was: "Is the Chrysler Building democratic—thrusting above our ocean of bricks like a frenzied swordfish? Did Dostoyevsky ask permission to write *The Brothers Karamazov,* or Rudyard Kipling to confess the world's sin and offer the world's prayer in his *Recessional?* Did Beethoven consult mankind about the Fifth Symphony?"

What Buttrick was saying is that democracy is not always at issue. It wasn't very democratic of Beethoven to write the Fifth Symphony by himself, without prior consultation with his friends or a vote of approval from a legislative body. Democracy should not be the question in creativity, neither should it be the question in preaching. "The stars do not apologize for invading our sky. There is in the prophet's soul an inevitable swing of the Spirit's tides, an oncoming as of starry hosts—he must speak his word. Not that his office can ever be his throne: it is his altar where life is laid down."[13]

---

[13]George A. Buttrick, *Jesus Came Preaching* (Grand Rapids: Baker Book House, 1970), pp. 9–10.

If the preacher uses his pulpit for the propagation of his political or social beliefs then he rightfully may be accused of being undemocratic. However, if he is the prophet of God, speaking the words of God, there can be no question of democracy. Democracy is based on equality and man can never have, nor does he deserve, equality with God. "All the inhabitants of the earth are reputed as nothing; and he doeth according to his will in the army of heaven, and among the inhabitants of the earth: and none can stay his hand, or say unto him, What doest thou?" (Dan. 4:35).

Some have suggested that preaching should be done away with and replaced by small discussion groups. There is no doubt that much good comes out of discussion groups. Dialogue between men is essential. But when man comes face to face with the truths and commands of God he doesn't say, "Well, let's discuss it," or "let's dialogue." When Isaiah saw the vision of God's holiness and heard the voice of the Lord say, "Whom shall I send, and who will go for us?", the prophet did not set up a discussion group to see who was best qualified to go. He said, "Here am I; send me." When the Philippian jailor came face to face with the reality of God, he didn't go to God's preachers Paul and Silas to dialogue. Acts 16:29-30 indicates: "He called for a light, and sprang in, and came trembling, and fell down before Paul and Silas, and brought them out and said, 'Sirs, what must I do to be saved?' " He wasn't concerned about whether or not the method of his salvation was democratic. He believed what was "preached" to him.

The question in preaching, then, is not, "Is it democratic?" but "Is it divine? Does it come from God?" Preaching is no more democratic than a magazine article, a television program, or a book. If what the preacher says is from God, who in His mercy and grace has allowed His Son to die for us, then there can be no question that what is said is for the good of the people. Let us not be concerned about the democracy of preaching. Let us rather be concerned about the declaration of preaching.

What conclusion can be drawn from this? John Killinger correctly concludes: "People are not tired of preaching but of non-preaching, of badly garbled, irrelevant drivel that has in so many places passed for preaching because there was no real preaching to measure it against."[14] How true. Preaching is not outmoded, just underachieved.

---

[14]John Killinger, *The Centrality of Preaching in the Total Task of the Ministry* (Waco, TX: Word Books, 1969), p. 21.

If you and I as preachers will recognize what preaching has been, and plan and perform our craft as excellently as the Lord desires us to, the bright days of preaching will be yet to come.

What Is the Place of Preaching?

Princeton Theological Seminary homilitician Conrad Massa once noted: "In the history of the church preaching has been neglected, ignored, debased, even almost totally forgotten, but never has its place been as seriously questioned by those who are genuinely concerned with the vitality of the church's witness as has been done repeatedly in this century."[15] If today's ministers are not absolutely convinced of the rightful place of preaching in the ministry, then the optimism of the preceding paragraph is unfounded.

W. E. Sangster, in his book *Power in Preaching,* titles his first chapter "Believe In It" indicating the necessity of the preacher being convinced of this method of ministry. He asks: "You believe in preaching? How much do you believe in it? No pulpit has power if it lacks deep faith in the message itself. The termites of unbelief may be working at our faith in the Gospel or at our faith in preaching. A bit of faith in both may survive in a man who goes on with a certain dutifulness in his work, yet only a bit. Haunted by the memory of the man who put his hand to the plow and looked back, he keeps in the furrow though he plows neither deep nor straight. ... An awful impoverishment falls upon the whole church if the preachers ... lose faith in preaching."[16]

In asking the question, "What is your concept of preaching?" H. C. Brown, Jr. says: 'Think high and preach well! Think low and preach poorly! It really is this simple."[17] What is the rightful place of preaching in the ministry? Notice the following aspects to the answer.

Preaching's Place In History

To understand the place of preaching in history we must consider both its positive and negative place.

1. Preaching's positive place in history is evidenced in that since the

---

[15]Quoted by Peter H. Eldersveld in "The Pulpit and Our World," *Christianity Today* (June 7, 1963), p. 3.

[16]W. E. Sangster, *Power in Preaching* (New York: Abingdon Press, 1958), p. 15f.

[17]H. C. Brown, Jr. *Sermon Analysis for Pulpit Power* (Nashville: Broadman Press, 1971), p. 20.

greatest of all preachers, Jesus Christ, walked this earth, God has never been without a preaching witness. Notice the following periods of history and those preachers who have dominated them:

APOSTOLIC AGE—The Apostles, Stephen, Philip, Timothy, Titus, Apollos, Barnabas.

ANTE-NICENE, NICENE, POST-NICENE AGE—Polycarp, Ignatius, Justin Martyr, Irenaeus, Tertullian, Origen, Augustine, Chrysostom.

PRE-REFORMATION AGE—Peter Waldo, John Wycliffe, Savonarola, John Hus, Thomas Cranmer, George Fox, Hugh Latimer.

REFORMATION AGE—Martin Luther, Philipp Melanchthon, Ulrich Zwingli, John Calvin, John Knox.

SEVENTEENTH CENTURY—John Bunyan, Richard Baxter, Samuel Rutherford, Roger Williams, William Penn.

EIGHTEENTH CENTURY—John Wesley, George Whitefield, Jonathan Edwards, David Brainerd, William Carey.

NINETEENTH CENTURY—Charles Spurgeon, Alexander Maclaren, Charles Finney, Dwight L. Moody, Adoniram Judson, David Livingston.

TWENTIETH CENTURY—George W. Truett, Robert G. Lee, Billy Sunday, W. A. Criswell, Peter Marshall, Billy Graham, Lee Roberson, Jack Hyles, Jerry Falwell.

2. Preaching's negative place in history is evidenced by the spiritual darkness during those periods when the Word of God was not strongly preached. The greatest period of preaching was that of the Apostolic Age. These men knew what their mission was, i.e. to make disciples. They knew they were the messengers of reconciliation and thus they went everywhere preaching, day and night. They gave themselves wholly to the task and vigorously preached the need for repentance. Thus, more progress was made during these years and more fruit produced than at any other time in history.

Contrary to this, however, were the centuries which followed. A monarchic episcopacy arose in the church and Rome grew in power. When Christian worship became cluttered with saints, idols, and pagan rites, the light of the Gospel was almost totally obscured. Preaching the Word had lost its importance and the power of the true church began to decline.

However, during the days of the Reformation, after it was again

preached that "the just shall live by faith," after the Bible was placed
into the hands of the common man and translations began to spring up
all over Europe, the light of the Gospel again grew bright. "When the
Reformation and the Revival come they have always led to great and
notable periods of the greatest preaching that the church has ever
known."[18] There seems to be a direct relationship between the faithful
preaching of the Word and the blessing of God on His church. On the
other hand, when the Word of God was not preached, the church began
to grow obscure and out of step with the needs of the people.[19]

Speaking almost prophetically, Jay Adams says: ". . . if revival
comes, if there is a great day coming for the church of Christ and for
the country, you may be sure of one thing: it will be a revival sparked
by preaching. This has been true of all past revivals of the Christian
faith. They have all directly involved the faithful preaching of the
Word, the preaching of the Christ who saves."[20]

Preaching's Place in Ministry

With regard to the total life of the ministry, preaching holds the
central place.[21] "Of the diverse forms in which the Word of God can
and does reach men, one in particular will hold our attention because it
occupies a central place, governs all other modes of disseminating the
word, and deals precisely with our subject. Namely, with the Word of
God, drawn from Scripture and preached in His name by virtue of a
divine charge, and with the content of the revelation proclaimed in the
preaching of the church."[22]

While it is very important that the pastor be a good manager, a
trained executive, an understanding person, a learned scholar, and one
who appeals to young and old alike, when a church calls a candidate
for an interview what do they ask him to do? Do they have him set up a

---

[18]D. Martyn Lloyd-Jones, *Preaching,* p. 25.

[19]For more information on the place of preaching in history, see the exhaustive three
volume set by Edwin C. Dargan, *A History of Preaching* (Grand Rapids: Baker Book
House).

[20]Jay E. Adams, *Pulpit Speech* (Philadelphia: Presbyterian and Reformed Publishing Company, 1974), p. 3.

[21]See John Killinger, *The Centrality of Preaching in the Total Task of the Ministry*
(Waco, TX: Word Books, 1969).

[22]Pierre Ch. Marcel, *The Relevance of Preaching* (Grand Rapids: Baker Book
House, 1963), p. 18.

sample calling program or show his executive skills? Do they ask if he is a Phi Beta Kappa? No, they ask him to preach. Granted, they will be interested in his ability to do calling and pastoral counseling, but their primary interest is, "Can he preach?"

"Preaching is the most distinctive institution in Christianity. It is quite different from oratory. Many succeed in the one, and yet are failures in the other. The Christian preacher is not the successor of the Greek orator, but the Hebrew prophet. The orator comes with but an inspiration, the prophet comes with a revelation."[23]

"Preaching is the central, primary, decisive function of the church."[24] It is the key to successful ministry. Paul S. Rees claims: "If the ordained man places the crown of primacy on any other head in the cabinet of his interests—visitation, group therapy, counseling, liturgy, administration, or whatever—it will be reflected in what he does in his study, with his Bible, on his knees, and in the pulpit."[25] To paraphrase Nathan Hale: "I only regret that I have but one life to give to my preaching."

Preaching is also basic to the pastoral ministry. It is the reference point to which the pastor looks for a common ground of understanding between himself and the one he counsels. Beyond that, preaching is a preventative force. When the pastor faithfully preaches the Word, he has far less counseling to do. A healthy congregation means less time spent on healing sick hearts and minds. A healthy congregation is, in large measure, produced by healthy preaching.

Preaching's Place in Worship

Sunday morning is usually reserved for what is sometimes erroneously called the "worship service." What makes that hour the worship service? Is it because the Lord's Prayer is recited? Is it because this service contains a pastoral prayer (sometimes designated by the teenagers as 'the long prayer')? Is it because of the hymns sung? All of these could be the case. But what really makes a worship service out of any service is the preaching. Unfortunately, most churches are either

---

[23]P. T. Forsyth, *Positive Preaching and the Modern Mind* (Grand Rapids: Eerdmans Publishing Company, 1966), p. 1.

[24]Pierre Ch. Marcel, *Relevance,* p. 18.

[25]Paul S. Rees, *How to Prepare and Deliver Better Sermons* (Washington D.C.: Christianity Today, 1970), p. 7.

heavy on prayer and liturgy or heavy on preaching and music. True worship is characterized when the two go hand in hand. Those churches which are heavily liturgical tend to have a ten or twelve minute sermonette. Others tend to have much praise and preaching but very little true worship. It is a fallacy to think that one can exist without the other. It is also a fallacy to think that worship can be divorced from preaching.

Preaching is not a function apart from worship and is not a one-man function. It is not the preacher alone who worships God through the message. The whole congregation does. Jesus had a company of disciples with Him as He preached. At Pentecost, Peter preached the Gospel to unbelievers, but it was in the company of the believing church. Thus, when it is done in the presence of the redeemed, preaching is a visible testimony to the saving power of God. In the words of P. T. Forsythe, the sermon is "the organized Hallelujah" of the church.

Preaching's Place in Scripture

"For Christ sent me not to baptize, but to preach the gospel: not with wisdom of words, lest the cross of Christ should be made of none effect. For the preaching of the cross is to them that perish foolishness; but unto us who are saved it is the power of God. . . . hath not God made foolish the wisdom of this world? For after that in the wisdom of God the world by wisdom knew not God, it pleased God by the foolishness of preaching to save them that believe. . . . But we preach Christ crucified. . . . Because the foolishness of God is wiser than men; and the weakness of God is stronger than men" (I Cor. 1:17–25). These words of Paul summarize Scripture's teaching on preaching. In essence, preaching is the God-ordained method of propagating the Gospel. This does not mean that other methods are to be excluded, but that preaching is the chosen method.

Natural man simply cannot understand how or why God uses bumbling men to communicate such a message. To him preaching seems valueless and foolish. The natural mind knows that if you want something done, force is the only answer. The preacher pleads with his congregation; the natural man laughs. The preacher makes an error in grammar; the natural man laughs. The preacher gets his tongue tied; the natural man laughs.

It is said that Spurgeon once preached what seemed to him one of his poorest messages. Because of his stammering and floundering he felt he had been a complete failure. By the standards of the natural mind he was. But Spurgeon was greatly humbled and fell on his knees and prayed, "Lord, Thou canst do something with nothing. Bless that poor sermon!" Having prayed that prayer he determined that the next week he would redeem himself by preaching a tremendous sermon. That he did. The next Sunday things went exceptionally well. Spurgeon went home pleased. Later he watched for the specific results of the two sermons. From the one that seemed a failure he later was able to trace forty-one conversions. Yet from the sermon of the second week Spurgeon was unable to trace a single convert or person helped. Understandable? Not at all. We simply do not understand why God blesses some sermons more than others, but He does, and that's reason enough to engage in it.

Phillips Brooks once said: "If we go back to the beginning of the Christian ministry we can see how distinctly and deliberately Jesus chose this method of extending the knowledge of Himself throughout the world. Other methods no doubt were open to Him, but He deliberately selected this. He taught His truth to a few men and then He said, "Now go and tell that truth to other men.' "[26] Mark 1:14 says: "After that John was put in prison, Jesus came into Galilee, preaching the gospel of the kingdom of God." Taking our cue from the Lord Himself, we today preach the Gospel of the kingdom of God.

Preaching was a method which the followers of Jesus used as well. Acts 2:14 reminds us: "Peter, standing up with the eleven, lifted up his voice, and said unto them, Ye men of Judaea, and all ye that dwell at Jerusalem, be this known unto you, and hearken to my words." With these words Peter began the great sermon of the day of Pentecost.

"As for Saul, he made havoc of the church, entering into every house and haling men and women committed them to prison. Therefore they that were scattered abroad went every where preaching the Word. Then Philip went down to the city of Samaria, and preached Christ unto them" (Acts 8:3-5). Notice that when the church was scattered they did not hide. They did not set up interpersonal relations groups. They preached. Preaching was constant. When Philip encoun-

---

[26]Phillips Brooks, *Lectures*, pp. 11–12.

tered the Ethiopian eunuch the Scripture says: "Philip opened his mouth, and began at the same scripture, and preached unto him Jesus" (Acts 8:35).

Upon his conversion, Paul had to join the others. On Mars Hill Paul encountered the scholars of his day. Luke tells us: "Then certain philosophers of the Epicureans, and of the Stoicks, encountered him. And some said, What will this babbler say? other some, he seemeth to be a setter forth of strange gods; because he preached unto them Jesus, and the resurrection" (Acts 17:18). Paul gives his reasons for being a minister in his first epistle to Timothy. I Timothy 2:5-7 declares: "For there is one God, and one mediator between God and men, the man, Christ Jesus; who gave himself a ransom for all, to be testified in due time. Whereunto I am ordained a preacher...." With Paul's background he would have made an excellent seminary dean in the "school of the Apostles," but he could not shake the call to be a preacher. It was the divinely-ordained method God had given to spread the Gospel. Hence, Paul instructed Timothy to *preach* the Word (II Tim. 4:2). Paul's chief concern for Timothy was that he be a preacher of the Word of God.

The place of preaching in Scripture is ultimately seen in Paul's counsel to the Romans. He says: "For whosoever shall call upon the name of the Lord shall be saved. How, then, shall they call on him in whom they have not believed? and how shall they believe in him of whom they have not heard? and how shall they hear without a preacher? (Rom. 10:13-14). Preaching is the prescribed method of God for enabling the lost world to hear the Gospel. There is no indication in Scripture or in the events of history that this method was ever abrogated or should not now exist as the God-ordained method.

Preaching's Place in Religion

Of all the religions of the ancient world, preaching was unique to Christianity. It is true that preaching has existed in other religions, but this was not an original function with them. Some heathen religious teachers, seeing the great power of preaching, have tried to imitate Christianity in this respect. Thus, the Roman Emperor Julian, commonly called the Apostate, directed the pagan philosophers to preach every week as the Christians did. This is no wonder. The early church was making terrific strides and multitudes, even among the Romans, were embracing the new religion. Thus, many pagans began to copy the Christian methods in order to keep pace. How different it is today, seeing so many Christians copying pagan methods in order to accomplish the same goal.

Other forms of religion today appear to have adopted a form of preaching. "In modern times there are said to have been in China, Japan, and India instances of the adoption of something like preaching. But so far as is known, preaching remains, both in origin and history, a peculiarly Christian institution." [27]

Preaching's Place in the Mass Media

It is a gross mistake to think that preaching and mass media are antithetical. As a pastor in New England I was frequently the speaker at the Monadnock Bible Conference in southern New Hampshire. This conference was about a two-hour drive from my home and on the way I passed a radio station in northern Massachusetts. I don't remember the name of the station, or even the town in which it was located. But I do remember one thing. I could not receive that station before I arrived at the city limits, nor could I receive it more than two miles out of town on the other side. However, while I was driving by the small station and the transmitter I received the station loud and clear. By definition, this would have been an example of mass media. Granted, it wasn't too "mass" but nevertheless it was part of the mass media. Yet Jerry Falwell, Jack Hyles, W. A. Criswell and many other pastors of our larger churches minister to more people every Sunday within the walls of those churches than that little radio station reaches via the airwaves.

I tell this experience to indicate that preaching is not to be pitted against the mass media as something inferior. Many times, in sheer numbers reached, it is far superior. But the two go hand in hand. As a matter of fact, preaching has for years been successfully using the mass media as a means of extending itself. The largest syndicated television network in the world today originates from the auditorium of the

---

[27]John A. Broadus, *On the Preparation and Delivery of Sermons* Reprint (Grand Rapids: Associated Publishers and Authors, Inc., 1971), p. ix.

Thomas Road Baptist Church in Lynchburg, Virginia, where Pastor Jerry Falwell is seen preaching to a local congregation.

It seems the world has sufficiently reacted to Marshall McLuhan's thesis that the medium is the message to put this whole question back into perspective. The medium is the medium and although the message is greatly enhanced by the type of medium used for its transmission, yet the message is not antithetical to the medium. One needs the other. Preaching is both medium and message but it is sometimes greatly helped by television or radio in that it is amplified and heard by many more than the confines of the sanctuary. Mass media is a great boost to the ministry of preaching and the church needs to use much more of it, especially television and cablevision. Nicholas Johnson of the Federal Communications Commission (FCC) indicated the great impact of television, especially on the young, when he said: "By the time he enters first grade, the average child has spent more hours in front of a television set than he will spend in a college classroom."[28]

Still one might argue that there is a greater medium than the preaching of the Word, and that is the printing of the Word. Books, magazines, newspapers, tracts, and leaflets all have been used mightily of God in the salvation of souls. Since it is far easier to print a thousand tracts than it is to preach a thousand sermons, one might well say that it would be a wise use of the Lord's money to simply concentrate on the printed Word and neglect the preached Word. After all, a book does not pick up a man's voice as do television and radio, and thus it is not a vehicle of preaching but a different avenue altogether of propagating the Gospel. TV and radio may not be antithetical to preaching, but what about printing?

It is true that printing is an effective way of getting the message into the hands of great numbers of people. However, we must do more than simply get the message into their hands; we must get it into their hearts as well. We need to convince them of that message. Printing has one less ingredient than does preaching and it is an important ingredient. Preaching is defined as the communication of truth by man to men. It consists of two elements, truth and personality, both of which are essential. The printed word communicates truth, but must do it without the invaluable aid of personality.

---

[28]Quoted in S. I. Hayakawa, "The Sorcery of Television," *Santa Monica Evening Outlook* (March 9, 1970).

Listen to the wisdom of Phillips Brooks:

"But even if we look at preaching only, it must still be true that nothing can ever take its place because of the personal element that is in it. No multiplication of books can ever supersede the human voice. No newly opened channel of approach to man's mind and heart can ever do away with man's readiness to receive impressions through his fellowman. There is no evidence, I think, in all the absorption in books which characterizes our much reading age, of any real decline of the interest in preaching. Let a man be a true preacher, really uttering the truth through his own personality, and it is strange how men will gather to listen to him. We hear that the day of the pulpit is past, and then some morning the voice of a true preacher is heard in the land and all the streets are full of men crowding to hear him, just exactly as were the streets of Constantinople when Chrysostom was going to preach at the Church of the Apostles, or the streets of London when Latimer was bravely telling his truth at St. Paul's."[29]

How true it is. Nothing surpasses the human personality in ability to convince men of their needs. In this modern age think of the stirring speeches of Winston Churchill, John F. Kennedy, Martin Luther King and others. Similarly, God has chosen "divine truth through a chosen person" as His method of making the message known. The Spirit-inspired Scriptures and the Spirit-inspired servant are the keys to a meaningful understanding of God.

"When a man who is apt in teaching, whose soul is on fire with the truth which he trusts has saved him and hopes will save others, speaks to his fellowmen, face to face, eye to eye, and electric sympathies flash to and fro between him and his hearers, till they lift each other up, higher and higher, into the intensest thought, and the most impassioned emotion—higher and yet higher, till they are borne as on chariots of fire above the world,—there is a power to move men, to influence character, life, destiny, such as no printed page can ever possess."[30]

Jesus could have chosen to write books so that His earthly ministry might have been broader, but "Jesus came preaching" (Mark 1:14). It is true that the only record we have of the New Testament is the written record, yet the power of that record is drawn from the person of Jesus Christ. Personality is always more powerful than print. Therefore, do not let print supplant your preaching. Use print, write books, print your sermons, but for maximum effectiveness, preach them.

---

[29]Phillips Brooks, *Lectures,* pp. 11–12.
[30]John A. Broadus, *Sermons,* p. ix.

The Primacy of Preaching

It should be readily seen by now that preaching occupies the most prominent place in the propagation of Christianity. Those objections to preaching fall away when one gains a proper perspective on the importance of preaching. It is because of preaching that we assemble ourselves together in the Lord's house. Private Bible reading is not sufficient to make a well-rounded Christian. Individuals miss much in the Bible that is brought out in preaching. Private Bible reading leads to preaching and preaching in turn leads back to private Bible reading.

John Calvin noted: "We shall see some fanciful fellows who think they have wasted their time by coming to the sanctuary to be instructed. Is not all of God's teaching contained in the Bible? . . . 'Why must there be so much preaching?' they ask. 'There are only two requirements in Scripture, namely, to love God and one's neighbor.' To the contrary! Saint Paul points out that, if we have only the Holy Scriptures, it is not enough for us to read them in private, but we must have our ears attuned to the teaching which is drawn from them, and they must be preached to us that we may be instructed."[31]

No radio or television can substitute for the preacher. The printed word, even the Bible itself, cannot substitute for the preacher. The personal element is lacking even though the truth is there. It is significant that even the motion picture industry relies on their stars making personal appearances to stimulate the public to attend the movie. We may use many avenues to propagate the Gospel, but the place of preaching in relation to those avenues must be one of primacy. The Warrack Lectures on preaching for 1954, delivered by Arthur A. Cowan of Inverleith Church (Edinburgh) were entitled, "The Primacy of Preaching To-Day."[32] Nothing has changed over these decades. Preaching is still of prime importance.

Can Preaching Ever Be Relevant?

One frequently heard criticism of the church is that it isn't relevant; it doesn't relate to the needs of this day. This criticism comes from all quarters and is sometimes very cynical.[33]

---

[31] John Calvin, Sermon on II Timothy 2:14–15.

[32] Arthur A. Cowan, *The Primacy of Preaching Today* (Edinburgh: T. & T. Clark, 1955).

[33] Consider the words to the Beatles song, *Eleanor Rigby:* "Father MacKenzie, writing the words to a sermon that no one will hear, no one comes near . . . ."

One must recognize, however, that relevance is, in most cases, a very relative thing. To be relevant depends on the conditions around you. As those conditions change you must change to meet them and thus you are said to be relevant. Yet if the conditions do not change, your changing will make you irrelevant to the conditions around you. If the church changes to meet changed conditions it has become relevant. If, however, the church changes while conditions do not change, it is irrelevant. Thus, the question of the preaching message of the church and its relevancy is a question of the conditions which surround the church and not the church or the preaching message itself.

It has been said that the Bible message may have been relevant for Old Testament or even New Testament times but it is certainly out-dated today. The question to be asked is then, "Are conditions today any different which would make the Gospel message irrelevant?" You might venture an answer in the affirmative. Clothes are different, styles are different, customs are different, therefore people must be different. But you are wrong. The Bible doesn't deal with clothes, styles or customs. It deals with man's sin and God's provision for man's sin. Yes, many things are different today but man's basic problem (separation from God because of sin) is still the same. As long as sin remains the universal problem and faith in Christ the universal cure, the Gospel message will be the most relevant message ever given. Jesus is the same yesterday, today, and forever. He is the center of the Gospel message which the church presents.

It is interesting to see that the minute the church attempts to contemporize its message by speaking out on the problems of pollution, welfare, and other issues (so as to be relevant), it is at that minute, by the very act of departing from the eternal truth of the Gospel, that the church and its message have become the most irrelevant. Even though conditions change around us, man's condition never changes. To change the church's message when man's sinful condition has not changed is not to become relevant but to become totally irrelevant. As long as sin causes soul-death and Christ offers eternal life, any message other than the Gospel message is a non-essential message.

This does not mean that the methods used by the church to propagate the Gospel cannot change. Someone has aptly said that the last seven words of the church are, "We never did it that way before." Just as change for change's sake is ridiculous, so too is tradition for tradition's sake. If there is a reason for doing something the way it has been done in the past, change is folly. The old country philosopher used to say: "If it works, don't mess it up." If change cannot bring about a better method, don't change. But when better methods are available, not to change to accommodate them is likewise folly. Just because the church never used audiovisuals before is no reason to rob the congregation of their benefit now. One must not confuse a change in method with a change in the Gospel message. Even if methods change, the Gospel message will never change.

One caution must be mentioned with regard to relevance. That caution is that the preacher must never compromise the Gospel message simply to appear to be relevant. You cannot effectively minister to all segments of society, for those which appreciate the fact that you are up to date generally do not sit down with those which think you are too modern. Therefore, you cannot compromise your message to minister to a specific group. To do so is to be untrue to that message.

If the Gospel message is changed to fit the young, changed to fit the aged, changed for a university meeting, changed again for a church meeting, you will soon learn that you have not communicated the Gospel message to anyone. You will go out of your mind like the chameleon crossing a plaid cloth. Change your methods, but don't tamper with God's message. Preach the Word and you'll always be relevant.

2

Your Remarkable Sound System

"The mastery of forceful speech is one of the noblest purposes to which a man can address himself" —*Newell Dwight Hillis.*

"In all that ever I observed, I ever found that men's fortunes are oftener made by their tongues than by their virtues, and more men's fortunes overthrown thereby, also, than by their vices"
—*Sir Walter Raleigh.*

You never hear anyone say, "Talk is cheap" after an election year. If our system of government proves anything, it proves the fallacy of that statement. Talk is imperative, but it certainly isn't cheap. Nearly every occupation today places a high premium on the ability to communicate well. Can you imagine an inarticulate door-to-door salesman, executive, congressman, missionary, telephone operator, tour guide, teacher, barber, or preacher? Not at all. People need to speak well to be understood. It would be an utter disaster for a child evangelism worker, church secretary, missionary, evangelist, or preacher to be unable to express his or her thoughts clearly and concisely.

Learning to speak well should be the desire of every individual. Big business has learned the value of this skill; many businesses send their executives to Dale Carnegie or other public speaking courses in order to improve their ability to communicate. The church should have an even greater concern for their personnel.

This chapter deals with what is generally called speech or public speaking, which is concerned not with what you say, but how you say it. The art of oratory has existed for centuries and has gained a place of great importance in the curriculum of most colleges, universities, and seminaries. We are told that the first American professorship in this field was established in 1806 when John Quincy Adams was appointed at Harvard University to occupy the Boylston Chair of Rhetoric and Oratory.[1] Presently, many universities have vast programs in speech and oratory. We live in the midst of a communications explosion. "The amount of communication that goes on is also fantastic. Surveys indicate that we spend some 75 per cent of our waking time in communication activity, that is, listening, speaking, reading, and writing."[2] The church must keep pace, in training, in abilities, in doing.

Why Study Speaking?

This chapter is actually a course on public speaking, preaching, and the science of sermon preparation. The natural question to ask on embarking would be, "What will I gain from a course in public speaking?" There are many answers.

By actually preparing speeches and sermons you will find that this exercise will improve the orderly process of your thinking. Speech training helps you to think more logically. This assertion can be proven.

"Dr. Charles Hurst studied 157 college sophomores, 70 with speech training, 87 without such training. He sought to describe the educational implications arising from any relationships between formal instruction in a basic speech course and increased readiness to undertake work at the next academic level. More specifically, the speech group showed a statistically significant gain in ability to demonstrate learning and reasoning on a standardized test of academic aptitude; the gain

---

[1]See Ota Thomas, *A History and Criticism of American Public Address* edited by William Norwood Brigance (New York: McGraw-Hill Book Co., 1943), pp. 196–197.

[2]Raymond S. Ross, *Speech Communication* (Englewood Cliffs, NJ: Prentice-Hall, Inc., 1965), p. 1.

experienced by the nonspeech group was not found to be statistically significant. A finding of interest to all gradepoint-conscious students was that improvement of the speech group in ability to achieve in classroom work, as measured by comparison of mean honor-point averages, was found to be superior to the improvement of the nonspeech group. In fact, the speech group showed a net gain as compared with a net loss for the nonspeech group. Hurst concluded: The data of this study clearly suggest that the basic speech course is an agent of synthesis, providing students with a schematic basis for orderly thinking and improved control of the multivariate phenomena constituting the total personality."[3]

What this means is that the study of speech can do far more for the student than simply improve his ability to speak. It can better his grades, his understanding of textbook material, his written papers, essay answers, and a host of other academic pursuits, simply by improving his orderly process of thinking. It is wise, then, for every student to have at least a basic knowledge of public speaking.

A second reason for studying public speaking is to remove impediments which would otherwise inhibit your presentation of the Gospel message. Dale Carnegie says: "The problem of teaching or of training men in delivery is not one of super-imposing additional characteristics; it is largely one of removing impediments, of freeing men, of getting them to speak with the same naturalness that they would display if someone were to knock them down."[4] Let it be known from the beginning that true success in preaching does not come from polishing the art but from the presence of the Holy Spirit and His enabling of the preacher. The preacher must be a God-enthused man. Without the sanctioning of the Spirit of God and His filling the preacher, all the native ability in the world will be of no avail in convincing men of the truth of the Gospel.

There are, however, people who say that formal training in public speaking is not needed. If the Holy Spirit is the key to preaching's success, then a person wastes his time in years of preparation and

---

[3]Charles Hurst, "Speech and Functional Intelligence: An Experimental Study of Educational Implications of a Basic Speech Course" (Unpublished doctoral dissertation, Wayne State University, 1961) quoted in Raymond S. Ross, p. 2.

[4]Dale Carnegie, *Public Speaking and Influencing Men in Business* (New York: Association Press, 1953), p. 147.

practice. Just "get out and preach," the argument goes. "Look at D. L. Moody. He was uneducated, used poor grammar, and dropped the endings from words. Yet he was used mightily of the Lord." Yes, that's right, but Moody is the exception, not the rule. Who knows but God how much greater things might have been accomplished by Moody had his speech been more acceptable. No, we need to rely on the Spirit but we need also to do what we can to aid the Spirit in fashioning our tongues as swords to make the message piercing.

In the Epistle to the Colossians Paul instructs his fellow believers in the Christian life. He sums up the general subject of Christian living in 3:17 when he says, "And whatsoever ye do in word or deed, do all in the name of the Lord Jesus, giving thanks to God and the Father by him." In essence what he is saying is this: Whatever we do or say, word or deed, we are to do everything with Jesus Christ in mind. His atoning sacrifice has been applied to our sinful lives and we have been reconciled to God. In response to this sacrifice, we are to give our all to Jesus. This means that in everything we do and everything we say we are to give the best to the Master. He must get the best that we can offer. Thus, if a good preacher can become a very good preacher by taking a course in public speaking and trying to overcome and remove his impediments, then he owes it to Jesus Christ to take that course. This should apply to every avenue of our lives. The cream of the crop, the best we have to offer should be given the Lord, and we need to do the very best we can for Jesus. Offer yourself as a more fit vessel for the Master's use. Do the best you can.

In light of this, a third reason why studying public speaking can be of benefit to you is that by adhering to the principles taught in this chapter a simple speaker may become a superlative speaker. There are some who say that by studying the principles of public speaking the speaker will become artificial. Nonsense. If you are an individual you will never be artificial. In fact, training adds to instinct, it does not take away from it.

Can you imagine a baseball pitcher relying purely on his instincts to pitch? Without training he would never make it out of the minor leagues. Good artists have talent but they receive hours of practice and instruction as well. A good singer doesn't just open his mouth and sing; training is needed. The famous orator Quintilian said "orators are made, poets born." We may hear someone say a person is a born speaker. That person may be born with a certain talent for speaking but he or she is certainly not a "born speaker." Not many can carry on an intelligent conversation the day they are born. Good speakers are not born, they are made.

Possibly the greatest reason for the public speaking course outlined in this book is to overcome our own ineptitude. Each student approaches this course with a different background of experience, but no one comes with a history of perfection. Have you a handicap? Thank God for it. It will probably help you. The apostle Paul had a thorn in the flesh and sought to have it removed. God planned otherwise. From Paul's perspective this ''thorn'' could do nothing but hinder his ministry, yet it helped him. When he asked God to remove his handicap God answered, ''My grace is sufficient for thee: for my strength is made perfect in weakness. . . .'' Thus, viewing his handicap from God's perspective, Paul continued: ''Most gladly therefore will I rather glory in my infirmities, that the power of Christ may rest upon me . . . Therefore I take pleasure in infirmities. . .'' (II Cor. 12:9-10).

You have probably heard of the great Demosthenes (384-322 B.C.) who was the most celebrated orator of antiquity. At the beginning of his life he had a harsh voice, weak lungs, and was very mush-mouthed. On coming of age, Demosthenes set himself to a rigorous study of rhetoric and practiced speaking as he climbed steep mountains. He also placed pebbles in his mouth to improve his articulation and shouted above the roar of the ocean to strengthen his lungs. In time he overcame his ineptitude and astounded the world at his ability in oratory. He had a problem; he overcame it.

It is said that Sir Winston Churchill had to overcome tremendous difficulties in learning to speak well. He had a lisp which was distracting to his hearers, and even in his younger years he stuttered. Yet his handicaps were overcome and Churchill's tongue pulled the British nation together during those dark war years like it has never been since.

Dwight L. Moody, the great evangelist, was advised by the officers of his church, as he began his preaching ministry, that since he would never succeed he should not try to talk in public. Many thousands are glad Moody didn't take their advice.

These men are not isolated cases. Many fine speakers have had to overcome inherent weaknesses. Moses was not a great speaker. Jeremiah was afraid. Peter was sinful. Wesley was diminutive. Councilor was deformed. Whitefield was afflicted with asthma. The list is endless. All of us have some sort of handicap and all of us, in some measure, can overcome it.

The Vocal Process

It will not be long until the student learns that in order to overcome ineptitude in speaking, special attention must be given to the voice. Public speaking is simply the proper use of the voice, coupled with the proper use of the body. The voice plays an important role in public speaking. That should be apparent, but many times it is not. Someone has said, "Let me hear his voice, and I can tell you what sort of man he is." This statement is greatly exaggerated, but it does contain an element of truth. By listening to a speaker's voice, listeners can tell if the speaker is angry, nervous, aggressive, sleepy, excited, or bored. Much of one's personality is largely determined by the sound of the voice. First impressions are made by measuring many things, one of which is the voice. Therefore it is important that we cultivate a good speaking voice. It is not the voice itself but the proper use of it that brings success to the speaker.

The first consideration to be given to the voice is that of the vocal process itself. It is important that the student understand what is going on as he speaks. Logically, the study of the voice and vocal delivery begins with a basic understanding of the mechanics of the vocal process. The vocal process or method by which speech is made can be studied in four parts: the energy source, the vibrator, the resonators, and the modifiers. Let us consider them one by one.

The Energy Source

Sometimes called the motor of speech, the energy source refers to the breathing machinery which produces the voice (phonation). Essentially this is a pump for compressing air and consists of: (1) the lungs, which contain the air; (2) the bronchial tubes, which converge into the windpipe or trachea and form a nozzle through which the compressed air is released; (3) the ribs and other bones, cartilages, etc. which house the energy source and give leverage to apply power to the voice; and (4) the muscles, which alternately expand and contract the lungs and consequently the stored air causing the compressed air to be expelled. Together these four elements produce the energy which sets the vocal process in motion. It is readily seen, then, that we should make every effort to see that our energy sources are operating efficiently. To insure this, the speaker must have good posture, good ventilation, bodily rest, and stamina. If our motor is weak, so will be our presentation. The minister of Jesus Christ cannot afford to present the good news weakly.

The Vibrator

What is commonly referred to as your Adam's apple is actually your larynx, and the vocal cords associated with the larynx are the vibrating agents of the vocal process. The larynx is located at the upper end of the trachea or windpipe and is supported by muscles which shift it up and down. This is why you may observe a tenor's Adam's apple moving up and down as he sings. That is the larynx. It consists of small cartilages which are joined together in such a way as to move like the bones of the arm. These cartilages are controlled by a number of small muscles. It is between the cartilages that the vocal cords are stretched. These are not really cords but a pair of membranes very much like thin lips. When a tone is produced, these cords come together until there is but a tiny slit between them. The compressed air of the energy source is forced up the trachea into the larynx and when that air hits the vocal cords it causes them to vibrate and thus produce sound. The tone of the sound is regulated by the muscles which control the tension of the vocal cords, and consequently, the size of the opening between them.

The Resonators

The unsung heroes of the vocal process are the resonators. The sound which is produced by the action of the energy source and is driven up through the vibrator would be thin and weak were it not for some method of building it up. This is the function of a group of air pockets or chambers in the head and throat, the resonators. The principal pockets are the upper part or vestibule of the larynx, the throat or pharynx, the nasal cavities which include the sinuses, and the mouth. These cavities do the same work that resonators do in musical instruments. They amplify the sound and modify its quality making it rich and mellow or harsh or whining. The changes of the size, shape, and texture of these resonators vary the tone qualities produced in the vocal process. For example, the size and shape of your aural cavity is greatly changed as you open your mouth or lower your tongue. The nasal cavity is controlled and changed by the action of the tongue and soft palate. You need not be reminded that when you have a head cold and your sinuses are swollen there is a drastic change in the sound of your voice.

The Modifiers

Now that the sound has been bounced around the resonators, it has become greatly intensified and is ready to leave the mouth. In leaving the mouth, sound has no meaning until it is precisely modified and delineated in conventionalized segments which we recognize as speech. The task of modification falls to the tongue, lips, teeth, jaw, and palate. These are the natural boundaries of the resonators mentioned above. Although these modifiers affect the tone of sound, their primary job is the interruption of the passing air and the consequent formation of consonants. The consonants are really voiceless, except for a few mechanical noises that accompany their movements, such as the hissing of an 's'. The voice is carried by the vowels. For example, the word ''bee'' receives all the voice quality and tone from the 'ee' and almost none from the 'b'. The 'b' is the 'ba' of the word and the tone is carried on the 'ee'. The modifiers simply interrupt the passing tone of the vowels. Faulty articulation is sometimes caused by faulty modifiers such as a broken tooth, cleft palate, hare lip, etc., but it is most often caused by lazy speech habits which can be corrected.

Vocal Variety

One of the greatest factors in poor preaching is monotony. The voice can be controlled so that it is exceedingly dynamic or exceedingly drab. There are certain attributes of voice that can vary and add interest to the sermon or speech. The minister can change his rate of speaking, he can adjust his volume, or he can speak at different pitch levels, all of which can have a profound effect on the reception of his message by the audience. In general, four variable characteristics of the voice are recognized: rate, pitch, quality, and force or loudness. Let's see how each can improve a minister's preaching, or the teacher's teaching.

Rate

Rate has to do with the speed of a person's speaking. In general, the rate of speech is in relation to the type of speech. For instance, you have probably heard an auctioneer rattle off the bids for a cow or a bushel of apples. You have also heard the sports announcer describing a "fast break" down the court during a basketball game. They were speaking rather rapidly. Contrast this with the pastor and his congregation repeating the Lord's Prayer. They speak rather slowly. The speed of talking ought to correspond to the thought expressed. Weighty or complex matters should be presented more slowly so that the audience has time to digest them properly.

For reading a narrative such as the story of the prodigal son in Luke 15, a fairly rapid rate is usually essential. Nothing spoils a good story like a dragging reader. In general, a rate in excess of 185 WPM (words per minute) is too rapid for normal speaking and a rate of less than 140 WPM is too slow. Some authorities have argued that since listening rates may be as high as 400–800 WPM, a speaking rate of 200 WPM is not unrealistic, but we should usually speak between 140 and 185 WPM.

In order to be an effective speaker one must vary the rate of his speaking. To do so involves more than merely speeding or slowing your speech. The rate of speaking also depends on two elements: *quantity* and *pause*. Quantity refers to the length of time used in actually uttering the word, the duration of the sound. Pause refers to the length of time spent in silence between each word. By using a long quantity a person would say, "t-ee-nnn, ni-i-inne, ee-iii-ght, see-ev-veennn, etc." instead of "ten, nine, eight, seven." The longer the quantity or pause, the slower the rate.

Quantity varies primarily to suit the mood of the message. Anything which is dignified or solemn would call for long quantity in expression. To say the Lord's Prayer or Lincoln's Gettysburg Address in a staccato would be absurd. Likewise, to give a play by play account of a basketball game in a long quantity would be just as ridiculous. "Weee-sst paaa-sss-ess to Rooo-biiinnn-sooonnn whooo gooeesss iinnn fooorr aaa laaaaay-uuup." The speaker can develop a feeling for proper quantity values by practicing aloud selections in which a definite mood is evident. When the true feeling of the selection has been absorbed, the speaker can then approximate the writer's feelings and develop a sensitivity to quantity values. Good speakers tend to have a longer average duration of words than do poor speakers. The poor speaker tends to staccato his speech consistently.

The proper use of the pause is vital. A speech or sermon can be made or broken by the speaker's use of the pause. The meaningful pause is no idle jest. Oral speech allows much more flexibility than grammar does in the written form of communication. By using the pause the speaker may indicate fine shades of meaning in the words and phrases he expresses. The entire mood of a sermon can be altered by the number and duration of pauses. Thus, it is important to know when to use the pause and how to use it correctly.

It is imperative that the pause be used between thought groups and not in the middle of them. Improper pausing only leads to improper emphasis and confusion in the audience. Pauses should also be definite. Haphazard use of the pause will again result in little or no emphasis and comprehension. Bear in mind that written and oral punctuation differ; not every comma calls for a pause, nor does the absence of a comma mean that a pause cannot be effectively used. This is especially true if the speaker is using poetry in his speech. Convention sometimes requires the poet to write his words to fit a certain metric pattern, but frequently his thought runs on to the next line. Therefore, it is not necessary to pause at the end of every line of poetry.

In speaking, pauses have certain meanings to an audience. A long pause after a phrase for emphasis is proper, but if you were to use a long pause after a phrase with little emphasis the audience would be sure you had lost your train of thought. Likewise, a short pause generally indicates to an audience that more is to come. The great use of the pause, however, is for emphasis. The pause will give the audience a chance to allow what you have said to "register" or "sink in." Pausing just before the climax of a story or illustration helps to heighten the suspense. A dramatic pause at the right moment will give the desired impression of sincerity and have a profound effect on the audience. Yet most speakers are afraid of the pause. They fear that their silence will focus the audience's attention on them and that words will fail them. The speaker must take great care in using the pause, but not shy away from it. It can be used to great value if used properly.

The greatest problem that exists with the pause is when it is used solely for the purpose of thinking of what to say next. These pauses are not planned; they just occur, and all too frequently. This has happened to every speaker. Words do not come to him so he must pause to think of what to say. However, the speaker does not like the silence of that pause so he fills it in. This is called the "vocalized pause." The most frequent fill-ins of the vocalized pause are 'and', 'er', and 'ah'. The last is the most widespread. Great fun is sometimes had in counting the 'ah's' of a speaker. In a thirty-minute speech or sermon, the 'ah' count can run into the hundreds. This is a habit which is most distracting and can be overcome. The best way to overcome such a distraction is for the student to have the problem pointed out to him repeatedly, and then for him to make a conscious effort to rid himself of that habit. It can be done and it must be done.

Pitch

The second variable characteristic of the voice is pitch. It does not take the listener long to determine that the four voices in a barbershop quartet do not sound the same; some are higher, some lower. This is a difference in pitch. When the compressed air of the lungs is pushed through the vocal cords, the frequency of the vibration of those cords determines the measurements of the sound wave. This frequency of sound waves in repetition is called pitch, the tonal level at which you speak. This level, however, is variable. If it were not variable you would be a "Johnny one note" all your life. The pitch of your voice can move up and down, which is what you do when you are singing. The range of the pitch of the average human voice is about two octaves. These two octaves may be used in singing, but they are rarely used in speaking. Beginning speakers especially tend to hit one level of pitch and stay there. This produces monotony and a preacher can thereby put his audience to sleep.

The general pitch level at which a person speaks is called the key. Almost everyone can span an octave or more, but most speak at one pitch level. Normally this level is established around the words which are most spoken, with a few excursions above and below this key level to add expression to our speech. To locate the key of your pitch level you must find a compromise between the high and low points at which you efficiently speak. This will be greatly determined by what is pleasing and generally accepted as appropriate by those who listen to you. The average voice will be found to perform best when you are speaking at approximately the mid-point of the lowest octave of the singing range. This means that a lower voice is more desirable to listen to than a high squeaky voice. For this reason, to seem more manly a gentleman speaker may attempt to lower his voice a little into the middle lower-half of his singing range. If he can do so through practice, fine. If he has to force his voice low and the audience quickly detects that he is speaking out of his key or natural pitch level, he has become a sideshow.

The idea is, however, to change the pitch of your voice to add variety to your speaking. This may be done through the use of vocal steps and slides. Let's look at an example. If we could draw a diagram of a speech pattern and you were going to say, "Ye must be born again!" it would look something like this:

$$\text{"Ye} \quad ^{\text{must}} \quad \text{be} \quad ^{\text{born } a}{}_{g}{}_{a_{i_{n!}}}\text{"}$$

Notice that a complete break in pitch level occurs between the first and second words. Your voice rises in emphasis of "must" and then comes back down for the verb "be" only to rise a little for the word "born." This word is somewhat emphasized over "be" but not as much as the word "must." The final word "again" begins a bit high but, since it is the last word of the sentence, begins to trail off and ends in the lower pitch level. To trail upward at the end of the sentence would imply the interrogative. Many speakers do this, to the dismay of the audience. We must always end on a downbeat in speaking.

The important thing to notice in our diagram of this speech pattern is the difference between the pitch levels of "ye" and "must." Notice that there is an abrupt change in the level of "must" as opposed to "ye." This abrupt change in pitch is called a step. The gradual continuous change of pitch in the word "again" is called a slide. Slides are frequently evident in expressing the meaning, "I didn't realize that!" by saying:

$$\text{"O} \quad ^{o}{}^{O}{}^{o} \quad \text{o oh!"}$$

The changing of pitch gives inflection to our speech, and inflection adds to the nuances of meaning. This avoids vocal monotony. It is a goal worth striving for. Once the technique of varying the key of our vocal range is understood and mastered by the use of steps and slides, we will find that our speech will have a certain rhythm woven into a pattern. This is not to say that we are speaking in a "sing-song" fashion, but that we speak as a pleasant melody. This is desirable. It makes our voices easy to listen to. By using these melody patterns the speaker can express sorrow and grief or cheerfulness and wit by merely changing the pitch of his voice. The speaker can develop a mood and turn the hearts of his audience to that which is right.

Quality

When you describe someone's voice as being harsh or mellow you are describing its quality. Voice quality, often referred to as "timbre" or "tone color," is a product of the resonators of the vocal cords. Just as the tone quality of a violin varies with the resonating space and texture of the resonators, so the human voice varies as well. Voice quality is determined by the initial tone produced in the larynx.

Armed with this information, unpleasant vocal qualities are quite easily distinguished. These unpleasant qualities are problems which may be overcome. Let us consider a few of the more common types of unpleasant vocal qualities and their causes.

Older books on elocution used to classify vocal quality by the terms guttural, pectoral, aspirate, falsetto, oral, nasal, normal, and orotund. Speakers would try to imitate the more desirable of these. However, they have now been seen to be pseudo-qualities and not to be desired. Yet some of them still exist today as unpleasant vocal qualities.

Nasality

Contrary to popular opinion, nasality is more often caused by too little nasal resonance than by too much. Most nasality results from failing to open the nasal passages enough. Consequently, nonnasal vocal sounds are given the same amount of nasality as nasal vocal sounds and no distinction is made. Say the word "button." After saying it a few times notice how your soft palate tightens up just before the explosion of the 't'. The palate is then relaxed to allow the 'n' sound to exit through the nose. The problem arises when the tension of the palate is retained during the production of the vowel sound as well as the consonants. A flat nasality results. This problem can be corrected by opening the mouth wider and exerting firm control of the tongue. If the tongue is allowed to become lazy and does not cut off that nasal tone at the proper time, we get a constant head cold sound. If this is a problem with you, try humming 'M-m-m-m' and 'n-n-n-n' in a prolonged manner until you can feel the vibration in your nose. Then, with your lips closed, continue to hum while you drop your jaw and feel the vibration throughout the mouth cavity. If your whole mouth is not vibrating you will receive a nasal tone. After the mouth is vibrating, open the lips and let the 'm-m-m-m' become an 'ah' and you will have 'm-m-m-m-m-m-a-a-a-ah'. Do this twice and put them all together and you have 'mama'. Practicing the elongated 'm-m-m-a-a-ah' will help get rid of nasality.

Harshness

You've probably heard speakers who sound like they ought to be in a gangster movie. Their problem is harshness or huskiness in their voice. This type of voice sounds raspy and very unmusical. It results from either tension in the throat or from forcing too much air through the vocal cords. You've probably experienced this type of voice after coming home from a football game. However, some experience it all the time due to a diseased or irritated condition of the throat. A chronic harshness of this type is organically caused and should have the attention of a physician. If a throat examination fails to disclose any pathological problem, then the harshness can be cured by relaxation and proper breathing.

Relax your throat and neck and softly repeat one syllable words like 'me,' 'bee,' 'run,' 'one,' etc. Keep up this exercise until all raspiness or breathiness if gone and your voice is clear. Then begin slowly to increase your volume until all raspiness is gone at your key level. When freed from the problem of harshness, try not to fall prey to it again. By giving your voice proper rest before speaking and by breathing correctly, you can avoid the stridently harsh quality of voice often referred to as "clergymen's throat."

Breathiness

"Hello, Daaaaaarrliing" might be all right for the movie actress but such breathy expressions are not appropriate for the pulpit or podium. Breathiness occurs when your vocal cords do not close sufficiently during the vocal process and an excess of unvocalized air escapes giving your voice a highly aspirate quality. Sometimes breathiness is caused by insufficient loudness. That is why a whisper is breathy. It allows too much air to escape. Apart from pathological reasons, breathiness is caused by overexertion, emotional strain, illness, etc. Again, this problem, like harshness, can be relieved by the proper method of breathing and better articulation.

Force

The final characteristic of the voice for vocal variety is force, or loudness. The first requirement any audience places on a speaker is that he be heard easily. Yet one of the chief speech culprits is poor volume control. Speaking too softly is an imposition on the courtesy of the listeners. It is an affront to their dignity and indicates an attitude of selfishness on the part of the speaker. To speak so that others cannot hear is the height of rudeness. A preacher that cannot be heard will not be. He will have no audience. That you must be heard cannot be preached too forcefully.

Speaking with adequate force is not only necessary so that the speaker may be heard, it is also necessary to give a favorable impression of the speaker to the audience. One who speaks softly with an inadequate amount of force tends to seem insecure. He does not convey the impression of confidence and vigor that a speaker needs. His audience will feel he is either unprepared to speak to them (and they will turn him off) or they will think he doesn't care whether they hear him or not (and they will turn him off). As before, this characteristic can be varied to inhibit monotony. It may be varied in *degree* and in *form*.

By degree we mean the amount of force applied, whether it be a whisper in low degree or a shout in high degree. By form we mean the manner in which that force is applied, whether applied gradually, abruptly, etc. Variation of force by degree is usually for the sake of emphasis. Increased loudness of a word or phrase will tend to make that word or phrase stand out. Likewise, by changing the degree of force, a drowsy audience can be awakened and enlivened. It should be remembered that to effect change in the degree of force or loudness does not always mean to get louder. A sharp reduction in sound is quite as effective as a sharp increase, if done properly.

As to the form in which force is applied, gradual application of force is called effusive form and is frequently used to convey a spirit of dignity, reverence, grandeur, and the like. When expulsive form is used, force is applied more rapidly and firmly with a vigorous stroke of loudness. Explosive form is expressed when force is violent and gives the feeling of anger, fear, or a sudden outburst.

Much of vocal variety is related to loudness or force. The relative amount of force applied to different syllables or words is called *stress*. Proper stress of a syllable or word falls within the accepted standards of pronunciation. Improper stress can greatly change the meaning of a word or phrase and can wreak havoc with the audience. Consider, for example, the shift in emphasis from the first to the second syllable of the word "refuse." Emphasis and contrast frequently require placing stress on a particular syllable or word. Consider Jesus' statement, "I am the way." If He wanted to stress that He alone was the way to salvation He would have said, "*I* am the way," or possibly "I am *the* way." If someone would have questioned the Lord asking, "Are you really the way" He would have stressed "I *am* the way." This stress is primarily a change in degree of force. Hence, variety in force or loudness can be an effective method of emphasis as well as an effective method of keeping an audience awake. As W. G. T. Shedd observes: "The principal, perhaps the sole cause of the success of the radical orator of the present day with his audience, is his force."[5]

One final caution is necessary in speaking to preachers of the variable characteristics of the voice. Most of the bad opinions of preaching have come as a direct result of bad preaching. It was said of Westminster Abbey, "Many persons sleep within these walls." This is true of many churches. The problem is that a "professional" voice has become prevalent in the pulpit. Some call it the "holy Sabbath day voice." Arthur Stevens Phelps calls it the "holy tone." A preacher who talks normally while out of the pulpit might take on a spiritual whine in the pulpit.

I can recall a well known evangelist who could put me to sleep in less than five minutes because of his monotone whine. Not only is this falsetto whine not necessary, it is not desirable. Yet it is common in many pulpits today. Why? For many older preachers this type of voice is a carryover from years gone by when preachers indicated their piety by a smug look and a "Sabbath day voice." Perhaps their voice is the only remains of the fervor which they once knew, or perhaps the habit

---

[5]W. G. T. Shedd, *Homiletics and Pastoral Theology* (London: Banner of Truth Trust, 1965), p. 72.

is just too intense, or perhaps they just don't care. Whatever the case, the spiritual whine is still there.

Young ministers have fallen into the same trap. Fearing the consequences of being themselves, they have imitated their elder counterparts and thus "whine". begets "whine." How is this condition stopped? Phelps says, "The cure for the holy tone is surprisingly simple: cease ranting or whining, and go to talking . . . Stop short, wait a minute, and then go on in a conversational tone of voice."[6]

I would add this reminder. You're at your best when you are yourself. Listen to yourself preach by recording one of your sermons. This will do a world of good for you. You will say, "Is THAT me?" By recognizing the problem you already have half corrected it.

The Voice and Volume

We have already discussed loudness or force under the variable characteristics of the voice. However, the problem of being heard is so acute that this discussion needs to continue. Probably the most important single factor in being heard is you and not your physical environment. Before we consider you, though, let us examine the problems of environment.

Two factors must be considered in knowing how loudly you should speak. They are the *loudness-to-distance ratio* and the *speech-to-noise ratio*. Each of us speaks softer than we think and the reason is very simple. Our ears are closer to our mouth than anyone else's ears and thus we sound louder to us than to anyone else. Since sound travels from its source in a spherical manner, that is, it travels in every direction, and since it is transmitted literally upon air particles bumping into one another, it is only natural to assume that the greater the distance from the energy source the sound travels, the weaker it will be. If we exclude outside factors, the loudness of the voice varies inversely with the square of the distance from your lips. Mathematically that is $I \propto 1/D^2$. This simply means that sound is weakened by distance and if it is not reflected from the walls and ceiling, your voice would be only one-sixteenth as loud 12 feet away as at a distance of three feet; and the listener 50 feet away would hear it only about one two hundred-

---

[6]Arthur Steven Phelps, *Speaking in Public* (Grand Rapids: Baker Book House, 1958), p. 75.

eightieth as loud.[7] The obvious conclusion is to speak up. If you do not, those in the back of the auditorium will never hear you.

Not only is the loudness of your voice affected by its distance from the receiver's ear, but it is also affected by the amount of noise in the room. Loudness is expressed in decibels (db).One decibel is roughly equal to the smallest difference in loudness which the ear can detect. Thus, the rustling of leaves in a quiet country lane is about ten decibels. The noise of an empty church is about 25 decibels. When an audience is placed in that church, even if they are as quiet as can be, the decibel level is raised to 42. Eighty decibels are likely to be recorded in a factory and some rock music is well over 100 decibels and may even damage the ear.[8] It is important for the speaker to know that he must do more than merely speak to be heard comfortably. Ease of listening is the speaker's aim, not maximum loudness. Speak loudly enough to be easily heard.

This evokes two more questions. "How can I know if I am loud enough?" and "How can I be loud enough if I'm not?" How can the speaker know if he is loud enough? Although very elaborate equipment is available to determine proper loudness, most do not have such equipment. Yet we do have very good equipment for determining if we are loud enough; we have eyes and ears.

Audience Analysis

There are three types of audience analysis to see if your message is being received. They are *prior* analysis, *present,* or simultaneous, analysis, and *post* analysis.

Prior analysis refers to what can be done before you speak to determine if your voice is loud enough or not. First determine the space of the room in relation to other rooms in which you have spoken. Is it larger, smaller, or about the same size? If it is larger you must allow for the additional distance your voice must travel and the additional

---

[7]Alan H. Monroe, *Principles and Types of Speech* (Chicago: Scott, Foresman and Company, 1949), pp. 129-130.

[8]In a study made by Charles Speaks and David A. Nelson of the University of Minnesota, ten rock bands were observed. It was noticed that the db reading of these bands ranged from 105-120 decibels. This is just 10 db's less than the maximum tolerable. Twenty-five of these musicians were interviewed and six of them were found to have suffered permanent hearing loss and another five temporary hearing loss. These findings are recorded in *Fight for Quiet* by Theodore Berland (Prentice Hall, 1970).

noise from people in the room. You also will want to be at the church or meeting place in time to try it out. See how much of an echo there is. See if there are a number of drapes or tapestries to "eat up" the sound of your voice. Is there wall-to-wall carpeting on the floor? Is there a balcony or over-hang? All of these factors will be of extreme value in determining how loudly you should speak.

Also, if there is a microphone system you will want to try that out as well. How far away from the mike can you stray? Must you speak directly into the mike? If it is a lapel mike, how is it fastened? Is there a "ring" to the mike when you speak? Learning to use a microphone well is an art. Someone who knows his microphone can add great effect by raising his voice without "ringing" the mike and then suddenly whisper and still he heard. Prior analysis can also be accomplished by placing someone in the back of the auditorium to see if you can be easily heard. Anything you can do beforehand to determine if you are going to be heard is of inestimable value.

Present analysis is done after the audience has arrived and you have begun speaking. It is now that your eyes and ears are most handy when analyzing whether or not you are being heard. You must look for the reaction of the audience. If they appear to be straining to hear you, they probably are not hearing you. If they seem to be "in a daze," they probably can't hear you. If they are sleeping, they aren't hearing you. In any case, you need to increase your volume or in some other manner increase your understandability.

Occasionally, someone in the back of the room will cup his hand over his ear to indicate that he cannot hear you. This will be helpful but it is not a wise idea to call attention to the fact that you are not being heard. For instance, it is never necessary to stop in the middle of your presentation and ask, "Can everybody hear me?" That is what your eyes and ears are for. You can determine if you are being heard without asking "foolish and unlearned questions" by being alert enough to notice if your audience is with you.

Post analysis is a time of learning. Especially if you are preaching in the same church every Sunday, after the service ask your wife or an associate if you could be easily heard. If the answer is negative then do something about it. Begin the process all over again. Go to the auditorium before the next service and practice speaking with more force. Then watch the people as you speak. If they are hearing you, fine. If not, make sure they do. Volume is a matter of learned behavior which can be changed. A most important rule for beginning speakers is, *you are never too loud.*

The second question to be considered is, "How can I be loud enough?" Obviously the most basic answer is to speak up. But this is not the only solution. You can be more easily heard through proper breathing, better articulation, and better pronunciation. Let us consider these three elements.

When Henry Ward Beecher was asked by a group of Brooklyn ministers what the qualifications for success in the ministry are, Beecher replied: "Brains, brass, and belly!" This does not mean that the bigger the belly the better the speaker. It does mean that to be a good speaker one must use the proper method of breathing. Mastering the correct method of breathing should be number one on our list of things to do for voice penetration and improvement. Since breath is the very foundation of the voice and the raw material with which we work, it is important to treat it wisely. The proper use of the breath will yield full rich tones. Shallow breathing will yield a thin weak voice, barely audible.

Diaphragmatic Breathing

Famous singers and speakers have for years maintained that the diaphragmatic method of breathing (belly breathing) is the proper method. "Diaphragmatic," you say, "what's that? Some newly discovered secret? Something it takes a life time to learn?" Quite the contrary. Most people do not use the diaphragmatic method in breathing, and those who do not have learned not to. That's right, we have learned not to use this method. If someone tells you to take a big breath of air, what do you do? You raise your shoulders, expand your chest, and pull in your stomach. Even though this is the most common method, it is all wrong. To take a big breath of air you should do it as you did when you were a baby, or even now as you do while you are sleeping.

Try it. Lie flat on your back and breathe deeply. Did your shoulders raise? Your chest expand? Your "tummy" pull in? Not at all. As a matter of fact, just the opposite happened. Lying flat on your back and breathing deeply makes the main activity center your stomach. It didn't pull in, it pushed out. Watch a baby. This is the method of breathing babies use, for it is natural. We all breathed that way as babies. Somewhere along the line we learned to breathe otherwise. When you are sleeping (like a baby), you breathe this natural method as well for you have reduced control over what you do and your natural instincts take over causing you to breathe properly.

Actually, what is happening with diaphragmatic breathing is this. The diaphragm is a thin muscle which forms the floor of the chest at the base of the lungs and the roof of the abdominal cavity. When you breathe properly, using the diaphragmatic method, this arched muscle (like an inverted washbowl) is pressed down flat by the incoming breath. This is why your stomach pushes out to meet your belt. Air enters your lungs and they in turn push upon the diaphragm, which in turn pushes upon the stomach. With diaphragm depressed, the lungs may fill the chest cavity. When air is exhaled, the diaphragm, ribs, stomach muscles, and chest muscles all work together to assist the lungs in expelling the air. That's proper breathing. Lung breathing alone is not only improper, it is harmful as well.

It can thus be seen why diaphragmatic breathing is so important. Since the diaphragm divides your body into two distinct compartments, the upper part (heart and lungs) and the lower part (abdomen, liver, intestines, etc.),if a person simply fills his lungs with air and does not allow the diaphragm to be compressed to permit the entrance of more air to the lungs, a speaker is only speaking with half the air he could. Half the air may mean half the force, and half the force will mean half the volume. Hence, the proper method of breathing will greatly increase your power as a speaker. It is a goal worth striving for.

Practice saying HO - HO - HO - HE - HE - HE, not speaking from your throat but from your belly. Each time you say "HO" your belly should bounce in to push out that air. As soon as you have uttered the sound allow your belly to bounce back out, taking in more air as you do. Practice, practice, practice. Remember, it has taken you years to learn the wrong method of breathing. It will take much practice to correct this. You must think of doing it correctly. Think and practice, think and practice. In so doing you will begin to breathe correctly and double your efficiency as a speaker.

The diaphragmatic method of breathing is advantageous for five distinct reasons. As we have already mentioned, it is the natural method of breathing. Second, it allows controlled breathing. With this added reservoir of air you need not be huffing and puffing in the middle of a word or sentence. The air you have can be meted out in the proper proportions and thus helps not only to conserve your breath but helps prevent breathiness as well. Third, this method of breathing tends to relax the neck. Tension in the throat and neck results in soreness and possibly the loss of voice. Fourth, this method gives you greater confidence as a speaker. You are not constantly worried about whether or not you are being heard. Your breath does not give out on you in the middle of your most important sentence. Your presentation will go much more smoothly. Finally, the diaphragmatic method of breathing is advantageous in that it allows you to put correct emphasis on words, phrases, and sentences. Greater emphasis comes with greater air. Raising the voice, whispering, etc. all take an increased amount of air which can best be gained through the proper method of breathing.

Articulation

Better articulation is the second element in being more readily heard. Articulation in general refers to a mobile joining of things together. This is why the bones and cartilage in your elbow are said to articulate. They work well together. When a football team is articulating it is winning games. When your lips, tongue, jaw, etc, are articulating you are speaking well.

Articulation can best be summed up in two words, *enunciation* and *pronunciation*. *Enunciation* refers to a distinctness of utterance. To enunciate properly you must give full value to both vowels and consonants. Good enunciation depends largely on the tongue. Gray's *Anatomy* declares that there are more than 400 separate movements of the tongue when speaking. It is imperative, therefore, that the speaker keep his tongue under full control. It was to this important problem that James devoted one-fifth of his book in the Bible in another context.

Someone has said that although it is your mind that determines what you say, it is your tongue that determines how you say it. By properly manipulating the tongue a person can become more than just an average preacher or orator.

Shakespeare's famous line is still worth quoting: "Speak the speech, I pray you, as I pronounced it to you, trippingly on the tongue. But if you mouth it, as many of our players do, I had as lief the towncrier spoke my lines. Nor do not saw the air too much with your hand, thus, but use all gently, for in the very torrent, tempest, and (as I may say) whirlwind of passion you must acquire and beget a temperance that may give it smoothness."[9]

---

[9]*Hamlet, Prince of Denmark,* Act III, Scene 2, lines 1–16.

It may be that to give proper enunciation to words and syllables you will have to exaggerate them a bit until you get used to enunciating properly. This is because in the United States we have become notorious for our sloppy enunciation. Thus, if we lay greater stress on our enunciation while we practice for the pulpit, we will use better enunciation while we deliver the message.

Have you ever taken stock in your own enunciation? How do you say, "He's got a lot of..."? The great majority of Americans will say, "He's gotta lotta...." If you do, your enunciation needs "a lotta" work. James Black is right in contending that, "It is not loudness so much as good articulation that makes a speaker heard." By clear enunciation of all words and syllables you have come a long way in making yourself heard.

In lampooning business bureaucracy, James Boren, president of NATAPROBU (National Association of Professional Bureaucrats) has formulated three bureaucratic laws. He pokes fun at business leaders by saying: "(1) When in charge, ponder; (2) when in trouble, delegate; and (3) when in doubt, mumble."[10] Boren's last law seems to characterize much of pulpit preaching today. Men who are barely on speaking terms with God and are uncertain of their message do tend to mumble.

However, this is not the biblical pattern. Speaking in Psalm 81, God says, "I am the Lord thy God, which brought thee out of the land of Egypt: open thy mouth wide, and I will fill it." We are exhorted in Proverbs 31:8-9 to "Open thy mouth for the dumb in the cause of all such as are appointed to destruction. Open thy mouth, judge righteously, and plead the cause of the poor and needy." In God's empowering of Ezekiel, the prophet is instructed: "And I will make thy tongue cleave to the roof of thy mouth, that thou shalt be dumb, and shalt not be to them a reprover: for they are a rebellious house. But when I speak with thee, I will open thy mouth, and thou shalt say unto them, Thus saith the Lord God..." (Ezek. 3:26-27). Notice that in each case the instruction from the Word of God was to "open your mouth." Simply in heeding this injunction from God's Word we would immediately see better preaching. If you learn nothing else from this study, learn this:

Open thy mouth and... say unto them, thus saith the Lord God.

---

[10]Quoted in *Time* magazine, November 23, 1970.

48 PRESCRIPTION FOR PREACHING

Just as important as enunciating words properly is pronouncing them properly. *Pronunciation* is simply expressing the sounds and accents of a word so they conform with acceptable standards. I suppose you could say that an acceptable standard would be governed by the educated people of your community. This is because every community exhibits a bit different pronunciation. What is acceptable pronunciation in Chicago may not be acceptable in Boston. Thus, the way you pronounce words should not just be governed by the area in which you reside but by those that speak properly in that area.

With regard to pronunciation it should be said at the outset that our's is not an easy language to master, especially for a non-native. There are variations in English. For instance, can you imagine a Frenchman or German accurately pronouncing these lines:

Though the tough cough and hiccough plough me through,
Through life's dark lough my course I'll still pursue.

As a student, I spent my last semester in seminary at the University of Strasbourg (France). Upon arrival I was moved into the men's dormitory and found myself to be the only English-speaking person on the floor. My French had to improve immediately. It was difficult but not nearly so as if the situation had been reversed; if a French student would have moved into an American university and begun studies, he would have been in real trouble.

This does not mean that proper pronunciation is impossible. Consult your dictionary and cultivate proper pronunciation. Use a self-pronouncing Bible to learn the pronunciation of Bible names. This is always a tough area. I can remember when I was a youngster, there was a man in our church who always knew the pronunciation of Bible names. When a difficult passage was encountered this man would just rattle off the names with great ability. It was only after I had gone away to college and had begun to learn pronunciation for myself that I realized this man wasn't pronouncing these names correctly at all. He would blurt right through the name and we were all impressed. This is the way with many preachers today. They have never learned the proper methods of pronunciation and so they hurriedly ramble over the Bible names.

Problems

There are several outstanding problems in proper pronunciation. One is the misplaced accent. Consult the dictionary to learn the proper accent of "gen-u-ine," "de-vice," "the-a-ter," "il-lus-tra-tive," "in-flu-enced," etc. A second problem is the pronunciation of silent letters, such as the "l" in salmon, the "t" in often, etc. These words are pronounced "sam-en" and "of-fen." A third problem is just the reverse; the addition of letters that are not there. For example the pronunciation of "el-em" for elm, "fil-em" for film, "em-ber-rel-la" for umbrella, "ath-a-lete" for athlete.

Still another problem is the subtraction of sounds; the pronunciation of "his-tre" for his-tor-y, "pich-er" for picture (pick-cher). There are also sound substitutions such as "jest" for just, "kech" for catch, "git" for get, etc. This is an extreme problem in the pulpit, one which takes a great amount of effort to overcome. Another problem is the reversal of sound or syllables. With this problem a speaker would say "kal'-verē" for cavalry (and vice versa), "pres-pi-ra-shen" for perspiration, "per-po-sal" for proposal, etc.

Perhaps the greatest problem in pronunciation (notice that there is a difference in pronunciation between the word "pronounce" and the word "pronunciation") is that of the notorious dropping of endings. Sometimes this occurs because we do not pronounce the whole word. We say "priess" instead of "priest" or "munss" instead of "months." Most frequently, however, the dropping of endings comes as a result of hurriedness and faulty understanding of the importance of our speech. How many times have you heard someone say something to the effect, "She was goin' to the store to do some shoppin' and hurrin' home to see if the kids were fighting.'"? It is uncanny the number of dropped endings that can be counted in one sermon or speech. You cannot rid yourself of dropping endings until you try.

The Inarticulators

There are four things that stand in your way to proper articulation and consequently inhibit your being heard distinctly. Personified, they are:

Larry Locked Jaw. Larry is the person who simply will not open his mouth wide enough. His jaw is frozen, locked tight, and barely

movable. Larry cannot be easily understood because, in the English
language, failure to open the jaws adequately is a serious crime; much
of the meaning of our language is conveyed by consonant sounds. If
the jaws are tight, Larry will have to talk through his teeth and thus the
tongue is not given proper movement. The result is that Larry's projection is almost nil, his resonance is curtailed, and his voice quality is
unnatural. Poor Larry, he can't get a church.

Lucy Lazy Lips. Lucy has a problem: flabby lips. Lucy's lips have
become fat and lazy. Lips are made of muscle and if they are not used
they become flabby. In her case the lips are so slack that they do not
adequately shape the mouth opening for proper articulation. Her bila-
bials (*b* and *p* sounds) and her labiodentals (*f* and *v* sounds) have
become mumbled. She tried to tell a flannelgraph story and all the kids
fell asleep. Poor Lucy Lazy Lips, there are many people like her, but
she has few friends.

Mickey Mushy Mouth. Poor Mickey, he thinks the only reason
God gave him a tongue is to eat ice cream. He doesn't know that he is
supposed to move it while he talks. The tongue has more to do with
distinct articulation than does any other organ. If jaws are moving and
lips are moving but the tongue is not, then all is to no avail. Since the
tongue position determines to a large extent the size of the resonators
and consequently the vocal quality, and since many consonants also
depend largely upon the precise action of the tongue, Mickey's vocal
presentation is in jeopardy since his tongue is inactive. His lazy tongue
prohibits him from saying "these." Mickey always says "dese."
Mickey wanted to be a Bible translator but nobody could figure out
what he was talking about.

Sammy Super Speed. Sammy's problem is that he simply talks too
fast. He would make a great auctioneer, but the gospel isn't auctioned
off, it is heralded, proclaimed, and given away. If Sammy would learn
to take his time, a great deal of indistinctness would be avoided. Yet he
hasn't learned. Oh, he knows he should speak more slowly, but he
isn't willing to make the sacrifice. He would have to swallow his pride
and admit that he has a problem. He would have to practice speaking
more slowly, and practice again and again. This would take time, time
that Sammy isn't willing to take to lick the problem.

You could be any one of these four or a combination of several. If
your jaw isn't flexible enough, your lips too lazy to move with every
vowel and consonant, your tongue lying helpless in its grave, or travel-

ing faster than the speed of a locomotive, you have a problem. But remember, problems can be overcome and that's why you are engaged in this study—to overcome your problems. Admit them, and then do something about them. *The New York Times* indicated that one man out of every seven who sought to become officers in the U.S. Army during the Second World War was refused a commission because of "poor articulation, lack of voice and imperfect enunciation." If this is your problem, you can lick it with the help of the Holy Spirit.

The Voice and the Conversational Mode

In light of the warning against talking in a "holy Sabbath day voice," the type of voice a good speaker develops should be described. In practicing fluency, poise, vocal variety, etc. it is vital that the student does not become artificial. You are a man, not a machine. You are not a computer or a robot and your voice and actions should not give the impression that you are. The maxim in philosophy may be "Know thyself," but in public speaking it is "Be thyself." You must develop a type of speaking that is not only you, but natural to those around you. Individuality is no good without a measure of conformity. In essence, you must be the same person in the pulpit as you are when you are out of it. You speak with more authority and restraint in the pulpit, but you still must be natural. This type of speaking is frequently called the *conversational mode*. It is a middle-of-the-road type of speaking, not too formal, not too informal. It is lively but not disrespectful; it is forceful but not military. In a word, it is conversational, the middle ground between high and low; it is speaking as you normally would but with greater gravity knowing that you are communicating the words of life.

This conversational mode or manner of speaking is something that most people have to develop. This is because they feel every time they address a group of people they are delivering a presidential address. We must take care not to handle the Word of God in an informal manner, but in a conversational way. Alan H. Monroe of Purdue University suggests six kinds of speakers who do not use the conversational mode of speaking.[11] Perhaps you will find yourself as one of the following.

---

[11] Alan H. Monroe, *Speech*, pp. 16-17.

The Elocutionist. This person is "one who permits himself to be carried away by the sound of his own voice and the graceful manipulation of his body, at the expense of the thought behind them." His sermon or speech is to display his talent as an orator rather than to accomplish the worthy goal of communication. He has "tears in his voice; there is a studied care about every step or gesture; and he bows; waiting for applause when he is through. But he usually lacks in sheer rugged energy, and while his audience may applaud his 'act', they seldom remember what he said."

The Verbal Gymnast. You've heard of a "play on words"; this fellow plays with words. He delights in using long, polysyllabic terms, for his purpose is to display his knowledge of the language. He isn't concerned with his audience understanding him, just as long as they are awed by him. Former British Prime Minister Benjamin Disraeli referred to one of them as a man who "is intoxicated with the exuberance of his own verbosity." Seeking to display his own learning, he fails to convince because he seems so unnatural and insincere.

Many preachers fall prey to this type, especially those that have labored long years in college, seminary, and graduate school. This investment in time, money, and sweat seems to find its only gratification in displaying one's education. It is not needed. An educated man does not have to flaunt it for he cannot hide it. A preacher of the gospel does not have to flaunt it for he cannot hide it. A preacher of the Gospel too great.

The Oracle. This is a speaker with a "know it all" attitude. He gives the impression of deep intelligence. Every word is pondered. Every statement is worth committing to paper. Every thought is a brilliant gem. The oracle rolls his eyes, hesitates before he speaks, and usually begins with a rather pompous, "It is my considered opinion that. . . ." Unfortunately, the quality of his utterance degenerates from that point.

The preacher is God's oracle, but only to the extent that he is God's spokesman. He neither possesses supernatural wisdom nor, for the most part, excessive human wisdom. He is the simple prophet of God, uttering the simple message of God's love for fallen man. Let's not put on "airs" in the pulpit.

Monroe says, "All three of these—the elocutionist, the verbal gymnast, and the oracle—fail to communicate because they are parading themselves rather than honestly trying to talk; such speakers are very much aware of the audience but are interested chiefly in the applause."[12]

The Hermit. This person is a relative of Mickey Mushy Mouth. He is one who constantly mumbles to himself, but for a different reason than Mickey. "He may have a wealth of good ideas, well organized and developed, but he looks off at the ceiling or floor, talks in a weak, monotonous voice, and in general makes no effort to be heard or understood. He gives the impression of not caring whether anyone hears him or not; and usually, audiences do not." The hermit suffers from an acute case of fear; it may not be evident in shaking hands and knocking knees, but nevertheless, fear is there. The hermit has the idea that if nobody hears him, then nobody will hear his mistakes. Actually the opposite takes place; his whole presentation is a mistake. We need to speak boldly because we have the message telling where spiritual beggars can find food.

The Culprit. The culprit is one who seems ashamed of what he says. He shrinks from his audience and refuses to raise his voice, on the apparent assumption that the fewer who hear him, the fewer enemies he'll have. Sometimes he apologizes verbally; always his manner is apologetic; he is never forthright in his statements because he hesitates to believe even himself. Neither the hermit nor the culprit uses the conversational mode. While they avoid personal display, they lack sincere communicative energy. In his book *The New Testament Image of the Ministry,* W. T. Purkiser gives a number of metaphors of the ministry that are found in the New Testament but culprit isn't among them.[13] On the contrary Paul says, "For I am not ashamed of the gospel of Christ: for it is the power of God unto salvation to every one that believeth; to the Jew first, and also to the Greek" (Rom. 1:16).

The Gibberer. The gibberer is unique unto himself. He is neither a showman nor a coward. "He is one who emits a continuous stream of words with little or no thought behind them. He fails to communicate because he has no central thought to communicate. He jumps around

---

[12]Alan H. Monroe, *Speech,* pp. 16.
[13]W. T. Purkiser, *The New Testament Image of the Ministry* (Grand Rapids: Baker Book House, 1970).

from one point to another until both he and his audience are dizzy with his meandering; he usually stops by saying, 'Well, I guess that's all I have to say.' ''[14]

The nerve of modern day preaching has now had a finger placed upon it. Many present day preachers are not just functioning with their minds in neutral and their tongues in gear. Their tongues are in gear, but their minds are muddled. They aren't sure of their message. They have no answer to the question, "Where is the word of the Lord?" (Jer. 17:15). Many preachers have become simple gibberers because they have nothing specific to say. If preaching is to be repaired, preachers must stop seeking words from philosophy, psychology, ecology, and all the other "ologies" and ask themselves, "Is there any word from the Lord?" (Jer. 37:17). If they find the answer for them is negative, the preacher should leave the pulpit and stop degrading the highest of professions.

The conversational mode of speaking will lead you away from each of the above, but only the Spirit of God will lead you into truth. Make sure you have the truth and then, using the conversational mode, go out and set some sinners free.

---

[14]Alan H. Monroe, *Speech*, p. 17.

3

The Wonderful
World of Words

*"I think things had better not be said at all, than said
weakly" —Jean François Millet.*

*"He gave man speech, and speech created thought, which is the
measure of the universe" —Percy Bysshe Shelley.*

We do not actually know how man first spoke, but the Bible indicates that it was not long after he was created by God that he did so. Genesis 2:7 indicates that man was formed out of the dust of the ground and the breath of life was breathed into his nostrils. Verse 20 of that chapter tells us that Adam gave names to all cattle and fowl and every beast. Verse 23 begins, "And Adam said. . . ." This is the first recorded incidence of human speech.

Talking is a most important factor in every society. It is said that a normal person utters about 25,000 words every day. But words are meaningless in themselves. Meanings are in people. Words are the all-important symbols which we use to convey those meanings. They are the convenient labels which help us to classify things. It should be evident that it is extremely important for us to use words properly. This is doubly true for those who use words in their vocation. This definitely includes the preacher or public speaker.

Let us consider a few vital factors concerning words and their use. To speak well, the following factors should be considered.

Choosing Words

Make an accurate choice. Mark Twain aptly declared: "The difference between the right word and the almost right word is the difference between lightning and the lightning bug." To say precisely what you mean, to express the most delicate nuances of thought, is not easy even for the professional speaker or writer. But difficulty and impossibility are not the same. Many such differences exist. For instance, "apparently" and "evidently" do not mean quite the same thing. "Intriguing" is not equivalent to "interesting." "Disinterested" is not synonymous with "uninterested." Each of these words has a distinct meaning and no two are equivalent. It may now be more easily seen that a good speaker must accurately choose each word he uses.

As a speaker, you cannot afford to use a word when you are not absolutely sure of its meaning. To do so is to invite disaster. Norm Crosby, a popular comedian, makes his living by using incorrect words which sound similar to the correct ones. For example, he might say: "The preposition of men to women in this country is deceasing every year. Women are becoming dormant over the men. Thus we men have placed the women on a high pinochle and we worship them as the early Greeks did Afro-nitie." You can see the resulting confusion. The comedian gets a laugh. If the preacher uses the wrong word, the chances are he will get the same reaction. If you don't know the meaning of a word, don't use it. Be accurate and you will never be embarrassed.

Use understandable words. We have already spoken of the Verbal Gymnast in connection with the conversational mode. He never uses a little word if he can use a big one in its place. This is a mistake. The end of public speaking is communication. If communication is not enhanced by large, polysyllabic words, then by all means don't use them. The 23rd Psalm has 118 words, 92 of which are of but one syllable. In the first 118 words of Hamlet's famous soliloquy, "To be or not to be,'' 99 of these are of but one syllable. Yet many preachers give their congregation the impression they are listening to a talking dictionary. Many people are confused by big words, but few are impressed by them. Don't play with words, express them. Anyone can use words to sound intelligent or cosmopolitan, but unless these words express that person's meaning, they are of no value.

Philip Broughton is credited with the sure-fire method of converting frustration with words into fulfillment. Mr. Broughton has compiled a lexicon of 30 carefully chosen words which he calls "buzzwords." They are:

Column 1	Column 2	Column 3
0. integrated	0. management	0. options
1. total	1. organizational	1. flexibility
2. systematized	2. monitored	2. capability
3. parallel	3. reciprocal	3. mobility
4. functional	4. digital	4. programming
5. responsive	5. logistical	5. concept
6. optional	6. transitional	6. time-phase
7. synchronized	7. incremental	7. projection
8. compatible	8. third-generation	8. hardware
9. balanced	9. policy	9. contingency

"The procedure is simple. Think of any three-digit number, then select the corresponding buzzword from each column. For instance, number 257 produces "systematized logistical projection," a phrase than can be dropped into virtually any report with that ring of decisive, knowledgeable authority. 'No one will have the remotest idea of what you're talking about,' says Broughton. 'But the important thing is that they're not about to admit it.' "[1]

In choosing the proper words, the characteristic of freshness is just as important as accuracy. Harold Macmillan, the former Prime Minister of England, has said, "The difficulty of speeches is that you are perpetually poised between the cliché and the indiscretion." Certainly there is no place for the indiscretion in preaching the Gospel, but there is little room for the cliché as well. Try to avoid the trite or overworked

---

[1] Quoted in *Newsweek,* May 6, 1968.

word or expression. It is disheartening to hear a phrase that is powerful but stripped of its significance by repetition.

How many times have you heard the following expressions: "We humbly bow before Thee," "Let us look to the Lord in prayer," "Without a shadow of a doubt," etc.? Have we no other means of expression? Why must we always be "cool as a cucumber" or as "busy as a bee?" Avoid overused adjectives and adverbs such as "most," "great," "very," and "lovely." Also, avoid overused expressions like "dead as a doornail," and "pretty as a picture."

What About Slang? Should I ever use slang? This question is frequently asked by beginning preachers and the answer is often wrong. Slang words and phrases are sometimes both acceptable and effective and should be used. The consideration is when and where to use slang. It would be out of place in the morning prayer or on a dignified occasion. You would probably not use slang while addressing a ladies' missionary society. However, the use of proper slang would be acceptable while speaking to college students or young people in general.

Three cautions must be made. First, be careful where you use slang. Make sure it would be acceptable to the occasion. Second, do not use vulgar or offensive slang. Avoid ethnic or religious slang. Finally, make sure the slang you use is up to date. Do you want to lose your audience? Just use an expression like "beatnik" or "twenty-three skiddoo." Slang changes frequently. If you're not sure the slang you plan to use is current, don't use it.

Words can make or break your presentation. If you use words that are unclear, obscure, technical, or inaccurate, no one will understand you and your time will be wasted. A proper choice will bring the following questions to bear on your words. *Are my words clear? Are my words concrete? Are my words simple?*

Clear Words

Are my words clear? Read the following quote from former United States President Woodrow Wilson.

My father was a man of great intellectual energy. My best training came from him. He was intolerant of vagueness, and from the time I began to write until his death in 1903, when he was eighty-one years old, I carried everything I wrote to him. He would make me read it aloud, which was always painful to me. Every now and then he would stop me. "What do you mean by that?" I would tell him, and, of course, in doing so would express myself more simply than I had on paper. "Why didn't you say so?" he would go on. "Don't shoot at your meaning with birdshot and hit the whole countryside; shoot with a rifle at the thing you have to say."

St. Augustine said: "*Veritas pateat, veritas placeat, veritas moveat*" (Make the truth plain, make it pleasing, make it moving). It is agreed among all writers on the subject of rhetoric that the first property of style is that of intelligibility. The Latin rhetoricians called this quality *perspicuitas,* or plainness. As this word indicates, a discourse that is *perspicuitas* can be "seen through" or is transparent. The Greek rhetoricians described this property with the word *enargeia* which signifies distinctness or clearness. Whatever these early rhetoricians chose to call it, today this quality is called clarity. It is imperative that what you say be clear, for preaching is more than just proclaiming; it is communicating. To stand up and preach without a hearer is useless. To stand up and preach with hearers who do not understand what you say is likewise useless. Preaching is communicating the mind of God to men, and this cannot be done without clarity.

Clarity is not only desirable, it is mandatory. Every preacher of the Word should strive for it, yet few really obtain it. The ancient Lycophron declared that he would hang himself upon a tree if he found anyone who could explain to him the meaning of his poem "The Prophecy of Cassandra." Unfortunately, many preachers could make the same claim about their preaching.

Achieving clarity is no easy matter. Richard Baxter once said: "It is no small matter to stand up in the face of a congregation and to deliver a message of salvation or damnation, as from the living God, in the name of our Redeemer. It is no easy matter to speak so plain that the ignorant may understand us; and so seriously that the deadest hearts may feel us; and so convincingly that the contradicting cavillers may be silenced."[2] At the outbreak of the Franco-Prussian War, General Von Moltke gave his officers some true advice. The General said, "Remember, gentlemen, that any order that can be misunderstood, will be misunderstood." In the pulpit, any truth that can be misunderstood, will be misunderstood.

---

[2]Richard Baxter, *The Reformed Pastor*. (Richmond: John Knox Press, 1956), p. 74.

To make your meaning clear is not easy, but it is necessary. It is necessary, for many words have other words similar to them but not identical. For instance, we may be able to sit in a luxurious chair and look out the window to see the luxuriant vegetation. Again, it would be acceptable to have a translucent door to a shower, but hardly a transparent door. Such similar sounding words demand that we make our meaning clear. Occasionally some words have more than one meaning. If you say that you "have a great volume" no one will know whether you have a large amount of something or a good book. Make sure that you have chosen a word or sequence of words to make your meaning clear.

"How can I make my meaning clear?" There are several ways. First, use an *illustration*. In doing so you have allowed light to come into your meaning. The use of illustrations is probably the best way of making what you say understandable.

Another way to make your meaning clear is to use *statistics*. Facts and figures have a way of clarifying a subject. Rather than say that the voter turnout on election day was large, you will convey greater meaning if you say the voter turnout was 96 percent. People can identify with that. They can understand that 96 percent is almost the whole. Your meaning will be clear and you will have communicated with them.

Two cautions must be mentioned here. The first, do not "beat" people with statistics or overuse them. Your audience does not want to hear a walking encyclopedia. You are a preacher of the Word, not a computer. Statistics are like anything else—overuse means abuse. Secondly, make your statistics realistic. No one can imagine a figure of three billion. Our minds cannot grasp such a sum. Try and choose some other method of indicating this figure.

This brings us to a third way to make your meaning clear. If those in your audience cannot understand the meaning of large objects or numbers, you may make your meaning clear by the use of *analogy* or *comparison*. These are most useful devices for making a point vivid and clear. By these methods you proceed from the known to the unknown. For example, a tiny molecule multiplied to the size of a pea would in the same proportion make a baseball the size of our earth. Hence, realizing the size of a baseball, one may gain a clearer understanding of the minute size of a molecule. The state of Alaska has a gross area of 590,804 square miles. Such a statistic has little meaning to people. Who can comprehend nearly 600,000 square miles? However, if you indicated to your audience that the coastline of Alaska and its islands is longer than the distance around the globe or that its area is greater than the combined areas of Vermont, New Hampshire, Maine, Massachusetts, Rhode Island, Connecticut, New York, New Jersey, Pennsylvania, Delaware, Maryland, West Virginia, North Carolina, South Carolina, Georgia, Florida, Mississippi, and Tennessee; if you indicated this, your audience would sit up and take notice. This is a more understandable use of the statistic. This is comparison. It will aid you greatly in making your meaning clear.

Another way to make sure that your listeners understand what you are saying is by *restatement* and *repetition*. Restatement is more than simple repetition, and it must be distinguished. Restatement is saying the same thing in a completely different way. By restatement you approach the information in a different way and by so doing you have created another avenue for the entrance of light and your subject to be illuminated.

Repetition and restatement are both greatly used in the Scriptures. The Old and New Testament writers indicate several ways in which the importance of a statement is made clear by repetition and restatement. For instance, when the Lord wanted His hearers to remember something, He would repeat, "Verily, verily." "Verily, verily, I say unto thee, Except a man be born again, he cannot see the kingdom of God" (John 3:3). This repetition of "verily" increased the emphasis of His statement.

Frequently a name was repeated twice to add emphasis to the statement following. "Saul, Saul, why persecutest thou me?" (Acts 9:4). Again, Saul had to take notice when his name was repeated. In the Psalms is frequently found the musical and liturgical term "Selah" which means to play forté or accent. This added emphasis gives a clearer meaning to what is said. "I remembered God, and was troubled: I complained, and my spirit was overwhelmed. Selah" (Ps. 77:3).

An example of restatement for this same purpose, to achieve clarity, would be Psalm 91:13. In this verse the writer, probably Moses, repeats himself but uses a different approach. "Thou shalt tread upon the lion and adder; the young lion and the dragon shalt thou trample under feet." Lion is repeated but in an embellished manner, adding the adjective "young." By so doing, the author has given greater emphasis to the fact that the one who dwells in the secret place of the most High can tread upon the lion, even the young lion at the peak of its strength. This restatement makes a clear picture of the absolute victory to be found by abiding in Christ Jesus.

The second analogy drawn in this verse is also a restatement. "Thou shalt tread upon the adder . . . and the dragon (or serpent, the most dangerous of adders)." Again, here is an embellishment for the sake of making the point clear. Both simple repetition and the embellished restatement have added to a clearer meaning of the promises of this psalm.

Illustrations, statistics, analogy, restatement, and repetition, all can be used to increase the understanding of your presentation. Whatever means you use, make your meaning clear, make it clear, make it clear.

Concrete Words

A second question you should ask yourself is, Are my words concrete? Theodor Beza once said of Calvin's sermons, *Tot verba, tot pondera,* "Every word weighs a pound." To be concrete you must shy away from the general. People do not appreciate generalities. It used to be that this was the only way to write. The old method of writing a biography was to speak only in generalities which Aristotle called "the refuge of weak minds." That day is past.

People today live in the concrete and the preacher must preach in the concrete. This is the way the great prophets and preachers of the Bible did. Jeremiah describes God as "rising up early and sending" the prophets to minister unto Israel and Judah. Although theologians would speak about this being "prevenient grace," Jeremiah puts it in the concrete. We must cultivate the concrete as well. To do so we must use great precision in language and vocabulary. There is no place for equivocal language in the pulpit, for people will be confused about what to believe.

Spurgeon mentions an anecdote to illustrate this point. From his book, *The Greatest Fight in the World,* he relates: "One day one of his minister friends was visited by a man who wanted to get some money out of him. He exclaimed to the minister, 'I am sure you would help me if you knew what great benefit I have received from your blessed ministry.' 'What is that?' said the pastor. 'Why, Sir, when I first came to hear you, I cared neither for God nor for the devil, but now, under your blessed ministry, I have come to love them both.'

"What marvel," Spurgeon continues, "if under men's shifty talk, people grow into love of both truth and falsehood!"[3]

Unless the speaker learns to be concrete and unequivocating in his statements, his congregation will be as wishy-washy as he is. If the communication process is to be fulfilled between preacher and hearer, the preacher must speak so as to be understood. If he does not learn to cultivate concrete ideas, phrases, and sentences, as well as doctrines and beliefs, he will not long be able to hold the attention of his audience.

Simple Words

Thirdly, we need to ask ourselves, Are my words simple? Many learned men have failed in the pulpit because they could not communicate in simple terms. The Gospel is a simple story of God's love and Christ's atoning sacrifice. It is virtually as simple as ABC. Yet the way in which it is presented is sometimes so complicated that hearers miss the message.

Strive to use simple words. There is nothing sacred about long theological terms. Your purpose is the communication of the good news of salvation and that's as simple as John 3:16. Besides, most people do not like terms or phrases which are long and involved. That's why more people read the *Reader's Digest* than Homer's *Iliad*. Jesus spoke in the most simple language possible. His method should be ours.

How does one assure simplicity in his presentation? The answer is by avoiding long words, complicated sentences, and theological jargon. It is not wrong to use a big word. If you choose to do so, however, make sure that you use a simple, understandable word with it. For example, if you say, "Jesus Christ is the propitiation for our sins," add to it, "that is, He appeased or satisfied God's wrath toward our sins." By so doing you have not only conveyed the meaning of propitiation, thus introducing an unfamiliar word, but you have also made known what Christ has done for us.

Also be careful about using long and complicated sentences. For example, you should never say, "Christ, having seen the pitifulness of our condition—and you know it is pitiful—and having known that He

---

[3]Charles H. Spurgeon, *The Greatest Fight in the World* (New York: Funk and Wagnalls, 1891), p. 38.

was the true Lamb without spot and blemish being appointed to be the sacrifice of atonement for our sins, willing to live but ready to die— which in fact He did—without a moment's hesitation and fully aware of what He was doing for us, died on the cross of Calvary.'' The subject is too far removed from the verb and, in general, this sentence is too long and complicated. Be simple. Jay Adams advises: "Learn to freckle your speech with periods."[4]

Again, do not use the technical jargon of the theological dictionary or systematic theology in the pulpit. If you cannot translate this jargon into simple words, you probably don't understand the theological concept which the word represents. In listening to the Apollo flights to the moon we all were reminded how jargon becomes a part of us quickly. Decades ago none of us knew what an EVA or a module was. During the 60s and 70s these terms became quite common. But notice that they were only common during coverage of the space flights by television and the press. Now we hear little of these terms. Always bear in mind that you are preaching to everyday people. Theological jargon is out of place everywhere but the college or seminary classroom, and sometimes there as well.

"Strive to be simple. Your audience is lost if you talk like the bureaucrats are said to have answered a New York plumber. The plumber wrote the National Bureau of Standards saying that he had found hydrochloric acid good for cleaning out clogged drains. The bureau wrote him: 'The efficacy of hydrochloric acid is indisputable, but the corrosive residue is incompatible with metallic permanence.' The plumber replied he was glad the bureau agreed with him.

"The bureau tried again, saying: 'We cannot assume the responsibility for the production of toxic and noxious residue with hydrochloric acid, and suggest that you use an alternative procedure.' The plumber wrote he was pleased that he and the bureau saw eye to eye. Finally, the bureau sent a message that came through: 'Don't use hydrochloric acid. It eats the @#$% out of the pipes.' "[5]

People get the message when it is simple, and they do not when it is not. This conclusion can be drawn from the preceding incident. To be an effective preacher of the Gospel you must come to the same conclu-

---

[4]Jay Adams, *Pulpit Speech* (Philadelphia: Presbyterian and Reformed Publishing Company, 1974), p. 123.
[5]Quoted in *Nation's Business*, July 1967.

sion. If your meaning is not clear, if you are speaking in generalities and not in the concrete, if your words are too complex to be understood by the common folk of your audience, no matter how well you may have prepared, no matter how well you may have expounded the Word of God, you haven't really preached. A pertinent paraphrase of I Corinthians 13:13 is: "And now abideth concreteness, simplicity, and clarity, these three; but the greatest of these is clarity."

In light of what has been said about choosing your words carefully, several key considerations will improve greatly your presentation with regard to words.

Picture Words

"In this process of interest-getting, there is one aid, one technique, that is of the highest importance; yet it is all but ignored. The average speaker does not seem to be aware of its existence. He has probably never consciously thought about it at all. I refer to the process of using words that create pictures. . . . Picture-building phrases swarm through the pages of the Bible and through Shakespeare like bees around a cider mill. For example, a commonplace writer would have said that a certain thing would be superfluous, like trying to improve the perfect. How did Shakespeare express the same thought? With a picture phrase that is immortal: 'To gild refined gold, to paint the lily, to throw perfume on the violet.' "[6] This quote from Dale Carnegie gives some indication of the importance of using a picture to indicate more clearly a thought. The best preaching is pictorial for it brings the hearer to not only hear the truth but to experience it as well.

Using picture words is not new. Written language began with hieroglyphic (picture) words. Many of the great proverbs, both biblical and non-biblical, use picture words to convey their meaning. For instance, when someone uses the expression, "Flat as a pancake," you visualize a pancake. "A bird in the hand is worth two in the bush" conjures up a picture of a hand with a bird resting in it. These expressions make use of picture words.

A good preacher subscribes to the *Readers Digest,* if for no other reason than to harvest the fruit of one section, "Toward a More

---

[6]Quoted in Dale Carnegie, *Public Speaking and Influencing Men in Business* (New York: Association Press, 1953), pp. 305–306.

Picturesque Speech.'' This is a haven for picture words. Some examples are: ''the day snailed by''; ''the wrinkled half of my life''; ''as involved as spaghetti''; etc.

The best types of picture words are the *metaphor* and the *simile*. The *simile* is an explicit comparison in which one thing is likened to another. It is usually introduced with the words *like* or *as*. For example, the Song of Solomon is filled with both similes and metaphors, and several fine similes are: ''His head is as the most fine gold. . . . His eyes are as the eyes of doves. . . . His cheeks are as a bed of spices. . . . His hands are as gold rings. . . . His legs are as pillars of marble . . . etc., etc.'' (Song of Sol. 5:11–15).

The *metaphor* substitutes the picture for the word, without the intervening comparison. Hence, the metaphor uses no *like* or *as*. The Song of Solomon likewise is sprinkled with the metaphor. ''I am the rose of Sharon, and the lily of the valleys'' (2:1). ''If she be a wall, we will build upon her a palace of silver: and if she be a door, we will enclose her with boards of cedar'' (8:9). Song of Solomon 8:10 contains both, a metaphor first and then a simile: ''I am a wall, and my breasts like towers. . . .''

An extended metaphor is called an *allegory*. The simile extended is called a *parable*. The Bible is replete with parables. This was Jesus' favorite form of picture words. He used it to great advantage in making clear His meaning. We can learn from Him.

Any type of picture word which can be used in preaching ought to be used. People understand a picture better than an explanation. After all, isn't that the essence of John 1:1–5,14 which says: ''In the beginning was the Word, and the Word was with God, and the Word was God. The same was in the beginning with God. All things were made by him; and without him was not anything made that was made. In Him was life; and the life was the light of men. And the light shineth in darkness; and the darkness comprehended it not. And the Word was made flesh and dwelt among us (and we beheld His glory, the glory as of the only begotten of the Father), full of grace and truth.'' The light was there and shining in darkness but no one understood it. So, Jesus Christ came in the flesh, something concrete, a picture word, so to speak. That's what the incarnation is all about.

Remember the wise old Arab saying: ''He is the best speaker who can turn the ear into an eye.''

Brevity

Someone has aptly said that the rule of thumb for public speakers should be: "Stand up. Speak up. Shut up!" This would alleviate the burden placed on many audiences by speakers who do not know when they have spoken too long. This includes most preachers. Shakespeare said: "Brevity is the soul of wit."[7] Some who speak and disregard brevity either have no soul for their audience or are witless.

Despite a fair measure of truth in Robert G. Lee's contention that "sermonettes are preached by preacherettes and they produce Christianettes," everyone has heard a sermon that was simply too long. Some have heard them so often that they just "tune out" the preacher after a certain length of time. This does not mean that the church is ready for the ten-minute sermon (although a skilled speaker can say far more in ten minutes than an unskilled one does in an hour). It does mean, however, that there is nothing sacred about preaching for 45 minutes or an hour. Most preachers preach about 25 to 35 minutes. Sometimes, depending on the preacher's ability, that is too long. Generally it is not.

There are several false theories about brevity which should be dispelled. First, many young pastors feel that if they are brief the congregation will think they have not prepared their message adequately. Nothing is farther from the truth. Much preparation is manifested in quality not quantity. I can recall having to write five-page papers in seminary. When the assignment was given I felt it would be a snap—only five pages. Once I began I realized I would rather have been assigned fifty pages. It is not easy to prepare a brief message or speech. It is much easier to prepare an hour message with little quality than it is to prepare a half-hour message filled with good exegesis, biblical truth, and apt illustration.

Never feel that you have cheated your people if you have a quality product but only half as long as a product of inferior quality. Someone once asked President Woodrow Wilson how long he took to prepare a ten-minute speech. The former President replied, "Two weeks." "How long for a speech lasting an hour?" continued the questioner. "One week," answered Mr. Wilson. "How long for a two-hour speech?" asked the inquirer. "I am ready now!" replied the President.

---

[7] *Hamlet, Prince of Denmark*, Act II, Scene 2, line 90.

Most speakers apparently feel that to say something significant you must take time to do so. Just the opposite is true. Thus, the second false theory about brevity, the theory that what is said briefly is also said weakly, is not true at all. Someone has said that "Whatever can be said in 50 words and is said in 75 is weakened by about 50 per cent." Wordiness is a favorite sin of the pulpiteer. What is needed is a concise statement of the love of God toward us and our responsibility to Him and to others. Yet our pulpits are filled with "beating around the bush," excessive wordiness, and pacification.

One of the greatest sermons ever delivered was Jesus' Sermon on the Mount and it can be repeated in five minutes. Notice the conciseness of Caesar's famous statement: "Veni, vidi, vici"—"I came, I saw, I conquered." Lincoln's Gettysburg address has only ten sentences. The entire account of the story of creation in Genesis can be read in less time than it takes to peruse the morning paper. Why? Because quality of speech is not equated with the quantity of speech. The only time quality is equated with quantity is when the speech is too long and the quality is too short.

A former editor of the *Saturday Evening Post* claimed that he always stopped a series of articles when they were at the height of their popularity. It was at this time that people were clamoring for more. This editor knew that "the point of satiation is reached very soon after the peak of popularity." Preachers, take note. Feed the sheep, but be brief enough to make them hungry for more. Remember the five B's of preaching: Be brief, brother, be brief!

Vocabulary

An important key consideration in choosing words wisely and accurately is your vocabulary. The minister of the Gospel should be ashamed if his vocabulary is limited. There is little excuse for a small vocabulary. English is the language we use to proclaim the riches of Christ and we should use it well. This demands an expanded vocabulary and a firm grasp of our mother tongue.

Dr. Charles W. Eliot, former president of Harvard University, declared: "I recognize but one mental acquisition as a necessary part of the education of a lady or gentlemen, namely, an accurate and refined use of the mother tongue." Increased ability in the use of the mother tongue means increased ability in preaching. This does not mean that every person with a great ability in using words will make a great preacher. Not at all. Great preachers are made by the Spirit of God. But it can't hurt to be able to choose words from a large vocabulary.

You can certainly understand how embarrassing it must be to stand before an audience and forget the word you were going to use. If that is the only word you know for the meaning you desire to express, you're in trouble. But if you know five synonymous words and you forget the one you wanted to use, there is no problem. Simply choose one of the remaining four words. A person with a limited vocabulary cannot do this. There is no need for this embarrassment if you build a good, well-rounded vocabulary and use it.

Words are like money; the more you have, the more you can do with them. The average unabridged dictionary contains nearly half a million words. The average college student has a recognition vocabulary of about 250,000 words. Yet by popular estimates, the average man gets along with approximately 2000 words in his vocabulary Many people consistently use as few as 300 words. Thus, the problem is acute. There is a vast unconquered wilderness in the dictionary. Few people rise above that 2000 mark as an average. There are a few exceptions. John Milton is said to have employed 11,000 words; William Shakespeare, 25,000.[8] Yet these are exceptions. Most people have a few verbs, some connectives to hold a sentence together, a handful of nouns, and a few greatly overworked adjectives.

How can one increase his vocabulary? There are several ways. First, every time you encounter a word with which you are unfamiliar, look it up immediately and write out the meaning. Use this new word for three consecutive days. Refer back to it from time to time if you have little occasion to use it regularly. Second, study the dictionary. Yes, that's what I said, study the dictionary. We've all heard jokes about someone reading the dictionary but not understanding the plot. It may sound like a tedious enterprise, but studying the dictionary is a most useful exercise. It is said that William Pitt and Lord Chatam studied the dictionary twice, every page, every word. Robert Browning read the dictionary every day. Abraham Lincoln sat in the twilight and read a dictionary as long as he could see. Do you suppose there is some connection between their effectiveness as speakers and this practice with the dictionary? There certainly is.

These men are not the exceptions but the rule. Every great writer or

---

[8]See Lester Thonssen and Howard Gilkinson, *Basic Training in Speech* (Boston: D. C. Heath and Company, 1953), p. 140.

speaker has engaged in such a practice. One of the most memorable occasions of my seminary years was hearing one of my professors, Dr. Gwyn Walters, pray in a chapel service. Dr. Walters is a Welshman. His vocabulary was not only large but very colorful. Since I was an underclassman at the time, I inquired of one of the upperclassmen as to how this man of God could speak so eloquently. The upperclassman told me that it was Dr. Walter's practice not only to study the dictionary regularly, but when he had to consult the dictionary to learn the meaning of a word, he would memorize every other word on the page. Some ministers and students could benefit from the same practice.

"How did Mark Twain develop his delightful facility with words? As a young man, he traveled all the way from Missouri to Nevada by the ponderously slow and really painful stage coach. Food—sometimes even water—had to be carried for both passengers and horses. Extra weight might have meant the difference between safety and disaster; baggage was charged for by the ounce; and yet Mark Twain carried with him a *Webster's Unabridged Dictionary* over mountain passes, across scorched deserts, and through a land infested with bandits and Indians. He wanted to make himself master of words, and with his characteristic courage and common sense, he set about doing the things necessary to bring that mastery about." [9]

Another way to increase your vocabulary is to study foreign languages. In college, seminary, and graduate school I had the opportunity to study French, German, Spanish, Latin, Greek, and Hebrew. From these languages I learned far more about English than any English course I had ever had. The reason is simple. There is a good deal of overlapping among the languages and the study of one helps in the study of another. Even if you have no opportunity to study other languages you may study the roots and prefixes or suffixes upon which English is built. By knowing the meaning of a prefix and a root you can at least make an intelligent guess at the meaning of the word. For example, if you have the word "contradict" and do not know what it means, but you do know that *contra* is a prefix meaning "against" and *dict* is a root meaning "to speak or say," then you simply put them together, and compose a plausible definition. The next pages list the most valuable roots, prefixes, and suffixes that will aid you in vocabulary development. By studying them carefully you can greatly enhance your vocabulary.

---

[9]Quoted by Dale Carnegie, p. 350.

LATIN AND GREEK AIDS
TO ENGLISH VOCABULARY

The Principal Greek Prefixes

Prefix	*Meaning*	*Example*
a-, an-	no, not; without	atheist
amphi-	both	amphibious
ana-	up	anathema
anti-	against	anticlimax
apo-	away from	apology
dia-	across, through	diagonal
eis-	into	isagogics
en-	in	endemic
epi-	upon	epidermis
ek-, ex-	from; out of	exodus
hemi-	half	hemisphere
hetero-	different	heterodox
homo-	same	homogeneous
hyper-	above	hyperacidity
hypo-	below	hypodermic
kata-	down, under	catacomb
meta-	after	metamorphosis
mono-	alone	monoplane
para-	beside	parallel
peri-	around	perimeter
pro-	before	prologue
pros-	to	prosperity
syn-, sym-	with	synthesis

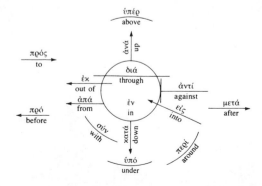

The Principal Latin Prefixes

Prefix	Meaning	Example
ab-	away from	abdicate
ad-, ac-, af-, at-	to, toward	admixture
ambi-	both	ambivalent
ante-	before	antecedent
bene-	well	benefactor
bi-	two	bivalve
circum-	around	circumnavigate
com-, con-, col-	with	competition
contra-	against	contradiction
de-	down; away	dehumanize
dis-	apart	dispossess
ex-	out of	export
in-, im-, il-, ir-	in; into	induct
inter-	between	interracial
intra-	within	intramural
mal-	bad	maladjustment
multi-	many	multicolored
non-	not	nonentity
ob-, oc-, of-, op-	toward	obtrude
per-	through	pervade
post-	after	postwar
pre-	before	precede
pro-	for; forth	produce
re-	back	reform
retro-	back	retroactive
semi-	half	semicircle
sub-, suc-, sup-	under	subterranean
super-	over	supernatural
trans-	across	transport
tri-	three	tripartite
uni-	one	unicycle
vice-	in place of	vice-president

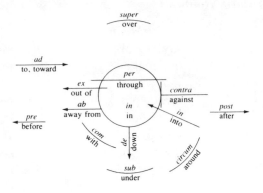

The Principal Greek Roots

Root	Meaning	Example
-anthrop-	man	anthropology
-chron-	time	chronology
-gen-	birth	genealogy
-geo-	earth	geology
-hetero-	different	heterogeneous
-bio-	life	biology
-homo-	same	homogeneous
-hydr-	water	hydroplane
-log-	word, science	monologue
-mono-	one	monogram
-morph-	form	anthropomorphic
-neo-	new	neo-evangelical
-ortho-	straight	orthopedic
-pan-	all	panorama
-phon-	sound	phonograph
-psych-	mind	psychology
-scop-	see, seeing	microscope
-tech-	skill	technology
-tele-	far	telescope

The Principal Latin Roots

Root	Meaning	Example
-dict-, -dic-	say, speak	dictation
-fac-, -fact-	do, make	manufacture
-junct-	join	junction
-pon-, -pos-	place, put	position
-scrib-, -script-	write	inscription
-spec-, -spic-	look, wee	spectator
-tract-	draw, pull	contract
-vert-, -vers-	turn	reverse
-voc-	call	vocation
-volv-	roll, turn	revolve
-mit-	send	transmit
-ven-	come	convention
-fer-	carry, bear	transfer
-vid-	see	videotape
-aud-	hear	auditory

The Principal Greek Suffixes

Suffix	Meaning	Example
-ic- -ics	pertaining to	ceramics
-ism	state	cynicism
-ist	one who	optimist
-ize	to render	eulogize
-old	like	spheroid

The Principal Latin Suffixes

Suffix	Meaning	Example
-able, -ible, -ble	capable of; fit	honorable
-ac, -ic	pertaining to	thoracic
-acious	having the nature of	pugnacious
-age	relating to	dockage
-al, -ical	having the character of	whimsical
-an	belonging to	clinician
-ance, -ence, -ancy, -ency	performs the root	endurance
-ant, -ent	one who	servant

-ar, -er, -or	pertaining to	globular
-ary	of the nature of	aviary
-ate, -ite	possessing	articulate
-action, -ition	state of	corporation
-cle	small	particle
-cy	state of being	normalcy
-ence	state of	existence
-esce	in process of	coalesce
-escent	growing	adolescent
-fic	making	soporific
-fy	to render	pacify
-ile, -il	pertaining to	percentile
-in, -ine	like	canine
-ite	one who	Manhattanite
-ity	state of being	scarcity
-ive	having nature of	pensive
-ment	a means	abridgment
-or	quality	ardor
-or	doer	speculator
-ory	pertaining to	auditory
-ose, -ous	full of	verbose
-sion, -tion	state of	tension
-tude	composed of	certitude
-ure	process	literature

Improper Grammar

You may ask, "When is it permissable to use improper grammar?" The answer is *never*. When the apostle Paul spoke of being "all things to all men," that he might "by all means save some" (I Cor. 9:22), he was not suggesting that good grammar could be abandoned when you preached to those who did not use it. Pay close attention to your grammar.

I cringe every time I hear a representative of Jesus Christ murdering the King's English. Be very careful about saying things like, "I seen him, he done it.'' Our duty to do the best we can for our Lord has already been discussed. This duty certainly extends to grammar. A man can preach a well-designed, thoroughly biblical message, and yet never reach his audience because of gross mistakes in grammar. Try to avoid grammatical mistakes, but if you make one, do not go back and call attention to it by correcting yourself. Just continue, but learn from that mistake and never do it again. An English grammar text should be within reach of your desk.

Occasionally, I have walked up to the counter of a department store and had the clerk ask me, ''May we help you?'' I've always been tempted to say, ''How many of you are there?'' This form of personal reference is very prevalent, even in the pulpit. There is a good chance that a preacher uses the editorial *we* because he doesn't want to appear conceited or proud. Yet using *we* instead of *I* doesn't alleviate that problem; you are still talking about yourself. If you are truly humble and are not trying to brag, there is nothing wrong with saying *I*.

Many ministers put on a ceremonial and sanctimonious air in the pulpit and begin to speak of themselves in a way which they would not dream of outside the pulpit. You would not say to yourself, ''It's time we go to our pulpit and preach our message.'' If you were overheard, your congregation would think you were seriously impaired.

Do not be too stiff and formal in your speaking. Remember, this is a speech or sermon you are delivering, not a book you are writing. There is a big difference. You needn't say ''need not'' or ''will not'' all the time. That is too stiff. Use contractions frequently. It will make your message flow.

It used to be the grammatical rule that a preposition was the one word with which you should never end a sentence. But times are changing and sentences generally sound better, not to mention make more sense, with the preposition at the end. Thus, it is not necessary that you frame your sentences as carefully in your mind, for if the preposition comes at the end of a sentence no one will criticize you.

An amusing incident in the life of Sir Winston Churchill was when he was once criticized by a young intellectual for ending a sentence with a preposition. Churchill hurriedly penned a note to his critic which in essence said: ''This is the sort of nonsense up with which I will not put.'' You are to be using the conversational mode and people end sentences every day with prepositions, so why shouldn't you?

Apologizing

One of the poems by Rudyard Kipling begins with the words, "There's no sense in going further."[10] This is the way many audiences feel after the opening apologetic remarks of a poor speaker. It is a serious blunder to begin a sermon or a speech with an apology. Haven't you heard speakers preface their speeches with the comment, "I'm no speaker . . . I'm not prepared to talk . . . I'm not adequate to face you . . . I don't know why the chairman asked me to speak . . . You are really scraping the bottom of the barrel when you asked me to speak" . . ., etc. Some speakers spend half their time saying that they are no speaker and the other half proving it. Such apologies are not required nor desirable. Don't undersell your speaking ability. It has a disastrous effect on your audience.

Most audiences start out with sincere respect for the speaker. If you admit in the beginning that you are no speaker or that you are not adequately prepared, that respect is destroyed. You have no basis upon which to be authoritative. Even if you say, "Thus saith the Lord," your audience won't believe you. They will fear you have not come prepared to tell them what the Lord says.

You must maintain a certain superiority over the audience while you speak. That does not mean you are superior to them. It does mean that you are the selected speaker and they are the listeners; you have some superior status, at least at the moment. Such apologetic beginnings do not convey sincerity or modesty, especially if you tell the audience you are no speaker and then you deliver a good speech. If you begin a speech by saying that you are not a speaker, you might better purposefully deliver a poor speech so that you do not make yourself a liar. To purposefully deliver the good news in a poor manner is nothing short of sin. So, you're caught in a vicious circle and the only way out is not to apologize in the beginning.

The orator Kleiser observed: "An apology is weakness on parade." How true. The speaker must operate from a position of strength, not weakness. Henry Ward Beecher never spoke disparagingly of himself or his sermons. He surmised that there were plenty of others to do it for him.

It is not necessary for speakers to make a big thing over a little cold.

---

[10]Rudyard Kipling, "The Explorer" line 1.

Don't preface your message by saying, "You'll have to excuse me this morning if I don't preach well." The cold will have little to do with it. You don't have to tell people you have a cold. After a couple of sentences they'll know and sympathize with you to a much greater degree than if you try to play on their sympathies. Your job is to preach, not apologize. Get to it. Don't waste our time with apologies. We don't want to hear them.

How to Err Gracefully

"What do I do when I make a mistake?" This question brings a variety of wrong answers. When most inexperienced speakers make a mistake they: (1) turn red; (2) stammer; (3) begin to apologize; (4) correct their mistake; and (5) lose their place in their speech. Most experienced speakers do none of the above. The reason is simple: most people do not notice the mistakes a speaker makes. Thus, by calling attention to your mistakes, in the vast majority of cases, you have for the first time made the audience aware of the fact you "goofed." If speakers would learn to only open their mouths at the right times they would be much better speakers.

Mistakes are mistakes only if people notice them. Otherwise, they are just a smile. Don't spend all your time correcting yourself. Just go on. Smile, look pleasant, but don't call attention to yourself. It is necessary that we learn from our mistakes. Philosopher Eric Hoffer says: "It is well to treasure the memories of past misfortunes; they constitute our bank of fortitude." It is not proper to simply forget past mistakes. They can help guide us from future error.

To get maximum attention, it's hard to beat a good mistake. Occasionally you will make such an error that you must correct yourself. For instance, if you immediately catch yourself saying something like, "John says in Romans . . ." then it would be wise to correct John to Paul. Such a mistake has the attention of the audience already. It is not wise, if you immediately discern that such a mistake has been made, to allow it to go uncorrected. However, changing "was" to "were" is a foolish habit if you have been talking in the plural. Such a mistake in grammar can only be compounded by calling attention to it and correcting it. Audiences are forgiving people. Allow them the pleasure of forgiving you now and again. For your sake, and the confidence of the audience in you, don't constantly correct your mistakes or make large gulping noises and facial gestures when you have erred.

4

Making Movements Meaningful

"Take care of anything awkward or affected either in your gesture, phrase, or pronunciation" —John Wesley.

"Action is eloquence, and the eyes of the ignorant are more learned than their ears" —Shakespeare.

Bodily Movement

All of us communicate nonverbally as well as verbally. This unconscious visible speech is with us every second. We constantly use bodily movement in our everyday conversation, as well as when we deliver a speech or sermon. It is a definite part of our communication system. We gesture with our eyebrows, glance at someone, shift positions in a chair—all of these actions mean something.

Every culture has its own body language. When our children learn English they also learn our Americanisms. A Frenchman both talks and walks in French. Englishmen cross their legs differently than do Americans. Sex, ethnic background, social class, personal style, and even religious beliefs tend to mold our movements. Sigmund Freud once wrote: "No mortal can keep a secret. If his lips are silent, he chatters with his fingertips; betrayal oozes out of him at every pore."

79

Nonverbal communication by bodily movement is spontaneous and cannot be totally hidden. Typical forms of nonverbal communication include: "Vocal intonation, selectively exaggerated articulation, throat-clearing, yawning, laughing, crying, decreasing and increasing volume, gesturing with arms and hands, facial expressions and changes of expression, bodily posture, speed of movement and movement pattern."[1]

A nervous speaker can smile and look perfectly calm, but just watch his hands and feet and you'll know the real story. Bodily action need not betray us however; we may use it to our advantage. Since it already communicates, let us learn to make it communicate what we want.

Cicero called this movement *sermo corporis,* "speech of the body." Movements are advantageous to the speaker in that they attract the eye of the audience and thus hold its attention. The eye instinctively follows a moving object, so a sleepy audience can often be awakened by the simple expedient of moving from one part of the platform to the other. However, continuous and aimless pacing back and forth will distract and detract from the effectiveness of the speaker's presentation. Thus, our bodily movement must be purposeful and controlled.

There are two kinds of bodily movement; that of the whole body, and that of parts of the body as they are independently used in gesturing. Technically, however, the term movement can refer only to the whole body. Bodily movement is sometimes referred to as dramatic action. Hence, when you accompany your speech with the proper action of stamping out a fire, dying, rowing a boat, etc., you are using drama.

The gesture is probably the most predominantly used body movement in stressing a point. This is undoubtedly because much dramatic action is out of place in the pulpit and gesturing is often adequate for the purpose of making the message known. This does not mean that a preacher cannot move about, in fact, he should do so, as long as it is not too frequent, too distracting, or too dramatic. He should always do his preaching, however, from the pulpit and not prancing around the platform.

---

[1]George A. Borden, Richard B. Gregg, Theodore G. Grove, *Speech Behavior and Human Interaction* (Englewood Cliffs, NJ: Prentice-Hall, Inc., 1969), p. 84.

Gestures

To gesture is as natural as to breathe. The ancient Greek authority on speaking, Xanthes, said: "Speakers who are contented just to speak do not take long to weary those that hear them." To prevent wearying the audience we must be natural and do what comes naturally via the gesture. Most who do not gesture have to force themselves not to.

A familiar story about the French philosopher/writer Voltaire concerns his preparing a young actress to appear in one of his tragedies. The multi-talented Voltaire tied the hands of the actress to her side with thread to stop any tendency toward over-gesticulation. When she began reciting the actress was calm; but soon, being carried away with her feelings, she threw her hands into the air breaking the threads. Ashamed of what she had done, the actress went to Voltaire and apologized. Voltaire simply smiled and said, "I intended you to break the fastening threads, when your enthusiasm made it irresistible." Being human, if we act in a natural manner, we must gesture. We cannot help it.

The purpose for gesturing is not simply for display. Its object is to deepen the impression you make by what you are saying. It is to heighten the message in the minds of the hearers. In John Bunyan's classic *Holy War,* you will recall that Prince Immanuel besieged all five gates in attempting to win Mansoul. That is, he appealed to all five senses, not just one. The speaker must do the same. Don't settle for the people hearing your words; make them see them as well.

Hand Gestures

There are basically two types of gestures: *descriptive* and *conceptive,* or reinforcing. Descriptive gestures are imitative. They are the gestures you use when you describe the size and shape of objects. They illustrate material objects and serve to designate form or dimension. A circular staircase would be very difficult to describe if you could not use your hands. When speaking of the height of a small boy it is only natural to hold out the hand, palm down, to indicate the boy's approximate height. To indicate the length of "the one that got away" almost always requires the two hands spaced apart with the palms facing inward. The descriptive gesture is any one which indicates, compares, or designates form, situation, or dimension. Since the possibilities are innumerable, it is impossible to catalogue descriptive gestures.

Some descriptive gestures have a bit of the conceptive element in them as well. Pointing with the index finger is a good example. To say, "Get out" is only half as forceful as saying it while pointing to the door. In such a gesture you not only indicate direction, you also back up your vocal command with the reinforcement of pointing. Placing the finger to the lips in a vertical manner is far more potent than simply saying "Shhhhhh." The shrug of a shoulder would lose much in the translation to word. Each of these gestures is descriptive, yet conceptual as well.

Conceptive gestures are gestures of impression and emphasis. They may be said to emphasize spiritual concepts in the way that descriptive gestures emphasize material concepts. They tend to reinforce the vocal. Some gestures of this type are as follows: pointing, clenching the fist, dividing, rejecting, receiving, pounding the pulpit, etc. A good speaker is one whose voice is sincere and firm, whose purpose it is to individualize his message and make you feel that he is talking directly to you, and who at the right moment points his finger directly at you. The pointing of the finger adds tremendous reinforcement to what is said. To give a feeling of great strength or determination, the speaker will want to use a clenched fist. In gesturing, this is a symbol of might.

Rejecting and receiving gestures should both be very expressive and thoroughly understandable. The placing of the palm out away from the body and a slight pushing away motion represents a rejecting gesture. For example, you may use this type of motion in illustrating or reinforcing the first half of the Biblical injunction, "Abhor that which is evil; cleave to that which is good" (Rom. 12:9). To abhor is to hate, to stay away from, to reject. Thus, indicate this by pushing away from you with your hand. "Cleave to that which is good" would call for a motion in which your palms would be facing you, pulling in toward your body. To cleave means to grab hold of, to bring to yourself. Indicate this with your hands.

Facial Gestures

There are the two principal types of gestures, descriptive and conceptual. You may have noticed that most of these gestures have had to do with the hands. This is only natural. Most gesturing is done with the hands. Quintilian said: "As to the hands, without which delivery would be mutilated and feeble, it can scarcely be said how many movements they have, when they almost equal the number of words." The hands are important, but there is one important area of gesture which most speakers totally overlook. That is the face. Many times more can be said in an expression on the face than an hour of speaking. In preparing himself for the task of speaking, the student must not forget the face.

Is it just an accident that when a photographer or an artist wants to capture the true feeling of a person that he brings his talents to bear on the subject's face? Not at all. The face is the most expressive and quickly altered part of our anatomy. Whether we like it or not, the face conveys meaning to our audience. Psychologist Albert Mehrabian has devised the following formula: total impact of a message = 7 per cent verbal + 38 per cent vocal + 55 per cent facial. If this formula is anywhere near correct, it means that as a speaker you must spend more time developing the voice of the face. The face graphically expresses our emotions and ideas.

Sincerity, or lack of it, is quickly seen in the face. We have all heard the expression, "It's written all over your face." In essence, when a speaker is addressing an audience or a minister is preaching to his congregation, what he is vocalizing is also more powerfully "written all over his face." The face can be wonderfully used in gesticulation. The wrinkles of the forehead tend to mean sincerity and concern. The smile gives a feeling of friendliness and causes a relaxed atmosphere.

Kinesics, the study of body language, has taught us much about the face. For instance, through this science we know that the eyebrow has a repertoire of twenty-three possible positions and that men use their eyebrows more than women do. A raised eyebrow can effectively aid in conveying the impression of suspicion. The face can in many ways convey the thought that your words are desperately trying to convey.

The greatest problem in facial gesturing, however, is in the lack of it. Many speakers seem to have extremely immobile faces. They have a "dead pan" look about them. They never smile, never raise their eyebrows, never gesture in any way with their faces. If you are one of these people, limber up your facial muscles. Begin to massage your face in a circular motion in front of the ears. Make a smile and then repeat it in rapid succession. Massage your temples and forehead. Do not allow the skin of the face to become strained or hard.

Practice your facial expressions in front of a mirror, but never practice them in front of your audience. Let them be natural there.

Recognize the fact that concentration tends to make many people frown. It is a natural practice. As you are concentrating on the delivery of your sermon your face will show the strain of that concentration. Be mindful of this and correct it with a pleasant expression and an occasional smile. If you don't, your audience will see your unintended frown, misinterpret it, and frown back at you. Cultivate a pleasant expression.

Eye Contact

Cicero said: "In delivery, next to the voice in effectiveness is the countenance; and this is ruled over by the eyes." The crowning feature of facial expression is eye contact with the audience. Good preaching requires good eye contact. "The late Charles Haddon Spurgeon is said to have addressed two thousand people as though he were speaking personally to one man."[2]

Read what some powerful men of God have, said on this subject: "There is power in the eye, no less than in the voice, to convey all varieties of emotion—indignation, surprise, determination, appeal" (Wilder Smith).[3] "Eye contact between preacher and listener should be as intimate and continuous as possible. This does not merely help direct the listener's attention; shades of meaning are conveyed that would otherwise be lost" (Webb B. Garrison).[4] "Don't once break eye contact with the people" (Ilion T. Jones).[5]

". . . The eyes we can in some respects control. We cannot by a volition make them blaze, or glisten, or melt; but we can always look at the hearers. And the importance of this it would be difficult to overstate. Besides the direct power which the speaker's eye has over the audience, penetrating their very soul with its glance, it is by look-

---

[2]Dwight E. Stevenson and Charles F. Diehl, *Reaching People from the Pulpit* (New York: Harper and Row, Publishers, 1958), p. 59.

[3]Wilder Smith, *Extempore Preaching* (Hartford, CT: Brown & Gross, 1884), p. 128.

[4]Webb B. Garrison, *The Preacher and His Audience* (Westwood, N.J.: Fleming H. Revell Co., 1954), p. 236.

[5]Ilion T. Jones, *Principles and Practice of Preaching* (New York: Abingdon Press, 1956), p. 167.

ing that he catches their expression of countenance, and enters into living sympathy with them'' (J. A. Broadus).[6] "Look your audience decently in the face, one after another, as we do in familiar conversation'' (John Wesley).[7]

The importance of good visual contact has been known for a long time.[8] The eye is itself "an organ of speech'' but is very frequently used improperly. Poor eye contact, not looking the audience in the eye, is usually caused by nervousness. The speaker is nervous and doesn't want to show that in his eye to the audience. Timidity is also a cause of poor eye contact. Many speakers are so timid that it is a chore for them to look you in the eye. Even when the timid person does look toward the audience, it is generally only for a very quick glance.

I knew a pastor (he now has left the pastorate after six churches in almost as many years) who never looked lower into the congregation than the chandelier. Parishioners used to twist their necks into unnatural positions simply to see what he was looking at. Since it wasn't they, they stopped listening to him.

Again, kinesics has taught us that in normal conversation, eye contact between two individuals lasts only about a second before one or both individuals look away. Not too intimate, is it? Yet the audience will stare you in the eye and you must force yourself to look into their eyes longer so that it will become natural to you. Eye contact is simply too important not to be practiced.

If you do not engage in constant eye contact with the audience they will accuse you of one of three sins. They will feel you are negative and do not want to present positive solutions to their problems; they will think you are timid, a characteristic in public speaking which is associated with cowardice; or they will think you are simply uninterested in them and are speaking, not for the purpose of communication, but for the purpose of "getting it over with." Whichever sin you are guilty of, your audience will not listen to you for long if you do not maintain visual contact with them.

---

[6]John A. Broadus, *On The Preparation and Delivery of Sermons* (Grand Rapids: Associated Publishers and Authors, Inc., 1971), p. 187.

[7]Quoted in Ross E. Price, *John Wesley on Pulpit Oratory* (Kansas City, MO: Beacon Hill Press, 1955), p. 19.

[8]See the important study recorded by Martin Cobin, "Response to Eye-Contact," *Quarterly Journal of Speech* XLVIII (December 1962), p. 418.

Characteristics of Good Gestures

It has already been mentioned that one problem with gestures is that they are suppressed. Many people do not use any gestures at all. A second problem with gestures is when they are used unwisely or wildly. Let us consider some of the characteristics of good gestures.

1. Gestures must be *natural*. Unnatural gestures are recognized immediately. Gestures should never be "laid on." You cannot plan ahead to put a certain gesture in a certain place in your speech. To do so is to be mechanical. You can imagine the embarrassment of the preacher who wrote the names of gestures in his notes at the appropriate places and as he read his Scripture he said: "Marvel not that I say unto thee, point to audience, Ye must be born again." Gestures must be natural. They must arise from within you and your expressive ability. Practice gesturing at home in front of your mirror, but never place your gestures in your sermon beforehand. You must get the natural "feel" of gesturing for the abandonment needed to be natural. This comes with experience.

2. Gestures must be *emphatic*. A halfhearted gesture is worse than none at all. Avoid meaningless gestures or artificial ones. Make each gesture a picture of the word or a reinforcement of it. Being emphatic does not mean being fast and furious. Jerky gestures only serve to confuse the audience. Also, being emphatic does not mean that you must frequently gesture with both hands. To do so would give you the appearance of Kwannon, the Oriental goddess of mercy who constantly waved her six arms. You aren't trying to get off the ground and fly, you are gesturing. Make each gesture meaningful and emphatic, not useless and halfhearted.

3. Gestures must be *varied*. As variety is the spice of life, so too the varied gesture is the spice of speech. Do not use the same gesture over and over again. As has already been quoted from Shakespeare: "Do not saw the air too much with your hand, thus, but use all gently, for in the very torrent, tempest, and (as I may say) whirlwind of passion you must acquire and beget a temperance that may give it smoothness."[9] Constant use of one gesture becomes very monotonous. Sometimes people use one gesture to such an extreme that they are remembered by it.

A survey of the American Presidents of the 60s and 70s will illus-

---

[9] *Hamlet, Prince of Denmark*, Act III, Scene 2, lines 8–16.

trate this. John F. Kennedy will always be remembered for the "pecking" motion he made into the air with his index finger. Lyndon Johnson will be remembered for his emotionless, expressionless face. Richard Nixon frequently patted his clenched right fist into the palm of his left hand or raised his arms in the double victory sign. Gerald Ford was characterized by a lack of gesturing. Jimmy Carter is remembered for his broad grin. Don't become associated with any one gesture. Avoid monotony. Vary your gestures.

4. Gestures must be *appropriate*. Your subject, your particular physique, your personality, your occasion for speaking, and most importantly, the size and nature of the audience must determine the appropriateness of gesturing. A very formal occasion, such as a funeral, worship service, or wedding ceremony generally calls for dignified gesturing. If you are short of stature you may want to use vertical gestures to give the appearance of greater height.

The greatest determining factor, however, will be the size of the room and audience. It is quite inappropriate to use large swinging gestures in a small room or before a small audience. In general, gesturing, as well as song leading, should not be greatly expansive unless you are meeting in a large convention hall or huge sanctuary. Keep fairly close to the body. But do not make small gestures in a large auditorium or they will simply get lost in the void. All things being equal, the larger the audience, the larger and unrestricted your gestures must be.

5. Gestures must be *coordinated*. Timing is very important in gesturing. Generally, the gesture should just precede the word it is to be coordinated with. Not long before, but just slightly before will allow the picture to linger longer than the word. Afterthought gestures give the appearance of being "laid on." Synchronize your verbal idea with your physical gesture. If they are not together, confusion and improper emphasis will result. Instead of being a dynamic speaker you will become a disastrous spectacle. Also, coordinate accepted areas with the direction you are pointing. Do not point down and say "heaven" or up and say "hell." Learn where objects and places are with relation to the church before you preach. Do not point to the back of the church to indicate the nearby highway that runs to the left of the church. Put your gestures together with your speech. Be coordinated as you speak.

Some *don'ts* might be helpful. Don't repeat a gesture until it becomes monotonous. Don't make quick or jerky gestures. Don't gesture with one hand only. Don't end your gestures too quickly. Sustain them for added effect. Don't be afraid to hold the gesture through an entire sentence. Don't force any gesture. Finally, don't copy the gestures of famous speakers.

The importance of positive nonverbal communication, meaningful eye contact, and timely gestures cannot be overstated. "A speaker's words may show strength, whereas his posture reveals weakness; the unsteady hand and the lack of eye contact may say more than the sentences spoken."[10]

Armed with a knowledge of the characteristics of good non-verbal communication, you should now view the gesture as the necessary accompaniment for making your meaning clear, forceful, and lasting.

Platform Manner

The speaker's platform manner is very important in the formulation of an audience's opinion of him. Is he courteous or crude? Does he participate in the congregational singing? Does he take part in those segments of the program which do not directly relate to him? Does he look like he is enjoying himself? These and a host of other questions subconsciously go through the minds of every audience. How you conduct yourself on the platform before you begin to speak may have a great bearing on the frame of mind the audience will be in. Do all you can to win their friendship and a faithful hearing even before you approach the podium or pulpit.

Related Factors

There are several related factors concerning platform manner which should be discussed. All of them are important and all mold your image before the audience. See how you measure up.

Dress

Like it or not, people judge you by the way you appear.[11] The influence of the fashion world has brought us the "anything goes"

---

[10]Thomas M. Scheidel, *Persuasive Speaking* (Glenview, ILL: Scott, Foresman and Company, 1967), p. 54.
[11]See John T. Molloy, *Dress for Success* (New York: Warner Books, 1975).

fashion. Well, anything may go, but people still will judge you by your appearance. The truth is, the first impression you make with your audience is not when you begin to speak but when you walk in the back door or onto the platform. Should we care whether or not the audience likes what we wear? If you are interested in getting your message across, you'll care. Anything may go in fashion, but it doesn't always go on the platform.

The watchword for platform dress is *appropriate*. Bear in mind that you are there to communicate a message. That is your only purpose. Always keep it in mind. Do not dress so flamboyantly that you call attention to yourself. In so doing you have distracted from your message. By the same token, do not dress so drably that people will ignore you. This works both ways. You need not be a fashionsetter, but don't detract from your message by wearing your 1949 suit either.

Good dressing involves paying attention to little things. See that you have a shine on your shoes. Make sure there is a crease in your pants. If your shirt, or blouse in the case of the ladies, is wilted or dingy, don't wear it. A crisp shirt is essential. The color is important too. In this day of flowered, frilled and fancy shirts, remember your message. Don't detract from it. Raspberry, orange, red, and chartreuse shirts are nice and add needed color to an otherwise dull appearance, but beware of wearing them in the morning worship service, to funerals, or other inappropriate occasions. White or a pastel color would be much more appropriate.

Choose your tie carefully and make sure it is tied well, tight to the neck, and centered between your collars. Ties are the first tipoff to your taste. Be appropriate. Do not call attention to yourself. Remember your message. Choose your socks very carefully. *Do not,* I repeat, do not wear white socks on the platform. Dark socks are always best, preferably black. Always wear over-the-calf socks. Nothing is quite so distracting when you cross your legs as a shiny shin showing between the top of the sock and the bottom of the cuff. Be careful also of wearing large shiny pins or lapel badges. Light striking these may flash into the eyes of the audience and distract them.

Much more could be said about dress, but the word *appropriate* is the real clue. When you are the invited speaker you may say that it's none of their business what you wear, but it is. They invited you, or they hired you as their pastor. They have an interest in you. Don't let them down. Don't let the Master down. Remember your message, that's the important thing. Do nothing and wear nothing that would get in the way of your message.

"Of course a man should keep clean. A bath Sunday morning and the use of a deodorant may be crucial to communication. And how about a man's breath? While a preacher with a twinkle in his eye said, 'Halitosis is better than no breath at all', it is clear that clean, fresh breath is a must. Toothpaste, gargle, and a breath mint will be helpful. . . . In short, avoid any offense created by poor hygiene, garlic, onions, or other odoriferous delicacies."[12]

Good grooming and proper dress have a lot to do with the way you feel. If you are neatly attired, brushed, combed, washed, and gargled, you have much greater confidence as a speaker. You know people will want to listen to what you have to say.

Dale Carnegie recounts that "when General Lee came to Appomattox Court House to surrender his army, he was immaculately attired in a new uniform and, at his side, hung a sword of extraordinary value. Grant was coatless, swordless, and wearing the shirt and trousers of a private. 'I must have contrasted very strangely', he wrote in his Memoirs, 'with a man so handsomely dressed, six feet high, and of faultless form'. The fact that he had not been appropriately attired for this historic occasion came to be one of the real regrets of Grant's life."[13]

Be appropriate and remember your message. Let nothing get in its way. There is no room in the ministry for a "Freddie the Fashion Hound," nor is there room for a "Sloppy Joe." Dress for the occasion. Do not overdress and certainly do not underdress. Do all things in moderation.

Posture

The most widespread physiological problem among teenage girls today is poor posture. Most of these girls grow into ladies with poor posture. Thankfully, some escape this fate, but some ministers have not. By posture we mean the stance of the speaker. Does he slouch? Does he look comfortable? Posture is an integral and important part of your general impression on an audience. Good posture involves the

---

[12]J. Daniel Baumann, *An Introduction to Contemporary Preaching* (Grand Rapids: Baker Book House, 1972), p. 188.

[13]Quoted in Dale Carnegie, *Public Speaking and Influencing Men in Business* (New York: Association Press, 1953), p. 166.

distribution of body weight in a poised and comfortable manner. Good posture involves the whole body. If any part of it is allowed to go out of control, all of posture is gone.

Good posture means that the body should be erect. A habitual stoop is not only unsightly but harmful to the organs of speech. It does not allow for proper breathing. Being erect does not mean that you are to look stiff. The pulpit is not a military post. Stand erect, but be relaxed.

In order to stand erect you must have a good foundation. This involves the proper use of the feet. The feet should be neither far apart like a soldier at parade rest nor close together so as to touch one another. If your feet are far apart you have no leverage. If they are close together you have no balance. Stand with the feet eight to ten inches apart, or whatever feels natural to you. One foot should be slightly ahead of the other to insure proper movement. Let the weight of your body fall on the balls of your feet, rather than on the heels. This will not only give greater movement but also prevents the possibility of "jiggling" up and down. Don't do it. You are not a jumping jack. Move, don't bounce.

One of the most common faults in posture is leaning on the pulpit. This practice of slumping down and "plopping" your weight on the pulpit is nothing but sloppy posture. It is a disgrace to the office of the ministry which you occupy. It tends to make you tired, for in leaning on the pulpit you generally stand on one foot. When only one foot has to support the entire weight of your body it becomes very tired. Thus, you have to switch to the other foot. It becomes tired and you begin a see-saw motion. Leaning on the pulpit also tends to tire the audience. If they see you stand erect with vigor and enthusiasm it will be contagious. They will sit erect and participate in your enthusiasm. However, if you lean on the pulpit, they will assume the same type of position in their seats and the whole audience will begin their own see-saw motions. Leaning on the pulpit is not only crude, it is disastrous to the comfort of all those concerned. Stand erect, you'll feel better during and after you speak.

Hands

"What shall I do with my hands?" is a common question. The answer is to relax them. Be natural with them. Let them fall to your side, palms in, when not gesturing. Or let them rest gently on the corners of the pulpit. Don't lean on them, just rest them. Don't desperately clutch the pulpit; be natural.

Many speakers feel extremely self-conscious about their hands. The Greeks have an ingenious device for keeping the hands busy while they talk. They can be seen fingering what looks to be a string of rosary beads but are in fact conversation beads. They are carried for the express purpose of giving the hands something to do during conversation. But you cannot carry conversation beads into the pulpit and you wouldn't want to anyway. Hands are a valuable asset to a speaker, not a liability. You must, however, be careful where you place your hands. For instance, to place the hands on the hips gives a sense of defiance which you do not want to portray. To place your hands around behind the hips tends to give the idea that you have a sore back. Hanging the hands on the lapel of your coat gives the impression of pride. To place the hands in the pockets of your coat is inelegant and to put them in the pockets of your trousers is crude. To play with change in your pocket is very distracting to your audience. The best thing to do about your hands is to forget them.

Walking

On Walking to the Pulpit. Because the way you approach the pulpit tells the audience something about you, tell them something good. Walk briskly but do not run. I have a close pastor friend who always runs to the pulpit. This may be just a habit; perhaps it is to impress the congregation with his eagerness to get into the message. Whatever the reason, it is wrong to run to the pulpit. It does not give the dignity demanded by approaching the Word of God. Remember, walk, don't run. Also, do not tiptoe forward timidly as if you were afraid of the audience. You need not be afraid. On the other hand, don't swagger like a bully or pompously strut with artificial dignity. The idea is to simply walk to the pulpit, but it is surprising how many speakers have not mastered this art.

On Arriving at the Pulpit. Do not begin talking before you get to the pulpit. Don't rush into your sermon or speech. To do so would mean that your first and very important statement will go unheard or unheeded by the audience. Take time to get comfortable in your stance. Get the "feel" of the pulpit. Look over your audience. Smile and make them feel at home. It is *now* when you either win or lose your listeners. Don't rush. Timing is tremendously important.

Don't take so long that your audience gets the impression you have forgotten what to say or are suffering from stage fright. Pause, breathe deeply, then begin.

On Walking from the Pulpit. When you are finished speaking, the temptation is to rush off. Yield not to temptation. Don't rush away too abruptly. If you do, your audience will get the impression that you are saying, "Whew! I'm glad that's over with." A good, forceful speech or sermon can be ruined by an untimely exit. I attended a church service once where a soloist sang so beautifully that he deeply moved the audience. This spell did not last long, however, for he tripped down the steps leading from the platform. Be careful how you leave the pulpit. After you have finished, pause, allow what you have said to penetrate the minds of the audience, then step down and walk firmly back to your seat. Don't walk pompously as a victor, but humbly as a servant.

Sitting

Sitting down is an art that has not been mastered by many speakers. Some who must sit on the platform ease into their chair while others appear like a camel painfully trying to come to his knees or a pig wallowing in the mire. The object of sitting is to sit. It should be done as painlessly and inconspicuously as possible.

The first prerequisite of proper sitting is to know where the chair is. That may sound facetious, but it is true. A poor sitter doesn't know where his chair is and thus he begins groping behind himself for something solid. When you approach the chair, know your distance from it. It will make sitting much easier.

A man who knows how to sit not only knows his distance from the chair but when he sits he feels the chair against the back of his legs. Until he feels the chair strike the back of his legs, he does not sit. Then, when he is sure the chair is there, he holds his body erect from the waist up, bends at the waist and at the knees, and eases himself into his chair with complete control of his body.

Sitting in a pulpit or platform chair requires added caution. Sometimes pulpit chairs seemingly have no bottom. It is embarrassing for a visiting speaker to sit in the pulpit chair that "sits" about six inches lower than he expected. Usually he tries unsuccessfully to suppress a look of terror, a blood-curdling scream, and an unrehearsed juggling act of all that he has in his hands.

If you are asked to sit in such a chair, and you have not had opportunity to try it out beforehand, sink gently into the chair, fully aware that the bottom may be lower than you think. Don't be caught off guard.

Crossing the legs for gentlemen is natural. If you do cross your legs,

cross them at the knee. Do not put your ankle on top of your knee. This
is unacceptable platform behavior. Ladies should refrain from crossing
their legs on the platform.

Much concern over sitting and standing can be abolished with a few
advance questions before coming to the platform. If you are a visiting
speaker, ask the pastor in which chair you will sit. This will save
conspicuous glances when you arrive at the platform. Then, do not sit
until the pastor does or everyone is on the platform that should be. Be
seated together. It will avoid your being a sore thumb if you sit and
everyone else is standing.

Platform "Junk"

Too much trumpery on the platform tends to clutter both the platform and the minds and eyes of the audience. Too much embellishment
tends to take the audience's eye from the speaker. Make your platform
like your presentation—simple. Remember your message. Let nothing
get in its way. If you are not speaking in a church and the platform is
cluttered with maps, banners, tables, stacked chairs, and other
paraphernalia, have all this "junk" removed before the beginning of
the program. Fire halls, auditoriums, lodges, etc. all tend to have this
type of distraction on the platform. Don't put up with it. Have it
removed.

Platform Lighting

A final consideration of platform manner is the necessity that people
see your platform manner. All the good manners in the world are lost if
the platform is so dimly lighted that the audience cannot see you.
Again, if you have control over the lighting, see that there is a light on
your face. This means a light from above and below. One or the other
alone will cast a shadow on your face and all your facial gestures will
be lost. People want to see who is speaking; they want to see your face.
Make sure the lighting is such that they can. Let your platform manner
be proper, fitting, and seen.

Fright

Perhaps the most devastating problem for the beginning speech student is the problem of speech fright, sometimes called stage fright.

Studies at various colleges revealed that 60 to 76 percent of the students were bothered by fright or nervousness when they spoke. Thirty-five percent said it was a severe problem with them.[14] If all the students were honest in their answers, the percentages would probably be higher. *The Book of Lists,* in its section entitled "The 14 Worst Human Fears," places *speaking before a group* at the top of the list.[15]

Much study has been done on speech fright because "there's a lot of that going around." It is reassuring to know that if you suffer from speech fright you are in good company. Abraham Lincoln said that he never lost his stage fright. He once observed: "I find speaking here in the House of Representatives and elsewhere about the same thing. I was about as badly scared, and no worse, as I am when I speak in court." Although William Jennings Bryan became a veteran orator, he admitted that when he began his knees actually knocked together. Mark Twain recalls that the first time he stood up to speak his mouth seemed as if it was filled with cotton and his pulse was speeding for some prize cup. Even the immortal orator Cicero claimed that all public speaking of any real merit was characterized by nervousness. Yet God directed the Apostle Paul: "Be not afraid, but speak" (Acts 18:9) and thus an investigation of speech fright is in order even if some great speakers are "in the same boat" as we are.

Does your hand quiver, mouth dry, stomach churn, knees knock, voice shake? If they do, you have all the symptoms of speech fright. Your mouth becomes so dry that you are nearly unable to speak. Your heart begins to beat abnormally and a sinking, churning feeling takes over in your stomach so that you feel like there really are butterflies in there. Your words become twisted and you find yourself saying things like "Mood Gorning, Gadies and Lentlemen." Such observable behavior patterns are reported in a study by Theodore Clevenger, Jr. and Thomas R. King.[16] They suggest three general factors or categories of symptoms:

---

[14]A. D. Baird and F. H. Knower, *General Speech* (New York: McGraw-Hill Book Company, 1949), p. 183.

[15]David Wallechinsky, Irving Wallace and Amy Wallace, *The Book of Lists* (New York: Bantam Books, 1977), p. 469.

[16]Theodore Clevenger, Jr. and Thomas R. King, "A Factor Analysis of the Visible Symptoms of Stage Fright," *Speech Monographs,* XXCIII, No. 4 (November, 1961), p. 296.

Fidgetiness	Inhibition	Autonomia
1. Shuffles feet	1. Deadpan	1. Moistens lips
2. Sways	2. Knees tremble	2. Plays with some-
3. Swings arms	3. Hands in pocket	thing
4. Arms stiff	4. Face pale	3. Blushes
5. Lacks eye contact	5. Returns to seat	4. Breathes heavily
6. Paces back and	while speaking	5. Swallows repeat-
forth	6. Tense face	edly
	7. Hands tremble	

There are several things which must be realized about speech fright.

1. Every speaker experiences it at the beginning of his speech or sermon. This should not discourage but encourage you. When you are relaxed your body has a certain level of what physiologists call *muscle tonus*. This is the level of activity of the muscles, the natural tension of the body. When you stand to speak, the tension of the body builds and the tonus get higher. You literally become more alive because the muscle tonus is higher. If this were not the case, you would be as dead in the pulpit as you are when you are sleeping. Therefore, some tension is not only good but necessary.

2. You should recognize that the tension which mounts before you stand to speak hits a peak when you step to the podium or pulpit. It always subsides after a few minutes and you feel more natural again. This doesn't mean you become dead. But it does mean that the muscle tonus has done its job; it has prepared you to enliven your speech which would certainly be dull and uninteresting if it were not for the nervous tensions which build beforehand.

3. You will always experience nervous tension to some degree as you speak. You never completely outgrow this nervousness because it stems from a feeling of failure. For the reasons mentioned in number two, it is a good thing we do not outgrow it. Some speakers look extremely calm. Many times they are. But other times they only appear calm for they are either hiding their nervousness or are using it wisely. If they are hiding it you will soon know, for they can't hide it forever. With experience in public speaking you will come to appreciate the natural nervousness that you have.

Reducing Tension

The question is: "What do I do with my excess tension and nervousness?" Well, you've already taken the first step by reading this far in

Prescription for Preaching. In his article, "Some Effects on Stage Fright of a Course in Speech," E. Henrikson discovered that students taking a speech course improved greatly in the ability to discard excess fright.[17] On a ten-point scale of speech fright intensity, Henrikson discovered that at the end of the speech course the student made an average gain in confidence of 6.67 points. A gain of 6.67 out of 10 isn't bad at all. Hence, by gaining understanding and experience through this study you have made great inroads into conquering fright.

Tension while speaking may be reduced by allowing tension to reach a fever pitch just before you rise to speak. Don't suppress your fears. Allow tension to build. It can only go so far and then begins to retreat. Allow it to reach its zenith before you stand. Then, after you begin speaking, several things may be done to relieve your tension.

First, be physically active while you speak. Actual physical movement tends to bring down tension. You are releasing and burning excess energy which your body has provided. The waving of the hand in gesturing, the stepping to the side of the pulpit to emphasize a point, the stepping back to pause, etc., all help you relieve tension. Also, gripping the podium or pulpit tightly once or twice will help to drain excess energy from your hands and keep them from shaking. Clinch hard and then let go.

Secondly, the use of any visual aid will benefit the drain of excess energy. Visual aids are valuable in themselves for their role in aiding the learning process, but they are just as valuable in providing something for the hands to do and controlling the emotions.[18] When you walk to a chalkboard and pick up the chalk and begin to write you have been physically active and have drained tensions as well as visualized something on the board. When you hold up an object to demonstrate it you tend to forget about yourself and concentrate only on the object. Thus, your nervousness leaves. A pastor does not frequently have opportunity to use visual aids, but he does have opportunity to gesture and use himself as a visual aid. By so moving, tensions are dispersed.

Swallow, breathe deeply, walk briskly to the pulpit, redirect the attention of your mind to something less "scary" as you arrive at the

---

[17]E. Henrikson, "Some Effects on Stage Fright of a Course in Speech," *Quarterly Journal of Speech*, XXIX, No. 4 (December, 1943), p. 491.

[18]An interesting treatment of the use of visuals in preaching is presented in a Master of Theology thesis by Laban Samuel Magbee presented to the Union Theological Seminary (Richmond, Virginia, May 1961) entitled, *Psychological and Biblical Basis of Visual Imagination in Preaching*.

pulpit, and you will be able to lick the problem of excess nervousness even before you begin to speak. Move about while speaking and you will continue the process of winning the battle over emotions.

Blanking Out

"What do I do if I blank out completely?" Well, don't cry. It happens to many speakers. To come apart simply because you have blanked out is a cardinal sin among public speakers. You probably have seen those of the junior church giving their speeches on Christmas or Children's Day. What do they do when they blank out? After making a funny face, they instinctively repeat the last line they do remember. You may do the same. By reviewing you may get some clue as to the general direction in which you were going when you blanked out.

Another suggestion is when you cannot think of what to say, simply summarize. By doing this you have time to remember what you have forgotten or have time to prepare something else. You may even quote Scripture if it is appropriate to the occasion and your general theme. However, do not be as the young pastor at his first wedding; when he blanked out and recalled the instruction to quote Scripture, he could but remember one verse: "Father, forgive them; for they know not what they do."

Whatever you do when you blank out, don't panic. Remain calm and try to remember where you were or where you were going. This is where it helps to have a good background of knowledge on your subject and a good, rich vocabulary.

Fear is the lack of two things: confidence and knowledge. In his book, *The Mind in the Making,* Robinson says, "Fear is begotten of ignorance and uncertainty." Abraham Lincoln once said, "I believe I shall never be old enough to speak without embarrassment when I have nothing to talk about." The greatest help in overcoming fear is a thorough knowledge of your subject. A certain amount of fear comes to you naturally, but that excess fear is quickly gone when you know the material to be presented. If you lack confidence in yourself or your message it will show up in the form of fear. Be confident.

5

The Speaker
and His Audience

"There is nothing more rare among men than a perfect orator. There is requisite to the orator the acuteness of the logician, the subtlety of the philosopher, the skillful harmony, almost, of the poet, the memory of a lawyer, the tragedian's voice, and the gesticulation of the most finished actors" —Cicero

"Whatever is in the sermon must be in the preacher first; clearness, logicalness, vivacity, earnestness must be personal qualities in him before they are qualities of thought and language in what he utters" —Phillips Brooks

St. Augustine once declared: "Shall I, as a Christian, be content to pursue the religious quest as a private hobby, and to develop my own spiritual life; or shall I concern myself personally for those outside, and take upon my heart deliberately the whole world's need for Christ? What I live by, I impart."

Apart from the Spirit of God Himself, and the Word of God, the most important element in the communication of the Gospel is the communicator himself—the preacher. You, pastor, are the greatest single human determinant to the success of the Gospel. You are the conductor of the heat of the Sun of Righteousness to a cold, cold world. You are the speaker, God's speaker. You had better be a good one.

The Marks of a Good Speaker

There are certain distinctive characteristics that are possessed by every good speaker. Some of these characteristics are inherent in a good speaker; others can be cultivated. Let's note seven marks of a good speaker.

Personality

Outside of preparation, personality is probably the most important human factor in good preaching. Notice that I said it is the most important *human* factor. Without divine enabling there is no such thing as good preaching. Yet one's personality does play an important role in successful speaking.

The Carnegie Institute of Technology once gave intelligence tests to one hundred prominent businessmen. On the basis of the results the Institute declared that a man's personality contributes more significantly to his business success than does superior intelligence.

A man's personality is, to a large extent, determined before his birth. Granted, sometimes his later environment molds his personality, but generally a man's personality is difficult to alter or improve. Personality is the whole combination of the speaker's being: his spiritual, physical, mental, social make-up. It involves his traits and tendencies, his temperament and his training, his mind and his manner. It is a hard thing to describe, but for a speaker it is extremely desirable to have a good personality.

Integrity

Nearly nineteen hundred years ago the famous orator Quintilian said that a good speaker must first of all be a good man. "How good we are as preachers depends—not altogether but (make no mistake!) primarily—on how good we are as men."[1] The preacher must be

---

[1]John Knox, *The Integrity of Preaching* (New York: Abingdon Press, 1957), p. 59.

intelligent and observant, but more than anything else he must be a man of integrity. In that people judge your message as much by what you are as by what you say, it is foundational that you have integrity of character. This is what the classical writers referred to as "ethical persuasion." People will listen to a man who is honest and sincere, who believes in what he preaches and whose life is consistent with what he preaches. Guard your integrity.

Buffon said: "The style is the man." If you adopt someone else's style, you have lost your integrity and have become another man. Be honest; be yourself. Dr. Alexander Whyte exclaimed: "We are too formal, we have too much starch in our soul. Starch is more deadly than sin. Your soul may be saved from sin, but scarcely from starch." Your own individuality and integrity as a person are things that will put sincerity in your speaking. Integrity is a most precious possession. Cherish it and be yourself. "A good name is rather to be chosen than great riches...." (Prov. 22:1).

Imagination

Napoleon said: "The men of imagination rule the world." It takes a certain amount of imagination to put together an interesting sermon. It takes imagination to deliver it in an interesting manner. To put yourself in the biblical writer's position takes a "holy imagination." By use of the imagination we can touch the feelings of our listeners, and ourselves gain a clearer visualized image of the message of God's Word.

"It is possible for the homilist to conjure up mental images which may add greatly to the effectiveness of a discussion. Such ideas will create an element of originality and surprise and add a fresh approach to the treatment of a subject. The use of the imagination in a sermon can therefore become a valuable ally to the preacher.... Two basic rules must always be applied, however, in its use; first, it must be exercised in moderation, and second, it should always be used with good taste; that is to say, we must avoid that which may be coarse or unrefined."[2]

Earnestness

Charles Haddon Spurgeon in lecturing his students said: "If I were asked, What in a Christian minister is the most essential quality for

---

[2]James Braga, *How to Prepare Bible Messages* (Portland, OR: Multnomah Press, 1969), pp. 139–140.

securing success in winning souls for Christ? I should reply, 'earnestness': and if I were asked a second or a third time, I should not vary the
answer, for personal observation drives me to the conclusion that, as a
rule, real success is proportionate to the preacher's earnestness."[3]

God has given us a great task. We must be earnest in our preparation
for that task. We must be earnest in study, never allowing ourselves to
take cheap shortcuts. We must be earnest in our speaking, seeing that
we do all we can to enable our hearers to understand the message.

Enthusiasm

Ralph Waldo Emerson noted: "Nothing great was ever achieved
without enthusiasm." The Gospel message will never be totally effective until this generation gets enthused about it. That was the secret of
the first-century church. They had God in them—*entheos*—from the
Greek "God in you." Enthusiasm is zeal. Zeal is an ardent devotion to
a task.

A little boy was selling post cards for ten cents each when he came
to a house, knocked on the door and explained to the lady of the house
that he was selling post cards to raise one million dollars for the church
missionary fund. The lady smiled and said: "That's a lot of money. Do
you think you can raise it all by yourself?" "No," replied the boy, "I
have another boy helping me." That is zeal, taking on all odds for the
accomplishment of the task.

The counsel of a great preacher with regard to earnestness is this. In
his book *The Reformed Pastor,* Richard Baxter wrote: "Whatever you
do, let the people see that you are in good earnest. . . . How few
ministers do preach with all their might. . . . Alas! we speak so drow-
sily or gently, that sleeping sinners cannot hear. The blow falls so light
that hard-hearted persons cannot feel it. . . . O Sirs, how plainly, how
closely and earnestly should we deliver a message of such nature as
ours is, when the everlasting life or death of men is concerned in
it. . . . What! speak coldly for God and for men's salvation? . . . Such a
work as preaching for men's salvation should be done with all our
might—that the people can feel us preach when they hear us."[4]

---

[3]Charles Haddon Spurgeon, *Lectures to My Students* Lecture VIII (Grand Rapids:
Associated Publishers and Authors, 1971), p. 145.
[4]Richard Baxter, *The Reformed Pastor* (London: Epworth Press, 1950), pp.
145, 106.

Enthusiasm must have a specific goal to which we may direct our zeal. Historian Arnold Toynbee once said: "Apathy can only be overcome by enthusiasm, and enthusiasm can only be aroused by two things: first, an ideal that takes the imagination by storm; second, a definite, intelligible plan for carrying that ideal into practice." The Word of God provides both the ideal (the salvation of lost souls) and the intelligible plan ("Come unto me . . . and I will give you rest.") What the Gospel now needs is preachers with genuine enthusiasm.

Concern

A good speaker does not perform before his audience; he ministers to them. The pulpit or podium is the place to meet the needs of the audience. People today are hurting, they are troubled. R. W. Dale advises: "People want to be comforted. . . . They need consolation— really need it, and so not merely long for it."[5] The preacher of the Gospel cannot be oblivious to the needs of his people. He must know his congregation as thoroughly as he knows himself. A good speaker researches the needs of the audience and then strives to alleviate those needs. He is concerned about the welfare of his audience, as he is of the welfare of the race.

Reproof, exhortation, and instruction are all a part of the preacher's responsibilities to his audience. But these do not exhaust his responsibilities. Chad Walsh once said: "The true function of a preacher is to disturb the comfortable and comfort the disturbed."[6] A good speaker never forgets this last injunction. Good preachers always remember the hurts of the world and are concerned that their message always include Jesus' invitation, "Come unto me, all ye that labor and are heavy laden, and I will give you rest" (Matt. 11:28).

Phillips Brooks' advice to preachers was: "There is nothing better in a clergyman's life than to feel constantly that through his congregation he is getting at his race. . . . Three rules seem to have in them the practical sum of the whole matter. . . . First, have as few congregations as you can. Second, know your congregation as thoroughly as you can. Third, know your congregation so largely and deeply that in knowing it you shall know humanity."[7]

---

[5]R. W. Dale, *The Preacher, His Life and Work* (Garden City, N.Y.: Doubleday, 1929), p. 107.

[6]Chad Walsh, *Campus Gods on Trial* (New York: Macmillan, 1953), p. 95.

[7]Phillips Brooks, *On Preaching* (New York: The Seabury Press, 1964), p. 190.

Persistence

"Much good work is lost for the lack of a little more"—E. H. Harriman. "Victory is will"—Napoleon. "Never despair, but, if you do, work on in despair"—Edmund Burke. Good speakers are frequent failures, especially when they are just beginning. Failure is no reason to quit. As Napoleon said, victory is will. A will to succeed is half the battle.

There once was a young man who was a candidate for the legislature in 1832. He lost. He won in 1834 but served only one term. He wasn't even renominated by his own party. He campaigned for Zachary Taylor for President of the United States in hopes that Taylor would appoint him Commissioner of the General Land Office. He didn't. He returned to his law practice. In 1854 he again ran for the state legislature and won but he soon resigned in hopes that the new Anti-Nebraska party would support him for the Senate. They didn't. In 1856 he was nominated for Vice President of the United States. He lost. In 1858 he ran for the U.S. Senate. He lost again. In 1860 he was nominated for the presidency as a "favorite son" from the state of Illinois. Later that year Abraham Lincoln was elected the sixteenth President of the United States.

Persistence pays. Never allow failures as a speaker to defeat you. Let us learn from them, but realize that God has a place for each of us in His vineyard.

The Speaker's Audience

To gain and hold the attention of an audience for any length of time requires no less skill than to pitch a no-hit, no-run baseball game. People just will not listen for a very long time to one speaker and if they do, their retention of what is said is very small. One of the greatest shocks in my pastoral ministry was the day I asked many of my parishioners at the door what my sermon was about that morning. No one could tell me. I had just finished preaching five minutes before and no one knew what I said. It was that day that I decided something had to be done to increase the "staying power" of my messages.

Psychologists tell us that an audience will usually forget 95 percent of what they hear. This means that your congregation will only remember about 5 percent of what you say. That's a pretty poor batting average.

The reasons that our congregations retain so little of what is said are, of course, legion. Listening is a difficult process, even under the most favorable conditions.

One factor is that human beings can comprehend speech at more than 300 words per minute without a significant loss in understanding. We generally speak about half that speed. Thus, the lag between speaking speed and listening speed contributes greatly to a wandering mind. Another reason that audiences do not retain much of what the speaker says is that the speaker is unclear or overcomplicated. We have already mentioned some remedies for these situations. Sometimes a speaker is just plain boring and the audience will not listen to him. The reasons are endless.

Whatever the case, we are concerned in this study with communication, particularly that of the Gospel. Since communication is the meeting of meanings and since you are attempting to get your message across to the listener, anything which disrupts the communication process must be weeded out.

Communication: A Circular Response

In order for the student to understand why he is not being received by his audience it is important for him to understand the fundamental nature of communication. James T. Cleland likens it to (in baseball terminology) the "homiletical battery" with the speaker (pitcher) hurling words to the audience (catcher).[8] But communication is more than that. It is a two-way street. There is a chain of events which must be completed for communication to take place. If that chain is broken anywhere, communication will break down and the message will be lost. Communication is a circular response and is not complete until, using Cleland's analogy, the catcher throws the ball back to the pitcher.

Robert S. Goyer explains the circular response as having five essential ingredients: generator, stimuli, projection, perceiver, and discriminative response. Goyer maintains that communication is dyadic

---

[8]James T. Cleland, *Preaching to Be Understood* (New York: Abingdon Press, 1965), p. 101 ff.

and illustrates this through the equation: P.R.M./G.R.I. = 1 (perceiver's response made over generator's response intended) equals the completion of communication when commonality of meaning is achieved.[9]

It is the duty of every speaker to do all he can to see that the circular response is completed. Since there is a continuous interaction between speaker and receiver it will be impossible for the speaker to completely control the communicative process. But he must do what he can to stimulate it.

A diagram of the circular response to a speech would appear as follows:

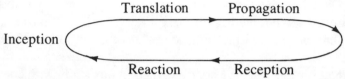

Translation   Propagation

Inception

Reaction   Reception

1. The first step is the inception of an idea in the mind of the speaker. He may have received that idea through observation, reading, listening to others, or illumination by the Spirit of God. Where he received the idea is of no concern now. The circular response begins with an idea that the speaker wants to transmit to others.

2. Once the idea is born, the speaker must translate it into language symbols of some kind: words, phrases, or sentences. Thus far these symbols are but mental concepts since they have not yet emerged from the mind of the speaker.

3. These mental symbols are made audible by nerve impulses from the central nervous system actuating the muscles of the lungs, the larnyx, jaw, tongue, lips, all the elements of speech.

4. These muscles react in a coordinated manner to produce sounds that are recognized as acceptable in speech. No longer are the symbols mental concepts but they are actual disturbances in the molecules of air surrounding the speaker.

5. As the air is disturbed, wave patterns are produced which carry the sound to the eardrums of the listener. This is accomplished by the bumping of air particles and the subsequent transmission of sound over the distance from the speaker's mouth to the listener's ear.[10]

---

[9]Robert S. Goyer, "An Inclusive Theory of Communicative Process," Western Speech Association 40th Annual Convention, San Diego, CA, November 25, 1969.

[10]It is important for the speaker to remember that listening is the other half of communication. One study indicates that the average person spends 9 percent of his

6. When the wave patterns of air reach the ear of the listener, communication is not yet complete. Here the waves of compressed and rarefied air are again translated into nerve impulses.

7. These impulses are then carried to the brain by the auditory nerve. When this is completed the listener has "heard" the sounds made by the speaker but has not yet understood these sounds.

8. The listener must now recognize these nerve impulses as symbols of language and understand that what he hears are, in fact, words and sentences.

9. After receiving these symbols and recognizing them as words and sentences, it is the duty of the listener to attach the proper meaning to these series of symbols.

10. Finally, the listener must react to what he has heard and understood. This reaction may take the form of a smile, a frown, questions, comments, etc.[11] At this point, when the listener reacts, the speaker observes his reaction and responds to that reaction. It is not until the speaker responds to the "feedback" of the listener that the circular response and communication itself are complete.

The process of communication is complete only when these ten steps have occurred. Once complete, this circular response is repeated. From this description of the numerous events which must take place before communication is complete, it is easily understood how a break or distortion anywhere along this chain of events can cause a breakdown. One of the great barriers to communication is the tendency of the audience to hear only what they wish to hear. Consequently, they believe what they want to believe regardless of what the speaker says. This is called autistic thinking, i.e. hearing what you want to hear. Communication cannot be completed when the listener has a closed mind. Hence, for the preacher of the Word, it is important to realize that sometimes communication can only be accomplished through supernatural aid. Until the Spirit of God has enlightened the minds of the audience, no matter how well you preach, they will not be as the Ephesians, "the eyes of your understanding being enlightened; that ye may know what is the hope of his calling, and what the riches of the glory of his inheritance in the saints" (Eph. 1:18).

---

waking hours writing, 16 percent reading, 30 percent speaking, but a full 45 percent listening. See Paul T. Rankin, "Listening Ability," *Chicago Schools Journal*, January 1930, pp. 177–179.

[11]Erwin P. Bettinghaus, *Persuasive Communication* (New York: Holt, Rinehart and Winston, Inc., 1968), p. 207.

Audience Disturbances

When disturbances occur and communication cannot be completed because of them, it is absolutely necessary that you rely on the Spirit of God to see you through. The list of possible disturbances is endless. It is difficult to categorize them as tolerable and intolerable. There are many borderline disturbances, such as the crying of a baby or coughing, which can be overlooked if they soon cease. However, some disturbances are so problematic that they cannot be ignored. Laughing or giggling, whispering loudly, misbehavior, and snoring cannot be overlooked. To ignore such rudeness is disaster for it will become contagious and habitual. It must be dealt with swiftly and effectively. The pastor is fortunate who has a wise usher who can deal with such situations as they arise. Sometimes in extreme cases a rude individual has to be removed from the auditorium. If this happens, don't be embarrassed. It is scriptural to let everything be done decently and in order, and that includes the church service.

Bible teacher David Cornell once told me of a great Irish preacher friend of his family who was being heckled by an old infidel in the balcony. After tolerating the infidel's insults as long as he could, this burly preacher, who had been a sailor before entering the ministry, calmly walked back the aisle, up the stairway to the balcony, grabbed the man, and bodily threw him out of the auditorium. As the preacher walked back the aisle to again take his place at the pulpit, a voice from the back of the room was heard to say, "Would Jesus have done that?" The burly preacher whirled around and without a moment's hesitation said, "No, He wouldn't have. He would have parted the devil from the man and cleansed the man; but since I couldn't separate them, I threw them both out."

Dealing with Disturbances

Two suggestions should be made in dealing with disturbances. First, try to tactfully work the disturbance into your sermon. By so doing you may embarrass a rude person into silence without embarrassing the whole audience. For instance, suppose you are preaching on the effects of sin on mankind and some teenagers are whispering in the back of the church. You are enumerating a catalogue of sins. Just include the disturbance by saying "Sin ranges from murder and theft, on the one hand, to whispering in church on the other hand." The guilty parties are embarrassed without your calling attention to the disturbance.

Secondly, if you must publicly mention a disturbance, stopping in the middle of your message, it is imperative that you do it tactfully. An occasional public reprimand is accepted by the audience if it is done properly. Remember your message. Let nothing get in its way, whether it be a disturbance or your correction of that disturbance. Above all, under no circumstances allow your anger to be shown. Nothing destroys a preacher as fast as losing his "cool" when he must speak to someone in the audience. Don't allow this to happen to you. Be firm but tactful. Don't be angry.

Preventing Disturbance

There are several things you can do to alleviate the problem of disturbances and make for better speaking conditions. You can group your audience if the church is not filled. Henry Ward Beecher said in his Yale lectures on preaching:

> People often say, 'Do you not think it is much more inspiring to speak to a large audience than a small one? No, I say; I can speak just as well to twelve persons as to a thousand, provided those twelve are crowded around me and close together, so that they can touch each other. But even a thousand people with four feet of space between every two of them, would be just the same as an empty room. . . . Crowd your audience together and you will set them off with half the effort.[12]

It is very difficult to speak effectively if everyone is in the back of the auditorium or scattered around. This makes for the possibility of greater disturbances; men and women in a large auditorium with few people around them tend to gain greater individuality, and with increased individuality comes increased disturbance. Also, if the audience is grouped together, they tend to lose some of their individuality and are more easily swayed by the speaker. An audience grouped together will respond in greater fashion. They will laugh when they are supposed to, sing with greater gusto, give more favorable "feedback"

---

[12]Henry Ward Beecher, *Yale Lectures on Preaching* (New York: Fords, Howard & Hulbert, 1887), p. 73.

to the speaker, and be more deeply moved by his words. It is much easier to get people to act as a body than it is to get them to act singly. Use this to your advantage. Cut down on disturbances and increase your effectiveness as a speaker by grouping your audience.

Something else you may do to prevent audience disturbance is to see that their environment is conducive to easy listening. Make sure that lights are not shining in their eyes. Attempt to have comfortable seats without being too comfortable which might aid the sleeping process. Make sure they can hear you properly, as well as see you properly. Most importantly, see that the air and temperature of the room are proper. The air must be fresh. If it is stale, so will be your message. You may be an extremely effective speaker, but if the air in the auditorium is musty or stale, your effectiveness will be reduced by half. See that the windows are opened enough to get the air moving.

For years I have taught classes at 7:00 A.M. Winter or summer, the first thing I always do upon entering the room is open the windows to allow the chilly morning air to flow through. This retards the tendency students have to believe that their being up and in class at that hour is just a bad dream. The brisk air awakens them and makes their minds alert. When their "feedback" indicates to me that this has been accomplished I then lower the windows.

It is said that for fourteen years Major James B. Pond traveled all over the United States and Canada as manager for Henry Ward Beecher, the famous Brooklyn preacher. Major Pond would arrive at the auditorium before the audience and rigorously inspect the lighting, seating, temperature, and ventilation of the room. If this old army officer found the room to be too warm or the air dead and could not get the windows open, he would hurl books through them smashing them open. This may be somewhat extreme, but it should indicate the importance of getting the air of an auditorium moving. Spurgeon once said: "The next best thing to the grace of God for a preacher is oxygen." Make sure there is plenty of it moving around in the auditorium in which you speak.

Most auditoriums today are air conditioned and the flow of air is automatically controlled. Yet the wise speaker carefully watches the "feedback" from his audience. He instructs his ushers or assistants to watch for church bulletins being used as fans, ladies putting on sweaters, or men taking off coats. All of these are clues to the improper flow of air.

Loving Your Audience

The most important element in speaking is not physical or mental but spiritual. It does not take an audience long, however, to determine whether or not you are speaking from a sincere heart. As soon as they detect that you are not, disturbances begin and communication ends. It is essential that a speaker have a genuine love for his audience. He cannot function well without it.

When a championship football team was asked why they won so many games the quarterback replied: "It's because we love one another." Without love there is no harmony. Without love there is no desire to do your best. A speaker will not endure the rigorous hours of preparation and practice needed to present an excellent speech if he does not love his audience. Jesus Christ is the prime example of a speaker who loved his audience. When His love was seen the audience was moved and stirred. We should exhibit that same type of love. As Dale Carnegie says: "If you want a splendid text on public speaking, why not read your New Testament?"

Love for an audience engenders respect for them. A speaker dare not "talk down" to his audience, particularly if his education exceeds theirs. Love puts men on the same plane. The speaker must make the audience feel that he is talking to them personally. He is not talking at them, but speaking with them. They are vital to him. A speaker that does not recognize the importance of his audience is a fool. The audience must be his first consideration after his Lord. It is his field to be cultivated, his game to be played; it is his raw material, his tree from which he can see fruit. The audience is essential to the speaker. Without them his time is wasted, his training is futile. As a public speaker, you must have a genuine love for those you serve, even as our Lord did.

Analyzing Your Audience

One of the best tools for audience analysis is the clever COLD SOAP grid devised by Jay Adams. COLD SOAP is an acronymic device for remembering the four arts of the preaching situation which are governed by four factors. Says Adams, "The four arts are: the art of researching content, the art of organization, the art of language usage, and the art of delivery. These four arts may be summed up by the mnemonic device C-O-L-D. The four factors with which they interact are the Scriptures, the occasion, the audience, and the preacher. These may be conveniently remembered by the word S-O-A-P. These four arts and factors can readily be recalled by simply remembering the two words COLD SOAP."[13]

By placing SOAP horizontally across the top of a grid and COLD vertically up the side of the grid the heterogeneous relationship between the elements is seen. For example, in the grid where the O of SOAP intersects with the O of COLD the speaker will interact the occasion for his speaking with the organization of his material.

This is but one method of audience analysis. Whatever system or method is used, the preacher must analyze his audience to determine his approach to presenting truth to them. He must be aware of their needs, heartaches, concerns, and desires if he is to minister to them. He must gather material accordingly, plan his sermon accordingly, and preach accordingly.

Adjusting to Your Audience

A speaker is not to be controlled by his audience, but, by the same token, he is not to be oblivious to their needs. Studies indicate that it is quite possible for a speaker to interpret the "feedback" clues given him by the audience and to adjust to the audience.[14] If the speaker determines, by present analysis and "feedback," that his audience is not receiving his message, he must do something about it. He cannot simply bull through his message without regard to the audience's reception of it. If he is not communicating the speaker must change his tactics or approach. To do so requires a fundamental knowledge of the types of audiences he will face. If he recognizes that not all audiences are the same, then he can appropriately adjust this style so that communication can be completed.

Professor Lloyd M. Perry properly recognizes the different types of audiences a speaker will face. The well known homiletician says:

---

[13]Jay E. Adams, *Pulpit Speech* (Philadelphia: Presbyterian and Reformed Publishing Company, 1974), pp. 6-9.

[14]Milton Dickens and David H. Krueger, "Speaker's Accuracy in Identifying Immediate Audience Response During a Speech," *The Speech Teacher*, XVIII (November 1969), pp. 303-307.

There are four types of audiences in terms of their interests and their attitudes toward the speaker and his ideas. These four are the apathetic, the believing, the doubtful, and the hostile audience. There are three reasons for believing anything. The first is that of the sensory in which we believe because we can see it. The second is that of authority where the individual believes because it was told to him. The final reason for believing is that of reasoning or argumentation in that it has been proven.

When dealing with a believing audience, one should emphasize the sensory material, use some authority material, and very little, if any, reasoning material. The doubting audience wants reasoning material, some authority information, but very little sensory material. The hostile audience demands much authority information, some reasoning material, and no sensory content. The apathetic audience presents a unique challenge in that one must get and hold its attention and then as soon as this is done it becomes one of the three preceding types and the appropriate approach must then be used.[15]

Audiences are capricious. Sometimes they are with you all the way. Other times it is most difficult to capture and hold them. They cannot be completely controlled by the speaker. This does not relieve the speaker from his duty of doing everything within his power to see that the audience receives his message and the circular response of speech is completed. Remember your message. It is your *raison d'etre,* your reason to be. You are the mouthpiece of God. If you do not capture that audience and win them over to your message, you will be most miserable for you have not fulfilled your purpose in life. Failures will come, but, with the help of the Holy Spirit, so will successes. Do all you can to aid the successful communication with your audience.

---

[15]Lloyd M. Perry, *Biblical Sermon Guide* (Grand Rapids: Baker Book House, 1970), p. 113.

6

Methods of
Presentation

"Of the three places where we hear most public speaking and reading—our courts of law, our theaters, and our churches—the place where we hear the best elocution is the first, and the place where we hear the worst elocution is the last" —Thomas Embley Osmun

"It is necessary to have something more than knowledge of the subject. You must have earnestness in its presentation. You must feel that you have something to say that people ought to hear" —William Jennings Bryan

At the risk of putting the cart before the horse, the various methods of presenting a sermon or speech will be discussed before the actual preparation of the sermon is discussed. Presentation naturally relates to words, movements, the preacher and his audience. Sermon preparation naturally relates to the component parts and approaches to homiletics.

There are basically four methods of presenting the material of your speech or sermon. They are: the manuscript, memorization, impromptu, and extemporaneous methods. What are the merits of each? What are the drawbacks of each?

The Manuscript Method

Probably the most difficult method of presentation is the manuscript method. In this type of delivery the preacher writes out his sermon in full prior to delivery and then he reads it verbatim to the congregation. An important message, such as a foreign policy speech by the President of the United States or an inaugural address, would ordinarily be of this type. Jonathan Edwards used this method when he painstakingly read his famous sermon, "Sinners in the Hands of an Angry God."

The manuscript method has several advantages. The speaker can deliberate over the exact words he wants to use. He can provide more accurate facts to support his case. He can predetermine the length of his sermon. The speaker can have greater excellence of style, being more precise, concise, and concrete. The sermon is in written form so it can be retained for delivery on another occasion or even published. The speaker has a greater freedom from speech fright for the words he is to say are written before him. Henry Sloan Coffin commented: "I know that many prefer me to preach without the manuscript; but I also know that I say more in a given number of minutes, say it with greater precision and in defter sentences than when I let myself go without it."[1]

There are some obvious disadvantages to this method. For a busy pastor, writing out several sermons in full each week saps time from other pastoral duties. The speaker also tends to become dependent on a written manuscript every time he is asked to speak. It is an effort simply to write out each sermon which adds to the difficulty. The speaker is compelled to follow the plan of the speech and can only with great difficulty stray from it. As to delivery, this method is probably the least effective. Eye contact is almost obliterated. Again, reading a manuscript tends to lessen the amount of gesturing and emphasis that a speaker can use.[2]

Henry Ward Beecher once said: "A written sermon is apt to reach out to people like a gloved hand; and an unwritten sermon reaches out the warm and glowing palm, bared to the touch." A sermon that is

---

[1] Henry Sloan Coffin, *Here Is My Method*, edited by Donald MacLeod (Westwood, N.J.: Fleming H. Revell Co., 1952), p. 58.

[2] See Charles R. Brown, *The Art of Preaching* (New York: The Macmillan Company, 1932), pp. 79-84 for complete discussion of advantages and disadvantages of this method of delivery.

well written is usually the type of sermon that is poorly delivered. You write differently from the way you speak. The manuscript method of speaking is appropriate on some occasions, as was mentioned, but is generally an ineffective way of speaking.

If you choose to use this method, at least make sure the print you are to read is large, distinct and legible so that you do not stumble over the words. It may be wise to type the manuscript rather than to write it out in longhand. Also, read and reread the manuscript until you become thoroughly familiar with it. Do what you can to improve your reading skills. You may even want to underline words to be enforced or accented. A simple, non-complex system of color-coded underlining is effective. Predetermine the type of emphasis you will give a certain thought or sentence and then code it with colored underlining. Do not allow this practice to become so complex that you have trouble remembering which color elicits which type of emphasis.

The Memorization Method

This method takes the manuscript method a step further. Not only does the speaker prepare his sermon in full manuscript form, but he memorizes it as well. This laborious task has all the advantages of the manuscript method. The speaker can use more elegant English, more accurately choose his words, he has his message prepared for publication, etc. There are some added advantages. By memorizing the sermon, the preacher can maintain near perfect eye contact. He is not tied to his notes for he has them in his head. He is also freed to gesture as he should, not having to hold his manuscript or having to turn the pages. Again, this method gives the impression that the speaker is skilled, gifted, and polished. He delivers an eloquent sermon with complete freedom from his notes.

There are great disadvantages, however, to this approach. This is by far the most laborious of all the methods. Not only does the speaker have to write out his manuscript in full, but his preparation time is multiplied many times in that he must memorize the manuscript as well. Although eye contact is good with this method, it is also somewhat artificial. The speaker tends to gaze or stare at the audience as he tries to remember what is to be said. The eye becomes glassy and stares over or through the audience. This method also eliminates the opportunity for interpolating thoughts which come to the speaker as he speaks. He is "trapped" by what he has memorized.

The memorization method does not lessen the fear of failure as you may expect. As a matter of fact, it heightens the dread of failure. You find yourself saying: "What if I forget?" "What will I do then?" Such dread usually brings about increased forgetfulness and memory lapse. This is a serious drawback. It is generally not used by good speakers.

The Impromptu Method

This is not a valid method for a preacher to use in his weekly preaching. The impromptu method is used when you are called to speak on the spur of the moment. You have had no advance warning and have had no preparation. Such delivery is called impromptu.

I say it is not a valid method for the preacher because he cannot plan to use this method (although inadequate preparation makes many preachers sound like they are using the impromptu method all the time). Yet the preacher is (as every Christian) "to be ready always to give an answer to every man that asketh you a reason of the hope that is in you . . ." (I Pet. 3:15). To speak for the Lord should never catch the preacher off guard. He may not be prepared as thoroughly as normal, but he can be prepared enough to say something for his Lord. No advantages or disadvantages will be discussed for this method as the speaker does not use it by choice. The impromptu method is strictly for those spur of the moment occasions when you are asked to "say a few words."

The Extemporaneous Method

This method of delivery requires the preparation of a thorough but flexible outline, without writing out the contents verbatim. Extemporaneous does not imply speaking without preparation. There is careful and detailed preparation, but it is not carried to the pulpit. The speaker prepares an outline which will trigger his thoughts remembering the preparation he has done in the study. It is to be distinguished from the impromptu method. In general conversation, the word *extempore* means without preparation, but never so with regard to speech.

This name is given to this form of delivery because the speaker is so well versed in his material that it appears as if he is delivering his speech or sermon "off the cuff."

There are definite and obvious advantages to this method. The extemporaneous method requires far less preparation than the memorization or manuscript methods. Less time is needed because of the quality of preparation, not because of the amount of preparation. One spends as much time in gathering and correlating material in this method as he does in the others. Time is saved, however, in that the material does not have to be written out in full. Further time is saved in that the speaker does not have to memorize verbatim this material. This allows the busy pastor to deliver a sermon with good content on Sunday and still have time to do his calling throughout the week.

Another advantage has to do with delivery. This method gives the speaker greater freedom to develop his own style. He is not boxed in by manuscript or memorization. Adaptability is another key advantage in this method. With the memorized manuscript there is little opportunity to adapt to the audience. If the speaker sees that his audience is not getting the message, he is helpless to assist them for he cannot rewrite his speech. With the extemporaneous method, however, he can simply shift his vocabulary, style, or approach to adapt to the audience and make sure they understand him and are listening to him. Greater expression is able to be given with this method. The greatest degree of sincerity is expressed with the extemporaneous method.

This does not mean that the extemporaneous method is without its faults. For instance, many preachers who use this method fall into the temptation of too little preparation. A skilled speaker can spend a minimum of time in preparation and make it sound like hours of preparation have gone into his speech. Also, by not writing out the sermon, a preacher has nothing prepared for publication if the opportunity arises. Even if there is little opportunity for publication, the next time the preacher wants to use that sermon he must repeat much of the laborious task of preparation.

There are also some drawbacks in regard to delivery. One great disadvantage is that of straying. The extemporaneous speaker sometimes has a tendency to follow a red herring. He too has the problem of using less elegant language for unless it is innate to him, or learned by him, such language rarely occurs on the spur of the moment. Occasionally the extemporaneous speaker may get trapped in an error and not be able to find his way out. The end result is usually worse than the original error.

Whatever problems the extemporaneous method of delivery may have, it is generally agreed that the advantages of this method far outweigh the disadvantages. Most skilled speakers use the extemporaneous method of delivery. The greatest amount of freedom is enjoyed by those who use this method. Therefore, usually the greatest results are produced by this method. It is safe to say that this is the most desirable type of delivery.

There is a variation of the extemporaneous method of delivery that has been successfully used by preachers for years. It is preaching without notes.

Preaching Without Notes

It should be noted from the outset that "preaching without notes does not mean preparation without notes. Indeed, carefully constructed notes are the basis of freedom from notes in preaching. Preaching without notes does not mean that there should be no notes on the pulpit. As a matter of fact, the preacher is well advised to have these notes with him whenever he preaches; if at any time he should need them."[3] Preaching without notes presupposes such a thorough preparation, such a logical outline, such an intense practice session that the preacher need not refer to his notes.

In his *Expository Preaching for Today,* Andrew W. Blackwood points out that note-free preaching was the method that Jesus and the apostles used. They spoke, "from heart to heart and from eye to eye."[4] Most of the great expositors of the Word have spoken extemporaneously and without notes. This was the method of Andrew Blackwood, John Broadus, G. Campbell Morgan, George W. Truett, Clarence E. Macartney, John Wesley, Faris D. Whitesell, Harold John Ockenga, and others. Dr. Ockenga, who for thirty-two and a half years was senior pastor of the historic Park Street Church in Boston, once told me that he always delivers his sermons in inverse order of their preparation. This means his Sunday morning message is last prepared and first delivered. This makes it fresh in his mind. He can thus preach

---

[3]Charles W. Koller, *Expository Preaching Without Notes* (Grand Rapids: Baker Book House, 1962), p. 10.

[4]Andrew W. Blackwood, *Expository Preaching for Today* (New York: Abingdon-Cokesbury Press, 1953), p. 159.

it without notes. He has maintained this practice throughout his ministry.

Speaking without notes is not exclusively used by preachers. Dale Carnegie says: "Although he was an excellent impromptu speaker, Lincoln, after he reached the White House, never made an address, not even an informal talk to his cabinet, until he had carefully put it all down in writing beforehand. Of course, he was obliged to read his inaugural addresses. The exact phraseology of historical state papers of that character is too important to be left to extemporizing. But, back in Illinois, Lincoln never used even notes in his speaking. 'They always tend to tire and confuse the listener,' he said."[5]

There are distinct advantages in extemporaneous speaking without notes. The impression of the audience is decidedly favorable toward the speaker. They feel he is speaking to them sincerely, as he would in ordinary conversation. With this type of extemporaneous speaking, eye contact is rarely broken. Thus, this method provides the ultimate in public expression with visual directness and sincerity. All the advantages of extemporaneous speaking and more apply here, because you do not even have to glance at your outline.

Several objections must be noted to this method of speaking without notes. Since one must become familiar or memorize the outline of his sermon to speak without notes, it becomes an added task in preparation. The pastor may not have adequate time to commit long passages of Scripture, poems, and an outline to memory. Again, it is objected that attempting to preach without any reference to notes is an undue burden on the memory. To have a single page of outline and Scripture is not so restrictive as to bring about such taxation of the memory.

Writing in *Christianity Today*, Irvin Shortess Yeaworth commented: "For many years I boasted of 'preaching without notes,' but there came a time when I realized I was using more mental energy trying to remember what came next than in giving convincing voice to the thoughts I wanted to communicate. Indeed, there were times when, weary of mind, I found that I was preaching not only without notes but also without ideas. . . . After all, according to the Chinese proverb, 'The weakest ink is stronger than the strongest memory.' "[6] On the

---

[5]Dale Carnegie, *Public Speaking and Influencing Men in Business* (New York: Association Press, 1953), p. 63.

[6]Irvin Shortess Yeaworth, "The Minister's Workshop: Preach Biblical Themes," *Christianity Today* (April 1, 1966), p. 35.

other hand, Gerald Kennedy says of preaching without notes: "It is worth all it costs, and many a fine preacher has surrendered a large percentage of his power to manuscripts and notes."[7]

It is a wise idea to attempt speaking without once looking at your notes, but if you need to glance at them on occasion, make sure you have something worthwhile looking at. Make your outline scanty, but make sure what you have will trigger your memory.

Memory

Whether or not a preacher uses notes in preaching depends on his memory. "There are two phases to every true sermon—creation and resurrection. It has first to be created in the study; then it has to be raised from the dead on the first day of the week."[8] Preaching without notes requires a good memory which most of us do not have. The obvious question then is: "How can I improve my memory?" You could buy books on memory improvement, but if the average preacher is given the name of a book on how to improve the memory, he would forget the title before he got to the store to purchase it.[9] However, each of us may abide by the natural laws of memory and thus our memories will be improved. The rules of these natural laws of memory follow.

1. **Impression.**   The first mandate of a good memory is that you get a deep, rich, and vivid impression of the thing you wish to retain. Without such an impression memory will be lost. Such an impression requires concentration. Henry Ward Beecher penned: "One intense hour will do more than dreamy years." To receive the proper impression of anything you must concentrate on it intensely. Notice that the emphasis is on quality of concentration, not quantity. If you are introduced to three people at a party the chances of your remembering all three names are slim. Thus, you must heighten the impression by asking that the name be repeated. Get an impression of the name. Concentrate on its sound. Repeat it in your mind. Even ask that they spell it. This will greatly deepen the impression. Be careful, however, that you do not use this spelling technique as a crutch by itself. I once

---

[7]Gerald Kennedy, *His Word Through Preaching* (New York: Harper and Brothers Publishers, 1947), p. 88.

[8]Dwight E. Stevenson and Charles F. Diehl, *Reaching People from the Pulpit* (New York: Harper and Row, Publishers, 1958), p. 57.

[9]See *How to Improve Your Memory* by James D. Weinland (New York: Barnes & Noble, 1957).

heard of a fellow who, when he could not remember a person's name he would simply say, "Do you spell your name with an 'i' or an 'e'?" He knew that many names have one or the other letters in them. Once when he asked this of a woman she became very indignant, angrily snorting, "I spell my name with an 'i' sir, it's Hill, H - I - L - L."

To deepen the impression, appeal to all the senses. As a child, Abraham Lincoln formed a reading habit which stayed with him for life. Each morning as he reached his law office in Springfield he stretched out and read the morning paper audibly. Said his partner: "He annoyed me, almost beyond endurance. I once asked him why he read in this fashion. This was his explanation. 'When I read aloud, two senses catch the idea; first, I see what I read; second, I hear it, and therefore I can remember it better.' "[10] When you are introduced to someone, repeat his name aloud to deepen the impression made on your memory. When you have an outline to memorize, read it aloud to make a deeper impression. If the initial impression is a good one, the process of memorization is at least a third won.

2. **Association.**   After the initial impression is made, the next mandate for a good memory is that of association. In explanation, memory Professor William James said: "Our mind is essentially an associating machine.... The laws of association govern, in fact, all the trains of our thinking which are not interrupted by sensations breaking on us from without. Whatever appears in the mind must be introduced; and, when introduced it is as the associate of something already there.... An educated memory depends upon an organized system of associations...."[11] The process of learning and remembering proceeds from the known to the unknown, from the familiar to the unfamiliar. In order to remember properly, a connection must be made between the new material to be memorized and that material which is already stored in the memory bank of your mind.

How does one proceed from the familiar to the unfamiliar? How is that connection made? The answers are numerous and each person will have to develop a technique of his own. Here are some examples. Supposing you are to remember someone's name. You are introduced to Mr. Brown who is a shoe salesman. In your mind he becomes Mr. Brown shoes. You don't call him that, but you remember not only his

---

[10]Quoted in Dale Carnegie, *How to Speak*, p. 79.
[11]Ibid, p. 85.

name but his occupation by that device. Mrs. Albright is a school teacher. Her job is to educate the children and make them "all bright." Thus you remember her name. The man standing in the corner with the mustache is Mr. Byrd. You remember his name for when you were introduced you silently said to yourself, "A bird in the hand is worth two in the bush."

What about remembering outlines by association? The same principle applies. Proceed from the known to the unknown. You have three main divisions to your sermon and you are speaking about the characteristics of the Word of God. You may say, "One characteristic of the Word of God is that it is credible; another characteristic is that it is authoritative; a third is that it is trustworthy." Notice that the three characteristics form an acronym: credible, authoritative, trustworthy (C-A-T). By remembering CAT you may easily remember the three characteristics of the Word of God.

Along this line, alliteration is very helpful. Again, speaking of the characteristics of the Word of God you might say: "One characteristic of the Word of God is that it is infallible; another characteristic is that it is inspired; a third is that it is irrefutable." In this instance, each of the characteristics begins with the same letter: infallible, inspired, irrefutable (I-I-I). This is a valuable aid to the memory, both yours and the congregation's. Do not stretch the point you want to make, however, just to fit it into an alliterative pattern. If you have to force it or use a word that isn't clear or aligned with the thought you are trying to express, then do not use it. It is an aid, not a necessity.

3. **Repetition.**   The final mandate for a good memory and the final natural law of memory is repetition. This may be the most important factor. Dale Carnegie reports that the large Mohammedan university of Cairo, El Hazar, allegedly has an entrance examination requirement that all incoming students repeat the Koran from memory.[12] The Koran is about as long as the New Testament, and three days are required to recite it! How is it possible for someone to remember something of such length? The answer is repetition.

Even the most difficult of outlines may be memorized by repetition. However, repetition in learning is again a question of quality as well as quantity. Certainly much repetition will get the job done. If you repeat something over and over you will eventually memorize it. But the way

---

[12]Ibid, p. 83.

you use repetition is important as well. Here the law of distributed effort is seen. Do not attempt to memorize something all at once. A man who repeats an outline over and over until he has it fixed in his mind is using more than twice the time and energy needed to memorize the outline as if he had repeated that outline at judicious intervals. Material studied for fifteen minutes a day for five days is more effective than five hours in a single day. Psychologists tell us that of the new material we learn, we forget more during the first eight hours than during the next thirty days. This means that it is a good idea to go over your outline repeatedly the day before you deliver it. Go over it and over it. Set it aside. Go over it again. Work on something else. Just before going to bed Saturday night, go over it again. Go over it the first thing Sunday morning. Then go over it just before the service. This type of repetition will produce results. You will be surprised what you can remember.

By using the three natural laws of memory and by marking your outline well, (indentation, underlining, capitalization, using numerals instead of letters, etc.) you will be able to effectively present your speech or sermon.

Your voice, your gestures, your eye contact, your method of presentation, are all combined in a package the congregation sees as you, the speaker. Improved manner can greatly improve the reception of the message which you have been given to communicate to others. Is it worth the effort to rid yourself of any idiosyncrasies or bad habits you may have acquired? If you seriously believe that the message of the Gospel is the most important news in the world, you will make yourself the best newscaster possible. Your manner of speaking will become improved with God's help and your desire.

7

The Mechanics of Preparation

"Because of the ease with which good speakers talk, some people mistakenly believe that such men spend little time in preparation. Nothing could be further from the facts. The very ease with which a speech is given often indicates the thorough preparation behind it" —Alan H. Monroe

"Men give me some credit for genius. All the genius I have lies in this: When I have a subject in hand, I study it profoundly. Day and night it is before me. I explore it in all its bearings. My mind becomes pervaded with it. Then the efforts that I make are what people are pleased to call the fruits of genius. It is the fruit of labor and thought" —Alexander Hamilton

The Importance of Preparation

The mechanics of the sermon can be divided into several elements, the first of which is the mechanics of preparation. In order for the student to realize the inestimable value of preparation, read what Martin Luther advised. *Bene orasse est bene studuisse* (To speak well one must prepare well). To have something to say requires hours of study.

127

Dr. John Henry Jowett correctly observed: "Preaching that costs nothing accomplishes nothing. If the study is a lounge, the pulpit will be an impertinence." A pastor cannot simply pray and then ask the Spirit to fill his mouth. It doesn't work that way.

Proper preparation produces perspiration. That may be hard to say, but it is true. Preparing a sermon properly is hard work. It can't be done in a Saturday night fever, nor in a Sunday morning flurry. We must have something to say. When the congregation asks: "Is there any word from the Lord?", we must be well prepared to give them God's Word.

What Really Is Preparation?

"There is a story of a young minister who, concerned about the apparent failure of his preaching, consulted Dr. Joseph Parker in the vestry of the City Temple. His sermons, he complained, were encountering only apathy. Could Dr. Parker frankly tell him what was lacking?" 'Suppose you preach me one of your sermons here and now', said Parker; and his visitor, not without some trepidation, complied. When it was over, the Doctor told him to sit down. 'Young man,' he said, 'you asked me to be frank. I think I can tell you what is the matter. For the last half-hour you have been trying to get something out of your head instead of something into mine'! That distinction is crucial. Wrestle with your subject in the study, that there may be clarity in the pulpit. 'For if the trumpet give an uncertain sound, who shall prepare himself to the battle?' "[1]

This incident illustrates the fact that many sermons are delivered without proper preparation. Many pastors do not prepare and it shows in their sermons. They have not realized that sermon preparation is more than gathering material. Granted, material must be gathered, but true preparation requires thinking, brooding, selecting, assembling, adding, subtracting, rethinking, reassembling, etc. In the preparation of the earth, the Spirit of God "brooded" over the face of the deep (Gen. 1:2). This same process must be ours in the preparation of speeches and sermons. We must mull over in our minds that which we want to say. This requires time.

---

[1]Quoted in James S. Stewart, *Heralds of God* (New York: Charles Scribner's Sons, 1946), pp. 123–124.

There are seven elements in the preparation of a speech or a sermon. They are as follows.

1. **Determine the purpose of the speech or sermon.** Unless you have the purpose of your sermon clearly and constantly in mind during preparation, it will sound as if you have no purpose when you deliver it. Frequently a speaker rises and delivers a speech and you have no idea why he ever rose. His purpose is not clear in his mind and certainly it is not clear in yours. It is not enough to merely pick a subject for a sermon, you must organize that sermon for a desired response. Keep asking yourself: "What is my purpose?"

2. **Analyze your audience and occasion.** Preaching on the concerns of the elderly to a teenage audience is less than wise. You must take your audience into consideration when preparing your message. Consider their ages, likes, dislikes, problems, and needs. Included in a check list for audience analysis by Loren Reid is: size, occasion for gathering, significant environmental factors, customs or taboos, nationalities, races, education, social level, economic level, attitude toward subject, attitude toward speaker, etc.[2] It is not wise to preach an Easter sermon on Christmas morning. Some preachers think this is "cute" saying that the Word of God is relevant all the time. But the people have been primed by the season to hear a Christmas message on Christmas Sunday. Don't disappoint them.

3. **Narrow the subject of your sermon.** It is not practical for you to speak on the subject of "God." Such a subject is too broad. You cannot say anything significant about God in one sermon unless you are selective about what you say. A narrowed subject is called a theme and will be dealt with in greater detail later.

4. **Gather sufficient material.** Once you have analyzed your audience and the occasion, picked a subject and narrowed it, you will begin to gather material for your theme. This is where the work begins. Material can always be found but only through intelligent research and laborious digging. When the material is gathered from many sources, primarily the Bible, it will have to be brooded over, correlated, brooded over again, added to, weeded out, assembled, etc. One of the hardest tasks of the preacher will be to discard material which cannot be used in this sermon.

---

[2]Loren Reid, *First Principles of Public Speaking* (Columbia: Artcraft Press, 1960), p. 60.

You cannot bring all the fruits of your labor to the pulpit. If you do you will sound like a preaching encyclopedia. Luther Burbank said: "I have often produced a million plant specimens to find but one or two superlatively good ones, and have then destroyed all the inferior specimens." The sermon needs this same type of weeding. Gather sufficient material but discard all but what is needed.

5. **Outlining the sermon.** It is extremely important that the material you have gathered be put into a logical form. This means you must engage in proper outlining. The outline must exhibit all the important elements of the sermon without being too detailed. The procedure of outlining will be discussed in greater length later.

6. **Wording the sermon.** This sixth element is one in which many preachers fall short. They feel they will be artificial if they word their sermons beforehand. Actually, if they don't, they will be very dull. People remember well what is worded well. It is not necessary for you to memorize every phrase or line of the sermon, but it is wise to lay your outline before you and "talk it through" several times. This way you compose orally what you have conceived in your mind. Such a practice will be a tremendous aid when it comes to actually delivering the sermon.

7. **Practice aloud.** The final element in preparation cannot be stressed too heavily. Effective delivery is not achieved simply by applying a set of rules to our speaking. Effective delivery is largely dependent upon practice. It takes practice to be natural before an audience. Study the careers of famous speakers and you will find they have one thing in common, i.e. all of them practiced.

George Whitefield was one of the most impassioned evangelists ever to deliver a sermon. He claimed he could not do justice to a sermon until he had preached it fifty times. After all, if a sermon is delivered better the tenth time, why should we not preach our Sunday sermon nine times in front of a mirror on Saturday? Singers practice. Actors practice. Football teams practice. Why shouldn't a preacher practice? It is not unspiritual to practice a sermon as you still pray for the power of the Holy Spirit when you deliver the sermon. In fact, it appears to be unspiritual not to practice, if practice makes us more effective in the service of the Lord.

A very helpful hint in the preparation of a sermon is to develop a reservoir of knowledge from which you may draw facts, figures, ideas, Scripture, etc. To develop such a reservoir requires that you be widely read. This will broaden your background of knowledge and make it possible for you to be conversant with a wide variety of subjects. It will require that you read the evening newspaper and listen to the evening television news; read popular magazines like *U.S. News and World Report, Time,* or *Newsweek;* read Christian periodicals (e.g. *Christianity Today, Moody Monthly, Christian Herald, Eternity,* etc.); read general material such as biographies, novels, fiction; read the classics. With a background of knowledge you will rarely be at a loss for what to say.

Sources for Preparation

Getting material for a sermon takes two approaches. First, you must be constantly gathering material with no specific sermon in mind. Second, you will need to do specific research for the sermon at hand. Where does one go to glean this material? There are many places.

1. **Scripture.** The most obvious place for the preacher of the Word to gather material is the Word of God itself. I say this is obvious, yet note how frequently Scripture is missing from the sermon. Our primary source for sermonic material must be the Word. This is true not only of specific preparation but also for general preparation. The daily reading of Scripture will provide the preacher with an unfailing supply of themes on which to preach as well as illustrative material. In preparation for the Sunday sermon the pastor is well advised to seek the explanation of Scripture by other passages of Scripture.

Christ's preaching is characteristic of the type of preaching we should use. He frequently used Scripture for His subject matter. As my former theology professor Roger Nicole points out: "More than ten percent of the New Testament text is made up of citations or direct allusions to the Old Testament. The recorded words of Jesus disclose a similar percentage."[3] With this example, it is surprising how many preachers do not rely on the Scriptures for their sermon material. Even many who have graduated from Christian colleges and seminaries are so sadly deficient in general knowledge of the Bible that they must look elsewhere for material. What a tragedy.

---

[3]Quoted in *Revelation and the Bible,* edited by Carl F. H. Henry (Grand Rapids: Baker Book House, 1958), p. 138.

2. **Systematic Theology.** This is an area in which few pastors find help for sermon material. Yet it is an area rich in such help. Next to the Scripture itself, the systematic theology text should be a prime source of sermonic material. Being acquainted with biblical truth gives the preacher confidence. A systematic theology text will present biblical truth in a logical fashion. This is important in the pastor's sermons.

3. **History.** Preaching material can be obtained from the history of the church as well as secular history. If the preacher is familiar with the events of history and the great empires of the world, his understanding of the Bible will be greatly enhanced. History is also a great interpreter of the providence of God. By looking at history we can see God's providential dealings with His people. Also, the great revival movements of history can add understanding to our preaching. A knowledge of history helps the preacher be aware of the timetable of God and the urgency of the preacher's task.

4. **General Reading.** Reading which is not historical nor biblical in nature can add much to our preaching. Devotional readings, poetry, prose, narrative, fiction, the arts and sciences, geology, archaeology, apologetics, the newspaper, magazines, etc. are all needed areas for the preacher to study. These extra-biblical areas add greatly to biblical preaching for they fill in the voids which are sometimes left between the main biblical facts of a sermon.

5. **Hymnals.** You've heard the expression, "they just don't make them the way they used to." Many people feel that way about today's hymns. Although there is much good Christian music found in our world today, much of what passes for "Christian" music is but a few experiential thoughts strung together by a chorus of "shoo-bee doo-bee doo's." But in the old hymns of the faith there is a lot of good preaching material. Read the hymns of Charles Wesley, Martin Luther, Philip P. Bliss, Isaac Watts, Alfred H. Ackley, William Cowper, and others.

6. **Personal Experience.** Preaching is the proclamation of Jesus Christ and His salvation for us. Acts 4:20 indicates, "We can not but speak the things which we have seen and heard." The preacher's own salvation experience is a strong area of sermon material. It has been said that a man with an experience is never at the mercy of a man with an argument. You need not argue for Christ, simply proclaim Him and your undeniable experience with Him. You need not apologize for a personal reference. After all, who knows you better than you. But be

careful not to punctuate your sermons with personal references. "A wise minister may bring strange grist to his mill from his own experience . . . only take one warning! The Session-clerk of an Edinburgh church used to say that the congregation made it a practice to send their minister to the Holy Land after 25 years' ministry and then they regretted it for the next 25. 'When I was in the Holy Land.' 'I once saw in Jerusalem.' 'I remember in Jericho.' You can imagine how stale and wearisome it becomes!' "[4]

7. **Biographies.** Very productive sources for preaching material are found in the biographies of great Christians. They will provide evidences of the hand of God on men's lives, the leading of the Holy Spirit, God's provision in the time of man's need, and faith that has been tested and tried. The biographies of Jonathan Edwards, Evan Roberts, D. L. Moody, Joni Erickson, David Livingston, A. J. Gordon, John Wesley, William Carey, David Brainerd, or Bob Jones, Sr. will all be inspiring and enlightening. They can provide material to which your audience may relate or empathize.

8. **Great Literature.** No less apropros for eliciting preaching material are the great books of literature. Here the classics are especially helpful. A gifted preacher will be even more effective as a herald of God's Word after he has read *Pilgrim's Progress.* He will be a better theologian after he has read *The Divine Comedy.* He will be better equipped to preach of God's remedy to man's need after he has read *Paradise Lost.* Many newer titles, on their way to becoming classics, are also beneficial to the preacher's preaching. All the works by C. S. Lewis, J. R. R. Tolkien, and others in that vein would be helpful. Whether sacred or secular, there is no end to the good reading of which the preacher or speaker may avail himself.

Borrowing

It is readily seen that not all of these sources derive their material from within themselves—they use other sources. This begs the question of using someone else's material in our sermons. May we borrow from someone else? Most certainly. In fact, many times we ought to borrow.

---

[4]James Black, *The Mystery of Preaching* (London: James Clarke & Company, Ltd., 1934), p. 78.

Borrowing can be of two extremes. Years ago in seminary a fellow classmate once said to me, "I'm not going to waste my money on commentaries. I'll just buy Greek and Hebrew lexicons and other aids and get into the Word myself." My immediate question was, "Does God give all wisdom to one man?" No, He does not. There is nothing wrong with sharing insights into the Scripture. A person is self-deceived if he denies himself the fruits of other's labors. This should not be the case. His own thoughts may be shallow or even incorrect. He needs the wisdom which God has given to others.

There is, however, the other extreme. This type of preacher never thinks for himself. He never cracks his Greek text. He never even reads the portion of Scripture which he has selected for Sunday's message until he reads a commentary. His whole life is wrapped up in what others have said. His sermons are one long quote after another. This is a very serious mistake. First, the congregation wants to hear what the Lord has to say through His Word, not what some commentator or theologian has to say. Secondly, such a practice engenders a shallow mind and in turn, shallow preaching. This approach to gathering sermon material should be shunned.

We should not hesitate to legitimately borrow from others, for they undoubtedly have done the same. Dale Carnegie reveals the following anecdote about borrowing which deals with the last line of Lincoln's Gettysburg Address—"and that government of the people, by the people, for the people, shall not perish from the earth."

It is commonly supposed that Lincoln originated the immortal phrase which closed this address; but did he? Herndon, his law partner, had given Lincoln, several years previously, a copy of Theodore Parker's addresses. Lincoln read and underscored in this book the words 'Democracy is direct self-government, over all the people, by all the people, and for all the people.' Theodore Parker may have borrowed his phraseology from Webster who had said, four years earlier, in his famous reply to Hayne: 'The people's government, made for the people, made by the people, and answerable to the people.'

Webster may have borrowed his phraseology from President James Monroe who had given voice to the same idea a third of a century earlier. And to whom was James Monroe indebted? Five hundred years before Monroe was born, Wyclif had said, in the preface to the translation of the Scriptures, that 'this Bible is for the government of the people, by the people, and for the people.' And long before Wyclif lived, more than 400 years before the birth of Christ, Cleon, in an address to the men of Athens, spoke of a ruler 'of the people, by the people, and for the people.' And from what ancient source Cleon drew his inspiration, is a matter lost in the fog and night of antiquity.[5]

It is evident that borrowing is widely practiced. Direct borrowing obligates the borrower to credit the source from which the material was borrowed. But indirect borrowing need not so obligate us. Oliver Wendell Holmes once said, "I have milked 300 cows, but I made my own butter."[6] The question is in what cases should acknowledgment be made to avoid plagiarism?

John A. Broadus observes:

> When the remark is obvious, or belongs to the common stock of religious ideas, so that it might have occurred to ourselves, although it happens to have been drawn from another, then it is often unnecessary to make any acknowledgment. When the idea is at all striking, so that hearers would give any special credit for it as a good thing, then we must not take a credit which is undeserved, but must in some way indicate that the thought was derived from another.
>
> In what cases shall we mention the precise source? When the author's name would give greater weight to the idea, or in some way attach interest to it. . . . Again, when we may hope thereby to lead some hearer to read the book mentioned. . . . Otherwise it is enough merely to indicate that the thought was derived from some source. Avoid a parade of honesty about acknowledging. . . . Let the acknowledgment interrupt as little as possible the flow of thought, detract as little as possible from the interest which the idea is likely to awaken. If it would decidedly interrupt or detract, then omit the acknowledgment, and the thing borrowed.[7]

It must be realized that we are speaking here of borrowing portions of texts, poems, sayings, etc. and not the practice of wholesale borrowing of entire sermons. We dare not plagiarize, but we dare not allow our blatant honesty to destroy the message we have to convey.

Dishonesty is not being advocated here, just common sense. As Broadus says, "avoid a parade of honesty." No one is impressed.

---

[5]Quoted in Dale Carnegie, *Public Speaking and Influencing Men in Business* (New York: Association Press, 1953), pp. 345-346.

[6]Quoted by A. W. Blackwood, *Pulpit Digest,* XXXIII, January 1953, p. 16.

[7]John A. Broadus, *On the Preparation and Delivery of Sermons* (Grand Rapids: Associated Publishers and Authors, Inc., 1971), p. 51.

Notebook and File

A pastor must prepare at least 150 messages every year, and even this does not include the Wednesday evening Bible study or a Sunday school lesson. It should be evident that this is a gargantuan task. To gather and correlate that much material every week is next to impossible. Besides, the less special preparation done for a sermon, the better the sermon. The best sermons are those in which thoughts have been gathered, stored, thought out, and illuminated long before the actual preaching occurs. This means the preacher must be gathering material constantly. The wise preacher gathers material for future use. He finds this material everywhere. This means he needs a notebook handy to jot down all those seed thoughts that come his way, all possible Scripture texts, all illustrations, all poems, etc.

Notebook

Richard C. Halverson suggests that for him, "a common daily record book, one page per day, is reserved for sermonic data and related materials. Sermon themes or topics, with Scriptures, are entered under the proper Sunday, leaving six pages in the day book for related ideas, illustrations, hymns, cross-references, and the like. This is my 'homiletical garden.' It is surprising how the garden grows. Often the sermons seem almost to prepare themselves."[8]

James Stewart suggests: "Again and again in your reading of the Bible, phrases, sentences, whole passages will leap out from the page, each of them positively thrusting itself upon you and clamouring 'One day you must preach on me! This is where your private notebooks come into action. When a text has once gripped you, do not let it escape. Jot it down at the head of a page, and underneath it any thoughts, illustrations, potential sermon divisions it may have brought with it."[9]

Most good preachers are in the habit of never being without their notebook. It does not have to be large, but it must be ever-present. What a shame to receive an inspiration and later lose it because you did not have opportunity to write it down. The notebook habit is a good one. It can greatly aid your sermon preparation.

---

[8]Richard C. Halverson in *How to Prepare and Deliver Better Sermons*, edited by Paul S. Rees (Washington, D.C.: Christianity Today, 1970), p. 12.
[9]James S. Stewart, *Heralds*, p. 154.

File

A file is just as important to a preacher as his library. The pastor will undoubtedly be more familiar with the material he has collected himself and put on file than with the books in his library. When you gather sermon material constantly you must have some place to put it. Throwing it into a cardboard box in the attic is not a good place. You need a file at your fingertips.

How did Dwight L. Moody prepare the sermons which stirred the spiritual lethargy of the last generation? He had no special secret. He claimed: "When I choose a subject, I write the name of it on the outside of a large envelope. I have many such envelopes. If when I am reading, I meet a good thing on any subject I am to speak on, I slip it into the right envelope, and let it lie there. I always carry a notebook, and if I hear anything in a sermon that will throw light on that subject, I put it down, and slip it into the envelope. Perhaps I let it lie there for a year or more. When I want a new sermon, I take everything that has been accumulating. Between what I find there and the results of my own study, I have material enough. Then, all the time I am going over my sermons, taking out a little here, adding a little there. In that way they never get old."

Filing

You will want to file the sermon you have preached. File it in chronological order with your other sermons. Be sure to keep a record of the sermons you preach. Record the following: (1) date; (2) title of sermon; (3) passage of Scripture; (4) location of sermon delivery; (5) name of pastor if it was not delivered in your own church; (6) hour of service; (7) number in attendance; (8) results from service; (9) comments on the service; (10) your reaction to the sermon and the service.

As your experience in preaching grows, so will your appreciation of a good filing system. It will prove to be vital to your ministry. Buy a good file, one that is well constructed, and use it every day, filing new material and drawing from previously filed material. In their book *Steps to the Sermon,* H. C. Brown, Jr., H. Gordon Clinard and Jesse J. Northcutt include a section entitled "Preserving the Sermon Material" which provides helpful suggestions here.[10]

---

[10]H. C. Brown, Jr., H. Gordon Clinard and Jesse J. Northcutt, *Steps to the Sermon* (Nashville: Broadman Press, 1963), p. 79ff.

Methods of Preparation

There are as many methods of preparing a sermon as there are preachers delivering them. In the preparation of this text I had correspondence with a number of outstanding preachers who are today successful pastors and evangelists. I asked each of them this question: "What is the most essential feature of good sermon preparation?" Their interesting and varied answers follow.

Dr. Leighton Ford

The answer of Dr. Leighton Ford was: "I like the prescription of the country preacher: 'I read myself full, think myself clear, pray myself hot, and let myself go'! With some, the greatest need is to think, read, and study until there is the real substance to what is to be said. With others, the most essential thing is to take time to achieve clarity of thought and expression. With others, it is to master the material so that it may be delivered easily. Basic to all is the biblical grounding." (Leighton Ford is the Associate Evangelist of the Billy Graham Evangelistic Association).

Dr. W. A. Criswell

With regard to general preparation, Dr. W. A. Criswell says: "When I began preaching, I thought I had to spin everything out of my own shallow, meager resources, like a spider makes its web. From every, any, and all sources gather material. Everything is grist for the preacher's mill. Newspapers, encyclopedias, magazines, books, experience, texts, everything." (W. A. Criswell is Pastor of the First Baptist Church of Dallas, Texas).

Dr. Jerry Falwell

"I take my responsibility as God's spokesman very seriously. I cannot prepare my people to hear from God until I have first heard from Him. For this reason most of my sermons begin, not in the study or in the office, but in my personal devotion time. Early in the morning, before my family rises, I get up and get alone with God. The sparks for my sermons are usually ignited while I am reading the

Word. Then they are burned into my heart while on my knees in prayer. This leads me to sermon preparation, but sermon preparation must follow that intimate contact with God in which I receive His message and His direction.

Usually my Sunday morning sermons are topical in nature. This is because there are millions of people looking in on the service at the Thomas Road Baptist Church by television. I have to keep their needs in mind as well as those of the congregation. On Sunday evening and Wednesday evening my sermons are textual in nature. This way I can treat those topics which are universal in scope and at the same time teach the Word textually to the local congregation." (Jerry Falwell is Pastor of the Thomas Road Baptist Church of Lynchburg, Virginia).

Dr. George Sweeting

"My Sunday morning sermons have always been expository. Each message is a unit and can stand alone. After studying the passage at hand, I prepare an outline, so that it is logical. Then I write down all the thoughts that come to me on that text or subject, drawing my illustrations primarily from Scripture. Often I will consult some commentaries for further light or verification. Then I will refer to my file for further illustrations, seeking to be exceedingly practical. Eventually, I write or type out the message word for word. Though I preach from extensive notes, I rarely have to refer to them. Special attention is given to the first two minutes as well as the conclusion. The final moments should be the hour of power." (George Sweeting, former pastor of Moody Memorial Church, is now President of Moody Bible Institute of Chicago, Illinois).

Dr. Harold John Ockenga

"The sermon preparation involves hard work. First there must be the message itself obtained from the Scripture; then the analysis of the passage which supports it; then the use of other Scripture by the way of analogy; then the use of theology; then of course, illustration and application. In my opinion, the greatest attention should be given to the outline of the message so that it is thorough, logical and an absolute unit in itself." (Dr. Harold John Ockenga, now the retired Chancellor of Gordon-Conwell Theological Seminary, was formerly the Pastor of the historic Park Street Church of Boston, Massachusetts).

Dr. Stephen Olford

"My primary method of preaching is expository. In seeking to ascertain what any given passage is declaring, I ask myself two questions: 'What is God saying to my heart?' and 'What is God saying to my church?' With these two standards before me I commence the actual research and writing of the sermon.

"In the preparation of a sermon I follow this plan: (1) The choice of a subject; (2) The construction of a skeleton, i.e. introduction, exposition, application and peroration. Such construction will carry three main headings (normally) with two or three subheadings. All these are carefully designed to relate to the main theme or subject and carry perfect sequence; (3) The collation of substance. This comes through the study of the text, meditation, reference to commentaries, textbooks, and the addition of suitable illustrations. I am usually in the study from 8:00 A.M. until 12:30 P.M. and spend at least two hours of this time each day in reading . . . (so) that ideas beget ideas, my vocabulary is expanded, suggestions are gathered for outlines, though I refuse to use other people's sermons or copy their style; (4) The composition of the sermon. When possible, I like to write out or dictate the sermon in full, giving special attention to the introduction and conclusion. I feel that the introduction should be designed to arrest attention, clear prejudice and place the subject in the right perspective. The conclusion should always demand a verdict of the audience. I use alliteration for my main headings and very often for subheadings. This aids my memory, as well as helps the listener to retain the essence of what I have said." (Dr. Stephen Olford was formerly Pastor of the Calvary Baptist Church of New York City).

It is interesting to note the variety of methods used in approaching preaching. Each of these men has a distinctly different style. Each of their ministries has been unique. And yet from these and other outstanding preachers of this last quarter of the twentieth century we can note special emphasis on specific areas of sermonizing.

1. Personal preparation of the preacher to preach the Word.
2. The primacy of expository preaching.
3. A thorough study of the passage.
4. Preparation of a logical outline.
5. Emphasis on the introduction and conclusion.
6. Emphasis on application and illustration.
7. Gather sufficient material.

Whatever method of preparation you choose in your sermonizing, be sure that it includes the above. These qualities are standard in successful preaching. They will be necessary for your successful preaching as well. For further information on methods of preparation see Clarence Roddy, *We Prepare and Preach*; Donald MacLeod, *This Is My Method*; H. C. Brown, Jr., H. Gordon Clinard, and Jesse J. Northcutt, *Steps to the Sermon*; or Charles W. Koller, *Expository Preaching Without Notes*.

8

Four Elements
in a Good Sermon

"There is absolutely no limit to the number of people who can stay away from poor preaching" —Charles W. Koller

"Before a speaker faces his audience, he should write a letter to a friend and say: 'I am to make an address on a subject, and I want to make these points.' He should then enumerate the things he is going to speak about in their correct order. If he finds that he has nothing to say in his letter, he had better write to the committee that invited him and say that the probable death of his grandmother will possibly prevent his being present on the occasion" —Edward Everett Hale

There are four great elements in a good sermon. In order to be a sermon of any quality, these four elements are absolutely essential. Without them, preaching is muddled, ineffectual and unintelligible. What are the four elements? They are *content, organization, arrangement,* and *consistency.* Let's consider them individually.

143

Content

The pastor is in his study; then comes the moment of truth. "Upon what shall I preach?" This question can be taken lightly or with great gravity. "It really doesn't matter what I preach on as long as I preach." Have you ever heard that? Nothing could be further from the truth. It does matter what you preach on. It matters greatly.

One of the great temptations of this day is to downgrade the pulpit by making it a forum for political and social discussion. It is here we receive discussions on current philosophies, economic problems, ecological worries, brotherly love, etc. How much better it would be to hear of Christ Jesus. If the Word of God is not preached, we cannot expect our "sheep" to go out into a world of spiritual "wolves" and survive. Speaking of sacred eloquence, W. G. T. Shedd says: "The pulpit is the place for the delivery of eloquence, and not philosophy, or technical theology." Many pastors who do not fall into the error of delivering lectures on secular psychology, philosophy, etc. do fall into the trap of delivering lectures on sacred psychology, philosophy, philology, etc. We are not interested in the Greek (although an occasional reference for clarification is good). We are not too interested in the psychology of living, but the author of life. Ecclesiastical lecturing is as bad as secular lecturing. Let us hear from the Word.

Preaching Christ

The Westminster Teachers' Quarterly related an incident several years ago. "On one occasion three people went into a church because they felt they needed spiritual help. The first was an unsuccessful businessman contemplating suicide. The second was a youth of extravagant tastes who, finding his wages insufficient, was planning to steal from his employer. The third was a young woman who had strayed from the path of virtue. The service moved along in a stilted, uninspiring fashion. Worst of all, when the preacher arose to deliver the message, he never spoke of Jesus and His love or presented the claims of the Word of God, but delivered instead a message on the theme, 'Is Mars Inhabited?' The hungry souls that needed 'bread' so desperately received only 'stones.' As a result, the businessman committed suicide, the boy went through with his evil plans and landed in the penitentiary, and the young woman returned to the street to continue her life of shame."

How important it is for us to follow the example of Philip as he went down to the city of Samaria and "preached Christ unto them" (Acts 8:5). When Philip preached Christ, the next verse indicates that, "the people with one accord gave heed unto those things which Philip spoke . . . and there was great joy in the city." Peace, joy, and comfort only come when Christ is preached.

Describing his Saturday walks with his friend Marcus Dods, Alexander Whyte commented: "Whatever we started off with in our conversation, we soon made across country, somehow, to Jesus of Nazareth, to His death, and His resurrection, and His indwelling." The subject of our sermons must be Jesus or something that pertains to Him. James Stewart declares: "If we are not determined that in every sermon Christ is to be preached, it were better that we should resign our commission forthwith and seek some other vocation."[1]

Describing the content of preaching today, Donald G. Bloesch says: "Much gospel preaching today is not informed by a knowledge of the Bible but by a fidelity to the religion of our forefathers. . . . Instead of being an exposition of a biblical text, the sermon often consists of a collection of proof texts that serve to buttress the party line of the denomination. If the sermon has a text, it is used more often than not as a point of departure for an inspirational talk on the Reformed tradition, the 'old time religion,' crisis theology, or the American Way of Life."[2]

The content of our sermons should be the same content as that of the New Testament church. Their's was the announcement of the correlation between the certain facts of history and their own personal experience. "That which we have seen and heard declare we unto you" (I John 1:3).

What were these facts of history? Essentially they were two in number, i.e. the crucifixion and the resurrection. Note that Paul says: "We preach Christ crucified, unto the Jews a stumbling block, and unto the Greeks foolishness . . ." (I Cor. 1:23). In the next chapter he records: "For I determined not to know any thing among you save Jesus Christ, and him crucified" (I Cor. 2:2). The preaching of Christ is insufficient without reference to His crucifixion and resurrection. The two are closely linked in Paul's mind.

---

[1]James S. Stewart, *Heralds of God* (New York: Charles Scribner's Sons, 1946), p. 61.

[2]Donald G. Bloesch, "Can Gospel Preaching Save the Day?" *Eternity*, (July 1969), p. 7.

In the Book of Acts they preached "Jesus and the Resurrection" (Acts 17:18). This is the second historical event which is to be preached. Paul continues in Corinthians: "Now if Christ be preached that he rose from the dead, how say some among you that there is no resurrection of the dead? But if there be no resurrection of the dead, then is Christ not risen; And if Christ be not risen, then is our preaching vain, and your faith is also vain" (I Cor. 15:12–14). Crucifixion and resurrection, the two are insolubly linked together and both are integral to the content of preaching.

Christocentric preaching does not limit the content of preaching. Edmund P. Clowney observes: "This preaching hems you in to Christ's fulness, limits you to all the riches of the wisdom of God, narrows your thought to the mind of Christ, and restricts your vision to one light of the eye, the glory of God in the face of Jesus Christ."[3]

The Whole Counsel

Although the crucifixion and resurrection are the primary contents of preaching, other related areas need to be preached. All biblical themes should be treated by the preacher. In his farewell address to the elders of the church at Ephesus Paul exclaimed: "For I have not shunned to declare unto you all the counsel of God" (Acts 20:27). This whole counsel concept has been battered and scarred through the years but nevertheless the principle remains. All the revelation of God is to be preached. The preacher must never allow his message to degenerate to his "pet peeves." Hobby horses are for kids, not for preachers. More than one good preacher has become fruitless for God because he has discovered some fringe element to preach on and has ridden it to death. Jerry Falwell frequently counsels young preachers: "Be careful not to fall into the ditches on either side of the road. Preach the death, burial, and resurrection of Christ. That's the Gospel."

Preaching the Word involves the command to "reprove, rebuke, exhort with all longsuffering and doctrine" (II Tim. 4:2). This is a day when reproof and exhortation are not popular. Preachers have become guilty of telling people what they want to hear instead of what they need to hear. When was the last time you heard a sermon on the horrors of Hell? How long has it been since you enjoyed a sermon on one of

---

[3]Edmund P. Clowney, "Preaching Christ" *Christianity Today*, (March 12, 1965), p. 7.

the great doctrines of the faith, e.g. justification, imputation of sin, redemption, etc.? II Timothy 3:16 indicates: "All scripture is given by inspiration of God . . ." and too frequently we end our thought there. But the verse continues, "and is profitable for doctrine, for reproof, for correction, for instruction in righteousness." Has it been a long time since you were instructed in righteousness or been reproved or corrected? Do you frequently hear sermons on doctrine? The answer is probably negative, for such preaching is not popular today. The Bible says, however, that Scripture is profitable for doctrine. Let the pulpit be a place for the exposition of sound doctrine as well as sound living.

James Montgomery Boice asks: "Where are the faithful teachers of the whole counsels of the Word of God?" He then answers: "Let the angry God be proclaimed, as well as the God of Love, and men's hearts will be stirred to repentance. Let the sovereign God be proclaimed, and some will bow before Him. They have done it before. They will do it again. Preach doctrine, and many will, out of a true sense of need, flee to the Saviour.'"[4]

Preaching is not a debate but a declaration of the mighty acts of God through Christ Jesus. It is not the propaganda of another religion but the proclamation of Christ's death and resurrection. No matter what the circumstances, preaching always should contain something about Christ's atoning death. Death and resurrection should be preached along with the associated events of Jesus' life and God's historical plan of redemption. Doctrine should be preached. It is no wonder that churches lose their young people when they go to high school and learn about astrophysics, calculus, and geometry and come to Sunday school for the annual rehash of David and Goliath. Growing Christians need meat; the more they grow, the more they need. The more we want them to grow, the more meat we must feed them. The whole truth of God's Word should be preached. We hear much about pastors preaching over the heads of their congregations, but the sad truth is most do not preach over the congregations' heads but under their feet. Such anemic preaching needs an inoculation of sound doctrine.

Do not neglect the Old Testament in your preaching. God's plan of redemption is there too. However, do not expect to get the whole counsel of God into one sermon. Joseph Parker commented: "There

---

[4]James Montgomery Boice, "The Great Need for Great Preaching" *Christianity Today* (December 20, 1974), pp. 8-9.

are those highly illuminated beings who expect a whole scheme of theology in every discourse. I trust they will be starved to death.'"⁵ Cover the whole of divine truth in your preaching, but not on any one Sunday.

Organization

Ronald Willingham says: "'Organization is the shortest distance between two points. A speech without organization is like a voyage without a set destination. Organization is a roadmap. It directs your course when speaking. It plots your starting place, your intermediate stops, and your goal or objective.'"⁶

There are three essentials in organization. Each sermon must have: (1) *aim;* (2) *unity;* and (3) *progression.* Without these three essentials there can be no organization. Like an arrow in flight, organization must have aim (the arrow's target), unity (the components that make the arrow aerodynamically sound), and progression (the movement of the arrow toward the desired end). Let's study these three essentials carefully.

Aim

Someone has said that most speakers aim at nothing and hit it. One of the most essential elements of organization is purpose, a general aim, a goal. Every step of sermon preparation should keep our purpose before it and every step should be checked against the end we are striving to achieve. If we lose sight of our goal we have failed. ''A fanatic,'' wrote Santayana, ''is one who redoubles his effort after he has lost sight of his goal.'' Every sermon begins with an aim and this aim should be written out by the preacher, word for word, and kept constantly before him.

John Henry Jowett put it this way. ''Let us clearly formulate the end at which we aim. Let us put it into words. Don't let it hide in the cloudy realm of vague assumptions. Let us arrest ourselves to name

---

⁵Joseph Parker, *Ad Clerum: Advice to a Young Preacher* (Boston: Roberts Brothers, 1871).

⁶Ronald Willingham, *How To Speak So People Will Listen* (Waco, TX: Word Books, 1976), p. 29.

and register our ends. Let us take a pen in hand, and in order that we may still further banish the peril of vacuity let us commit to paper our purpose and ambition for the day. Let us give it the objectivity of a mariner's chart: let us survey our course, and steadily contemplate our haven. If, when we turn to the pulpit stair, some angel were to challenge us for the statement of our mission, we ought to be able to make immediate answer, without hesitancy or stammering, that this or that is the urgent errand on which we seek to serve our Lord today. But the weakness of the pulpit is too often this: we are prone to drift through a service when we ought to steer."[7]

Whatever our purpose may be, we must maintain it throughout the sermon preparation and the presentation. The purpose of a sermon must be a noble one. It cannot be "to entertain." That may be a worthy purpose for some speeches, but not for a sermon on the Word of God.

Our purpose must be specific as well. Much of preaching today is muddled because it has degenerated to "pulpit talk" or discussion starters. Such sermons begin anywhere in general and usually end up nowhere in particular. Pick a target. Plan for it, prepare for it, and preach for it. You will find that you have not varied from the purpose of your theme.

Unity

The second element of a well organized sermon is unity. As you gaze at DaVinci's *Mona Lisa* or *Last Supper* you do not see a mass of different colors. These paintings are composites of many colors or characters but we are conscious of receiving only one impression. That is because there is a unity to each painting. The impression received is not of separate parts but of a unified whole. Sermons must exhibit the same element.

Like the Master's seamless robe, each of the divisions and parts of a sermon must fit together, not as a patchwork, but as a whole. If one of the component parts does not fit, it should be discarded. "There is no real unity when merely several sides of a subject are elaborated, such as the preacher may happen to choose at the time. There is no genuine unity in an essay-sermon with a number of interesting sub-heads for the

---

[7]John Henry Jowett, *The Preacher: His Life and Work* (Grand Rapids: Baker Book House, 1968), pp. 147–148.

sections of thought that have been selected. Nor is there a unity when a theme is treated under parts that merely tell us more or less of what is in that theme. We can speak of real unity only when a theme is divided into its component parts. Putting it in the simplest way, unity is: (1) that there is one thing, the one named by the theme; (2) all the parts of that one thing, each in its place, none missing. A sermon of this type is a unit in the true sense of the word.'"[8]

To insure unity in the sermon the preacher must select one theme and only one. One single idea has been the success of great master-pieces of literature (*Pilgrim's Progress*), art (the *Mona Lisa*), music (Beethoven's *Moonlight Sonata*). Even campaign slogans such as "I like Ike" or mottos such as "E pluribus unum" exhibit only one theme. Strength comes when there is unity. Weakness comes from division.

You cannot successfully preach on the temptation of Jesus and the murmurings of the children of Israel in the same message. It just can't be done. These two parts don't fit into the whole. Likewise, you cannot preach on Jesus' childhood and the childhood of Moses. Even though you speak only of childhood, there is no unity. Similar ideas or thoughts don't make for unity. Only a single idea in its component parts is a unity.

You cannot speak of two events associated with the theme. For example, it is folly to announce that your next Sunday morning's sermon will be entitled "Jesus' Death and Resurrection." Death and resurrection are related but are too complex to adequately treat in one message. You would be well advised to speak on one or the other in a single sermon. Don't compound your theme; make it a single unit and the sermon itself will become a single unit.

Progression

The sermon continually has to be moving toward its goal or interest will be lost. Progress is akin to unity. As a matter of fact, it is only by progress that unity is achieved. Progress is unity in development; it is a movement toward complete unity.

---

[8]R. C. H. Lenski, *The Sermon, Its Homiletical Construction* (Grand Rapids: Baker Book House, 1968), pp. 78–79.

The secret of attaining progress is a simple one. Determine just where you want to go, then go there directly. Determining where you want to go is the general aim and going directly is progress. Unity is reaching the goal without turning to one side or the other.

Arthur Steven Phelps asks the question: "How can one idea, once presented, progress?" and then answers: "In four ways . . .

> First, there must be progress in interest. Avoid being too interesting in the introduction, as you avoid a dull one. Do not serve the dessert first. Save the most interesting thoughts and illustrations for the last. Work for climax. . . . Study for their climacteric the two greatest stories in literature, The Prodigal Son and The Good Samaritan. There is no falling-off in the interest in the application.
>
> Second, to attain progress in interest, there must be progress in thought. . . . Your thought on any subject grows in width and depth as you pursue the central idea in your mind before putting pen to paper. . . . As each thought is elaborated sufficiently to make sure that it is clear to the hearer, and so driven home that he will retain it, more valuable and profound thoughts will be expected and received by him in the logical chain of reasoning that carries speaker and hearer from height to height as they ascend in company. Every idea is necessary both to the one that precedes it and to the one that follows it.
>
> Third, with progress in interest and progress in thought, the speech that wins attention will have progress in emotion. Save the things that move, that touch the heart, until the evolution of your thought is ready to use them. Let your audience feel the storm gathering. A congregation feels like Livingstone: 'Lead me anywhere, so it be forward.'
>
> Fourth, it may be assumed that if there be progress in reflection and sensation, there will be progress in delivery. Advice to remember is to 'start slow.' Let your delivery take fire as you go along. Progress in delivery will include (a) the voice, in the two factors of volume and speed. It will involve progress (b) in facial expression, as a skillful actor shows in his features. . . . (c) There will be also progress in gesture, like the parts of a machine responding to the push of inward power.[9]

Sequential Steps to the Sermon

Every good sermon must possess the same organized sequence that good speeches possess. This sequence is in the form of "steps" which

---

[9]Arthur Stevens Phelps, *Speaking in Public* (Grand Rapids: Baker Book House, 1958), pp. 122–123.

need to be followed in order that the desired response will be achieved. It is vitally important that the preacher organize his sermon so the congregation will respond psychologically in the prescribed manner, so that his end will be gained. Alan H. Monroe has noted five such steps:

 1. **Attention Step.** The function of this step is to arrest the attention of the audience. The attention must not only be gained but favorably gained.

 2. **Need Step.** Describing the problem or establishing the need is the function of this step. The congregation must be convinced of their need of a Savior, their need to witness, etc.

 3. **Satisfaction Step.** After establishing a need, fill it. Your purpose here will be to get the audience to believe that you have the answer to fill their need.

 4. **Visualization Step.** It is here that the congregation will 'see' themselves enjoying the benefits of having a Savior or of witnessing. They visualize the results of the satisfaction step.

 5. **Action Step.** The function of the final step is to get the congregation to do something about what they visualize as true. It is here that they say, 'Yes, I will do or believe this.' ''[10]

Once a preacher has a goal in mind, a purpose for preaching this particular day, and has organized his message into a unified whole which will progressively increase in thought and persuasion, and once the above five steps are clearly seen in the organization of his sermon, he will have little problem in achieving the end he has in mind. With the direction of the Spirit of God in the minds of his hearers and the proper organized preparation, the message will become a logical presentation of the Word of God moving toward a definite goal. This is what is so needed in preaching today. The famous Irish patriot, Daniel O'Connel, said: "A good speech is a good thing, but the verdict is the thing." How true. Preach for a verdict, a definite goal. Plan it well in advance and guide every step of preparation and presentation toward that goal.

---

[10]Alan H. Monroe, *Principles and Types of Speech* (Chicago: Scott, Foresman and Company, 1949), Preface ix.

Arrangement

The third element in a good sermon is the arrangement of the sermon. A sermon needs an outline just as a man needs a skeleton. Shedd says: "The evils of sermonizing without skeletonizing are many and great . . . if he (the preacher) neglects the practice of skeletonizing, he becomes rambling and diffuse. Having no leading idea branching off into natural ramifications by which to guide his mental processes, they run and ramble in every direction."[11]

Many times the only difference between a good sermon, one with great persuasiveness, and a sermon lacking in such power is a difference in arrangement. Lack of arrangement is probably the single most common fault of preaching today. Some sermons remind the congregation of the beginnings of creation; they are like the early earth, "without form and void."

As a builder, the preacher gathers his materials for the sermon and then proceeds to build a structure as in a building. This structure is suited to a specific design which will fit the present purpose of the sermon. When the builder builds a building he makes several floors, each equipped with entrances and windows. The preacher builds a sermon with several divisions, each equipped with entrances and windows (illustrations). When the builder is finished he has several levels, each with sublevels or divisions, but just one unified building. Likewise, the preacher finishes with several divisions, each with subdivisions, but ends up with but one unified sermon.

In this same vein, Henry Grady Davis lobbies for specific structure and arrangement in sermons: "Speeches can of course be knocked together with a saw and hammer. There is always much lumber of moral and religious platitudes lying around—prose, verse, stock anecdotes, glittering generalities, all over the place—kites in the wind of fashionable thought. A man can cut, splice, and nail it together exactly as he would build a doghouse. But sermons are not doghouses and preachers are responsible to build mansions for the Kingdom of God. Every sermon should be a masterpiece to the glory of God."[12]

---

[11]W. G. T. Shedd, *Homiletics and Pastoral Theology* (London: Banner of Truth Trust, 1965), p. 186.

[12]Henry Grady Davis, *Design for Preaching* (Philadelphia: Fortress Press, 1958), p. 82.

There are a number of advantages in having arrangement (an outline) to the sermon.

Advantage to the Preacher

When a preacher has a well-arranged sermon it assists him in working out the little details of the message. They fall naturally into place. He will also have far less difficulty in delivering his sermon if the preacher outlines it properly. If he is to use the memorization method, he will be aided by arrangement. If he is to preach extemporaneously without notes, arrangement aids him. Whatever is logically and clearly outlined will be easier to memorize and retain.

Advantage to the Sermon

Arrangement adds to the beauty of the sermon. Have you ever seen the beautiful gardens at Versailles? The symmetry makes the gardens beautiful even in winter when the fountains are not flowing and the flowers are not blooming. So it is with the sermon. Harmony in arrangement turns a dull sermon into an interesting one.

Again, good arrangement makes a sermon more persuasive. Progressive arrangement is the key to persuasion. To cut a diamond you do not chisel here, there, and everywhere. You progressively tap away in a specific arrangement of blows. Likewise, a sermon needs arrangement to be effective.

Advantage to the Congregation

It is absolutely essential that the preacher arrange his sermon so that the congregation can follow him. Good arrangement will help keep the audience with you. If a good outline makes it easier for the preacher to remember his sermon, it will certainly make it easier for the audience to remember it. Without good arrangement the audience will come away saying, "My, what a blessing that was," but what a shallow Christian experience is produced from little "blessings" without real learning and exhortation from the Word. The congregation has a right to receive instruction, rebuke, reproof, correction, and exhortation as well as a blessing from the sermon. To accomplish this demands clear arrangement. Clear arrangement will engender a remembering congregation. Without specific arrangement the congregation will soon forget the message and the sermon will be of little lasting value.

Good arrangement necessitates a good outline. A good outline is one in which each division contains but one statement of truth and the subdivisions and subpoints are logically subordinated under each main division. Also, the logical relationship between main divisions, subdivisions, and subpoints should be shown by indentation and the use of numerals. The mind does not think in terms of letters, such as a, b, c, but in terms of numerals like 1, 2, 3. Therefore, indent subordinate statements, but make sure always to number them.

Consistency

The final essential element in a good sermon is consistency. When you use a noun in main division one, do not use a verb in division two, and a sentence in main division three. An example of inconsistency in outlining is:

I.   God is Love
II. God deals in justice
III. Holiness is an attribute of God

How much better to be consistent and say:

I.   God is Love
II. God is Justice
III. God is Holiness

Give the audience a break. Make it easy for them to remember what you say. Make your outline rememberable. Here is an example of a sermon with main divisions and subdivisions which is gleaned from II Timothy 4:1-8. Notice the subordination of the subdivisions, the enumeration of the subdivisions, the alliteration (where possible) for easy memorization and audience retention, and the consistency in using nouns, verbs, etc. The introduction and the conclusion have been excluded because we are presently only concerned with the body of the sermon.

II Timothy 4:1–8

I. PAUL'S CHARGE, verses 1–2.
    1. Definition of a charge. vs. 1.
    2. Description of the charge. vs. 2.

II. PAUL'S CAUTION, verses 3–4.
    1. Caution against false doctrine. vs. 3.
    2. Caution against false teachers. vs. 3.
    3. Caution against false religions. vs. 3.

III. PAUL'S CONCERN, verse 5.
    1. That Timothy endure afflictions. vs. 5.
    2. That Timothy evangelize. vs. 5.
    3. That Timothy prove his ministry. vs. 5.

IV. PAUL'S CONFIDENCE, verse 7.
    1. That he fought a good fight. vs. 7.
    2. That he finished his course. vs. 7.
    3. That he kept the faith. vs. 7.

V. PAUL'S CROWN, verse 8.
    1. The purpose of the crown: righteousness. vs. 8.
    2. The person of the crown: the Righteous Judge. vs. 8.

Dr. D. Martyn Lloyd-Jones relates a delightful true story about a quaint old preacher who preached on the text, "And Balaam arose early and saddled his ass." Lloyd-Jones says: "After introducing the subject and reminding his hearers of the story, he came to the divisions. 'First,' he said, 'we find a good trait in a bad character,'— "Balaam arose early." Early rising is a good thing; so that is the first head. Secondly, 'The antiquity of saddlery—"he saddled his ass." Saddlery is not something modern and new, it was an ancient craft.' And then the inspiration seemed to have vanished and he could not think of another heading. Yet he felt that he must have three heads to the sermon, otherwise he would not be a great preacher. So the divisions of the sermon were eventually announced as—'A good trait in a bad character.' 'The antiquity of saddlery.' 'Thirdly and lastly, a few remarks concerning the Woman of Samaria.' "[13]

---

[13]D. Martyn Lloyd-Jones, *Preaching and Preachers* (Grand Rapids: Zondervan Publishing House, 1971), p. 208.

These main divisions not only fail the test of consistency, but of logic as well. Such a practice is not praiseworthy and should never be employed. With preaching like this it is no wonder there is need of a prescription for preaching.

Content, organization, arrangement, and consistency are the four essential elements in a good sermon. Don't be caught without them.

9

The Component Parts
of a Sermon

*"Sermons should have real teaching in them, and their doctrine
should be solid, substantial, and abundant. We do not enter the
pulpit to talk for talk's sake; we have instructions to convey
important to the last degree, and we cannot afford to utter pretty
nothings"* —Charles Haddon Spurgeon

*"Study carefully what you have to say, and put it into words by
writing or by speaking aloud to an imaginary person. Arrange
your points in order. Stick to your order. Divide your time among
your points according to their importance. Stop when you are
through"* —Edward Everett Hale

In his *De Arte Rhetorica* (iii. 13), Aristotle enumerates four parts to
oration. Those four parts are: the introduction, the proposition, the
proof, and the conclusion. In his famous speech/book *Acres of
Diamonds*, Russell Conwell advises three steps to oratory, namely: (1)
state your facts; (2) argue for them; and (3) appeal for action. Whether
you follow Aristotle's list of four, Conwell's list of three, or Monroe's
five steps of attention, need, satisfaction, visualization, and action, the
component parts of the sermon are much the same. Every speech or

sermon needs an introduction, body, and conclusion. These parts are sometimes referred to as the functional elements of speech.

Introduction

Motto: Well begun—half done. The introduction is a component of extreme importance. To see the need of a good introduction one need only look at a book. It is significant that every well written book has a preface, every oratorio has a prelude, and every major work has an introduction. Likewise, the day does not begin with instant light but is given an introduction via the sunrise. Many books of the Bible have introductions as well. The purpose of an introduction to a sermon is as follows.

(1). The introduction secures the good will of the hearers.
(2). The introduction awakens the interest of the hearers.
(3). The introduction provides an entrance into the theme.
(4). The introduction prepares the audience for what follows.

The main purpose of the introduction is to develop interest in what is to follow. It is the introduction which captures the minds of the audience. If the introduction fails, the entire sermon is a failure. Thus, arousing interest is vital.

In his book, *The Art of Preaching,* Charles R. Brown says: "The clock has nothing to do with the length of a sermon. Nothing whatever! . . . A long sermon is a sermon that seems long. . . . And the short sermon is the one that ends while people are still wishing for more. It may have lasted only twenty minutes or it may have lasted for an hour and a half. If it leaves the people wishing for more, they do not know nor care what the clock said about the length of it.' "[1]

Such interest must begin with the introduction. The first few minutes are crucial. The introduction should not only be brief but completely void of dull and inane remarks. This is not the place for irrelevant trivia. It is the place for information, but in a minimum quantity. Just enough information should be given to whet the appetite of the audi-

---

[1]Charles R. Brown, *The Art of Preaching* (New York: The Macmillan Co., 1932), p. 97.

ence. It is the place to gain the undivided attention of the congregation. It holds a vital place in the sermon. The introduction " . . . should be in accord with the interest, objectives, and feelings common to your hearers. ''[2]

Types of Good Introductions

What are some types of good introductions? Let me suggest a few.

1. **The Text.** Obviously the best place to start a textual sermon is with the text itself. The reading of the text is a proper way to begin an introduction, especially if the text is one like I John 4:20: "If a man says, I love God, and hateth his brother, he is a liar; for he that loveth not his brother, whom he hath seen, how can he love God, whom he hath not seen?"

2. **The Context.** If you are speaking about Paul's statement in Galatians 1:10, "For do I now persuade men, or God? or do I seek to please men? for if I yet pleased men, I should not be the servant of Christ," you must explain the difficulty Paul encountered in establishing his apostleship in some Christian quarters. Everywhere he went the apostle was hounded by Judaizers and false teachers. He had to firmly vindicate his apostleship to the church of which he said, "I marvel that you are so soon removed . . ." (Gal. 1:6). Thus the context reveals why he made such a statement in verse ten.

3. **The Subject.** If the sermon is a topical one you might begin by explaining something about the subject. For instance, if your theme is the unknown god which Paul spoke about on Mars' Hill, you may inform your congregation about the subject of mystical idol worship in the ancient Near East. This not only educates the congregation but also provides a useful point of reference for incidental information presented during the sermon.

4. **The Historical Setting.** It would be difficult to give a sermon on Daniel chapter one without explaining the warfare between Judah and Babylon. The successive Babylonian invasions of Palestine need to be delineated and distinguished. The change in the world's balance of power when Nebuchadnezzar defeated the Egyptians at Carchemish in 605 B.C. needs to be explained. In this case an understanding of the historical setting is definitely needed and makes a perfect introduction.

---

[2]Wilbur Gilman, Bown Aly, and Loren Reid, *Fundamentals of Speaking* (New York: The Macmillan Co., 1951), p. 69.

5. **Bible Customs.** Speaking of Jesus' encounter with the woman of Samaria at the well of Jacob should begin with some mention of the ancient custom of gathering water at the community well, the center of conversation in Palestine. Why was the woman at the well so late? What was the reason the women came to the well and not their husbands? Relating the customs of Jesus' day to this twentieth-century world is an invaluable way to begin a sermon. There are sufficient "manners and customs" books available today to give the preacher more material than he will ever need.

6. **Geography of the Bible.** Baffling to Bible students for years has been the reference in the parable of the good Samaritan, that "a certain man went down from Jerusalem to Jericho, and fell among thieves . . ." (Luke 10:30). A glance at the map would indicate that Jericho is northeast of Jerusalem and one would naturally say, "a certain man went *up* from Jerusalem to Jericho." However, an explanation of the geography of the Bible lands indicates that from Jerusalem (about 2,550 feet above sea level) to Jericho (about 825 feet below sea level) is a drop in elevation of about 3,375 feet in a distance of seventeen miles. This explains the going down to Jericho. One must descend the wilderness mountainsides to the sprawling Jordan Valley to reach Jericho from Jerusalem.

7. **The Occasion.** Perhaps you are speaking at an Easter sunrise service. The very occasion itself would provide a beginning point for the sermon. That early morning resurrection was but one in a long series of "early in the morning" events (cf. Abraham—Gen. 22:3; Moses—Gen. 8:20; 9:13; Joshua—Josh. 6:12; David—I Sam. 17:20; etc.). God does significant things early in the morning. Also, mention of the fact that Christ did most of His preaching in the open would be a point of identification for an introduction at an open-air sunrise service. The occasion makes the perfect introduction.

8. **The Quotation.** Frequently preachers will begin with a famous quotation or saying. An example would be the famous quotation of H. G. Wells: "Religion is the first thing and the last. Until a man finds God and has been found by Him, he begins at no beginning and works to no end." What an attention getter!

9. **The Illustration or Story.** This method provides for the maximum amount of immediate interest. Nothing gains attention like a good story, especially a personal one. It makes the congregation feel like they are a part of you, the speaker. Likewise, an illustration is a

thought-grabber. It sets the tone for what is to follow. Don't allow the story or illustration to be too lengthy or interest will wane. That which could be a great introduction could be instead a disaster if interest is not captured and held. Make the introductory illustration or story crisp, poignant, and powerful.

10. **The Startling Statement.** This is what Dr. H. A. Overstreet called the "shock technic" for it jars the attention of the audience and compels them to listen. Such a biblical statement is Psalm 22:1: "My God, my God, why hast thou forsaken Me? Why art thou so far from helping me, and from the words of my roaring?" Other startling statements would be: "God doesn't want you to die prematurely!" or "Preachers who do not believe the Bible to be God's infallible word ought to get out of the ministry and start making an honest living!" One must be careful not to overdo this approach, however, to avoid grandstanding.

11. **The Rhetorical Question.** An effective method of gaining interest is the rhetorical question. You are almost assured of getting the attention of the congregation if you begin your sermon by asking: "What do you think the consequences would be if you fell asleep in church this morning?" Everyone has heard such questions as: "If you died today, do you know where you would spend eternity?" Questions automatically arouse the interest of an audience. Rhetorical questions are not designed to be answered, but frequently, much to the chagrin of the preacher, they are answered. When such an answer is blurted out, be prepared to handle it or, if you can, simply ignore it.

12. **The Humorous Anecdote.** Humor or a funny experience always gets a speech off to a good start. There are two things that should be remembered about using humor in the pulpit. First, if you tell a humorous anecdote, make sure that it is really funny. If it falls flat, you have defeated the purpose of an introduction. Secondly, the preacher must be careful of the type and amount of humor used in association with the Word of God. Good taste should be used and humor should not be overdone. The house of God is not a night club, nor is the sermon a comedy routine.

Characteristics of a Good Introduction

What are some characteristics of a good introduction? Consider the following.

1. A good introduction is a brief introduction. Of course you will want to proportion it to the length of the message, but in general it should be brief. This is the worst place to string out your material.

2. A good introduction should not be stereotyped. Variety is the key. Don't always use the same words or expressions such as, "Now, to begin with . . ." or "By way of introduction. . . ." Such expressions were worn out long ago.

3. A good introduction will not be over-ornate. It should be kept simple. Hear the advice of the homilitician Lenski: "Do not become ornate in the introduction. At times a 'fine' introduction must be written out in order to get it out of the preacher's system. Write it, and then solemnly consign it to the wastebasket. All introductions should be direct and simple."[3]

4. Do not allow the introduction to become too cluttered or over-loaded with material. Remember this is the introduction, not the discussion of the text or theme. This segment of the sermon is only to lead into the body of material. It should be kept light.

5. Do not allow the introduction to be too good. This might sound strange, but it is true. The introduction must not be the climax of the sermon. Remember, you have the entire sermon to go and it must have good progression. Don't be so dramatic in the "intro" that everything else about your sermon seems dull by comparison.

6. Thoroughly prepare your introduction. A frequent mistake among preachers is to begin making an outline with the single word *Introduction* and then continue immediately to outline the body of the message without returning to prepare the introduction. The introduction is of such importance as to require equal thought to that given the body of the sermon. Think it through, plan it out, then outline it as you would the discussion. Having thoroughly prepared the introduction, commit it to memory.

Read the advice of Charles R. Brown in his Lyman Beecher Lectures of 1922–23. Dean Brown declared: "The man who preaches without manuscript reaches levels of joy in his preaching which I am sure the preacher from manuscript knows not of." But, Brown continues, "in my own practice, while I never use a manuscript in preach-

---

[3]R. C. H. Lenski, *The Sermon, Its Homiletical Construction* (Grand Rapids: Baker Book House, 1968), p. 301.

ing, there are five sentences in my sermon which I always write out in advance and know by heart—the first one and the last four.'"[4]

What Dr. Brown has said is good advice. You should strive to have the thoughts and statements of the introduction at the very tip of your tongue. They must be fresh, alive and immediate. If you hesitate here the congregation will lose confidence in you, and even if you have something of great import to say in the body of the message, you will not be heeded. Therefore, commit to memory the main thoughts of the introduction or even memorize the entire introduction itself to insure that what you say will not be trite or irrelevant. Writing out and memorizing the introduction is not what Professor Lenski was condemning above. He condemned the "fine" or fancy introduction. To be thoroughly prepared in the introduction and have these words ready to go is just good common sense.

Body

After the introduction is successfully finished and the congregation is eager to listen to the speaker, he may then proceed to the body of the sermon. Although this main partition of the sermon is viewed by various homiliticians as being composed of a varying number of aspects, yet most would agree that at least three are involved. These three are the *explanation,* the *argumentation,* and the *application.*

Explanation

Whether you are preaching a topical sermon, an expository sermon, a textual sermon, or any combination of these three, it goes without saying that there will be some amount of explanation needed in the presentation of the sermon. There will always be words, Scripture verses, concepts, doctrines, and phrases which need to be explained. Thus, having presented the theme of your sermon and having read the text (if the sermon calls for a text), your next task will be to explain that theme or text.

---

[4]Charles R. Brown, *Art of Preaching,* p. 87ff.

The explanation of the theme or text can be accomplished in several ways. Probably the most prominent is that of *exposition*. By exposition is meant the exposing of certain data relevant to the text or included in the text such as would enable as detailed an explanation as possible. By exposition the preacher can present the truth contained in a text and expose those details which will enable his congregation to grasp the importance of the text or theme.

Another popular method of explaining a theme or text is by *division*. By dividing a text into its obvious components the preacher can show the interrelationships among these components and give the sequence or logical progression of the principles involved in the text. Given a knowledge of the "approaches" described in chapter 10 of this book and a little "homiletical horsesense," any preacher will be able to correctly "divide" the Word.

A third method of explanation is *exegesis*. By the use of exegesis a preacher can bring to bear on his theme the original meaning of the words of Scripture. Thus those hard to understand passages become more understandable through an exegetical explanation. To exegete a passage is to sift through it as a miner would pan for gold. All the nuggets are extracted and carefully examined. Thus the whole is understood by a close examination of the parts. The text becomes more meaningful as the words and phrases of the text are exegeted and become more meaningful.

Interpretation is the final method of explanation. The interpretation of passages of Scripture, rightly done, gives a great deal of assistance to the understanding and comprehension of the audience. Interpretation, however, must be faithful to the text and in the mainstream of Christian thought. False or faulty interpretation will lead to confusion and result in misunderstanding. Often the explanation of a text is aided by an explanation of Bible customs which pertain to that text. For example, an understanding of the lonely and protective life of a shepherd in Palestine will give greater appreciation to Psalm 23. Knowing the background to a Scripture passage or the customs of the time will give rise to a more accurate interpretation.

By this and other methods the explanation of a passage can be achieved. However, we must recognize that mere explanation does not make good preaching. The added elements of argumentation and application must be applied.

Argumentation

By argumentation we mean the arriving at proper conclusions by a process of reasoning. *Argument* means to persuade, convince, prove, discuss, or refute. Although argument is a necessary element in preaching, as is evidenced by the logical preaching of Paul, the preacher must realize that argument alone is not preaching. To preach is not to argue but to testify and proclaim. It is not our purpose to persuade men by the cunningness of our argument or our ability to debate. We are to preach Christ crucified. Nevertheless, our preaching must be logical and the arguments presented for belief based on sound philosophical principles.

In general, we should always argue from the known to the unknown. This is one of the reasons why the preaching of Jesus was so successful. The common folk heard Christ gladly because they could understand His arguments. He used arguments which concerned wheat, corn, water, and other things with which they were familiar. When we argue in the sermon, we will probably use one of the following forms of arguments.

Testimony

An ancient yet very valuable form of argument is the argument from testimony. Personal testimony is the best. However, many times the preacher must rely on the testimony of others. In this case, the preacher must be sure the one advancing the testimony is of high integrity, that the facts presented by the witness are of high character, and that the facts are attested to by other witnesses. The Bible is replete with personal testimony and answers to such questions as: "What think ye of Christ?"

Cause and Effect

This means that every effect is produced by some cause and every cause has a corresponding effect. You may give the effects such as the Christian Church, the empty tomb, the appearances of Jesus after His crucifixion, or the Lord's Day and ask for the cause. The cause obviously is the resurrection of Jesus Christ. Conversely, you may advance the cause such as the new birth and ask for effects, (e.g. a changed life, love for Jesus, a new moral standard, a desire to love and serve God, etc.).

PRESCRIPTION FOR PREACHING

Deduction

Deduction is reasoning from a known principle to an unknown, from the general to the specific, from a premise to a logical conclusion. An example: "All men are mortal; all Greeks are men; therefore, all Greeks are mortal." This type of argument in sermonizing may easily fall prey to the fallacy of the illicit minor as if often does in philosophy. That is, if the minor premise (all Greeks are men) is untrue, the conclusion will be false as well. As you develop your biblical deductive argument, make sure that each premise is true.

Induction

Induction is the reasoning from particular facts or individual cases to a general conclusion. Having found that certain things are true of individual objects, we then conclude that the same thing is true of the whole class to which these individual objects belong. In essence, this method of argument tells us: "Jesus Christ has changed the life of John and Mary, and He can do the same for you."

Refutation

There are times when a preacher must refute a false doctrine or church rumor; it is at these times when this form of argument becomes extremely helpful. By sound doctrine the preacher must "exhort and convince the gainsayers. For there are many unruly and vain talkers and deceivers . . . whose mouths must be stopped" (Titus 1:9–11). Refutation is used only when errors exist. The preacher should not create an error in order to refute it. Refutation consists basically of the use of *reductio ad absurdum,* reducing the substance of the doctrine or rumor to absurdity.

Authority

One of the greatest forms of argument is based on authority. Of course, foremost in this respect is the greatest authority, the Bible itself. For Christians, arguing matters of faith and practice can best be handled by use of the authoritative Word of God. This is our final court of appeal in the Christian life. Even for the unsaved, arguments from authority combined with other arguments are helpful.

Analogy

This form of reasoning brings to bear the similarities between two or more things. It frequently uses the correlative conjunctions "Just as . . . so also'' or ''not only . . . but also.'' Hence, the preacher, using this form of argument, might say, ''Just as Christ is the head of the church and loves her, so also the husband is the head of the wife and must love her.''

Experience

It is said that the best argument for answered prayer is answered prayer. To the two on the Emmaus Road, the best argument for the resurrection of Jesus Christ was our Lord's appearance to them. The best argument for the possibility of living a faithful Christian life is someone who lives a faithful Christian life. For you, the best argument of salvation is your own salvation experience. Argument from experience is the strongest of all possible arguments. Remember, the man with an experience is never at the mercy of a man with an argument. Use your Christian experience as an effective argument for Christ's saving power.

Illustration

''The sense was dark—'twas therefore fit with simile to illustrate it''—William Cowper. According to the etymology of the word, *illustrate* means to light up, throw light upon, give luster to, illuminate. It has been correctly said that the illustration is to the sermon what a window is to a building. That is, the illustration lets light into a sermon the way a window lets light into a dark building.

The illustration has been a form of illumination in speech nearly as long as speech has existed. The earliest languages made use of the illustration in the very symbols which they used. For instance, Egyptian hieroglyphics were based upon the illustration principle, picture words. The second letter of the Hebrew alphabet is another example. The *beth,* ב, not only means house but is in the shape of a roof. The Japanese word-symbol for the word *west* is ⊕ which is a picture to represent the sun sinking behind a tree. Even the Greek delta Δ forms a similar picture. Thus, the illustration is very much a part of language and its symbols.

The Value of Illustrations

Illustrations explain truth. Many times the truth which you present from the Word of God is too profound to be understood by the audience. Other times the audience is too ignorant of the Bible to comprehend biblical truth. It is then necessary that light be shed on the subject, light which can be understood by the congregation. This light may come from an example, exemplification, or a case in point, by presenting something similar or analogous. However it comes, it will be present for the purpose of explaining what has already been said. The function of giving clarity to the sermon is probably the primary function of the illustration.

Illustrations prove truth. A favorite form of argumentation is illustration. Not only do illustrations explain the truth of the Word, they also may be used to prove that truth as well. This is generally done by the argument of analogy. Romans 6:4 is an example. "Therefore, we are buried with him by baptism into death, that as Christ was raised up from the dead by the glory of the Father, even so we also should walk in newness of life." This illustration of Christ's death and resurrection is used to prove the truth that when we are buried with Christ in baptism we should be raised from the baptism to walk in newness of life, even as Christ Jesus walked anew in life. The proof of our changed life and godly walk is given by the analogy to Christ's own death and resurrection to newness of life.

Illustrations emphasize truth. Once a truth has been explained and proven it must yet be emphasized before it will be believed. Thus, the preacher may use an illustration to show the importance of the truth which he has explained and proven. For instance, if the preacher wants to emphasize the importance of witnessing for the Lord Jesus now, not putting it off until some future time, he may use the following illustration.

> While we admire Abraham Lincoln and honor his memory, there is one thing in which we cannot hold him up as a shining example—and that is in regard to his putting off a public confession of his faith in Christ. Lincoln read the Bible, prayed, and had high moral principles; yet is has often been debated whether he was a true believer. The question arises largely from his reluctance to join any local church and thus become identified with the people of God. He attended the First Presbyterian Church in Springfield, Illinois, but hesitated when asked to make confession of his faith. Although he had a specially assigned pew, and contributed regularly to the church's expenses, he did not join. He said little or nothing about his personal salvation and hope of Heaven. But it is now known that for months he was under deep conviction concerning these matters.

The history of the New York Presbyterian Church, Washington, D.C., was recently researched, and among the documents found in the archives was a letter signed by President Lincoln. It stated that he had given due consideration to the question of his soul and was finally ready to give a public confession of his faith in Christ. The letter was written on April 13, 1865. His reception into the church was set for Sunday, April 18. However, on April 14, 1865 (one day after he wrote the letter), Abraham Lincoln was assassinated.[5]

Illustrations ornament truth. If your style of preaching tends to be barren and uninteresting, the illustration will enable you to become more elegant in style. It is no sin to be elegant and interesting as long as the truth is plainly presented. Many preachers need far more elegance. However, it should be warned that we use illustrations in order to make our style of preaching more interesting and not simply to make it ornamental. Remember your message. If your style is too ornate and you call attention to yourself, something must be changed. However, if your style is dull and uninteresting, this too will inhibit your message. Illustrations help to overcome this problem. Do not, however, allow illustrations to become an end in themselves.

Illustrations clinch truth. By this we mean that an apt illustration is a powerful tool in bringing about conviction. In this respect an illustration can be used effectively at the close of a message or speech to draw together the truth of that message. If the audience has been listening to the message and you have explained and proved the truth of the Word, then it is only natural to give that truth a final emphasis. A final illustration is an excellent way to clinch their understanding and to bring them to a decision. Thus, conviction is often brought about by what has been called the "sledgehammer of illustration."

Illustrations preserve truth. It is sometimes very easy for the congregation to forget most of what the pastor has said within a very few minutes of his message. Probably all pastors have had the experience of someone telling them that they have forgotten what the pastor said but remembered the message for they could not forget the illustration he used. Good anecdotes or story illustrations are far more easily remembered than the arguments of a sermon. This should have some bearing on the way a sermon is brought to a close. Allow your con-

---

[5]Quoted by Henry C. Bosch in *Our Daily Bread* (Grand Rapids: Radio Bible Class).

gregation's memory of the truth you presented to be aided by a well-timed, well-chosen illustration.

Ten Characteristics of Good Illustrations

It must be abundantly clear that the use of illustrations in preaching is not only desirable but many times necessary. Here are ten suggestions for the wise use of illustrations.

1. Illustrations should be *selective*. Be careful not to use every illustration that occurs to you. After a person has had a great deal of pastoral experience he has an abundant supply of illustrations for every occasion. It is a great temptation to use too many illustrations. You must be selective. You cannot allow your sermon to be built around illustrations. Never tell a story or give an illustration just for the sake of having one. Let your illustrations be windows and not the building itself. Generally, one illustration per main division is sufficient.

2. Illustrations should be *relevant*. Make sure your illustration actually illustrates what you are talking about. You must question your illustration. "Does it really do the job?" "Does it illustrate what I am speaking of?" If the answer to these questions is negative, then the illustration must be disregarded no matter how good it is. If you give an illustration which has little or no bearing on the truth you are presenting, your audience will become confused. Illustrations are to illustrate truth. Make sure the truth illustrated is the same truth which makes up the content of your message.

3. Illustrations should be *simple*. It is a serious fault to tell such a long or complicated story that the congregation can't remember which truth you are applying the illustration to. Make illustrations so simple that even a child can understand them. If the illustration is overly complicated or too lengthy it tends to become so prominent that it robs the message of its priority.

4. Illustrations should be *comprehensible*. It is folly to use an illustration of the workings of a computer if you are ministering to a farming community. Likewise, illustrating crop rotation to an urban church is not wise. The illustrations which are used must be understood by the congregation in order for the truth to be enlightened. Thus, a technical illustration which no one can understand is no illustration at all. No light has been let in. Illustrations drawn from a region remote from the life of your congregation will bring no response from them at all. Make sure the illustrations that you use are of the type with which your congregation can identify.

5. Illustrations should be *accurate*. If the illustration is worth telling, it is worth telling accurately. The facts must not be exaggerated or distorted. The preacher must not say: "I once knew a man from Texas, or was it Nevada? Well, it was one of those places...." If you are going to tell a story, get the facts straight first.

6. Illustrations should be *believable*. Do not resort to wide-eyed, ridiculous, sensational illustrations. Illustrations which are far-fetched only discredit the truth you are presenting. If there is some question about the believability of your illustration there will soon be some question about the believability of your truth. Do not assume that your congregation is gullible enough to swallow everything you give them. Make sure your illustrations are not incredible, unless you can show cause why the incredible should be believed.

7. Illustrations most definitely should be *true*. One great fault with illustrations is when they are misused. I know a pastor who used to take illustrations from a daily devotional booklet and use them as his personal experience. His congregation, however, read the same devotional booklet. One week they would read about a man with a unique experience and the next Sunday their pastor coincidentally had that same experience. This must never happen. Do not take illustrations which did not happen to you and make them personal. That is lying.

8. Illustrations should be *tasteful*. Illustrations using the grotesque or bizarre are out of place in the pulpit. Cleverness in illustrations can never compensate for good taste. If they do not exhibit a certain refinement, do not use them. Vulgarity and irreverence are not to be permitted. An occasional bit of humor can be used effectively, but if the audience is "roaring" they have lost the thought of the truth which you have been attempting to shed light on. Remember your message.

9. Illustrations should be *told,* not talked about. By this I mean a preacher should not spend his time and our time telling us that he is going to give an illustration. It is not necessary to say "Now, let me illustrate that." You need not announce illustrations. If they throw light on your subject you will get the job done without useless announcing.

10. Finally, illustrations should be *told well*. Just as you should practice your message and the Scripture reading, it is wise to practice your illustrations as well. Get the facts straight and get them down pat. Unless it is statistical or other difficult information, never read your illustration. Just as something is lost in a sermon that is read, so something is lost in an illustration that is read. Windows cannot let light in if

they are rigidly barred. Neither can illustrations cast any light on a sermon if they are uninterestingly read.

James Stewart relates the following of George Whitefield.

> There was a day when the flaming prophet of the eighteenth century, George Whitefield, was preaching to a vast throng on the power of saving faith. 'The pride of reason and worldly wisdom,' he declared, 'would lead the soul downward to inevitable destruction: only faith in Christ led heavenward.' To drive the point home to his hearers' minds, he used an illustration. He begged them to imagine a blind man, with a dog, walking on the brink of a precipice. So vividly did the preacher describe the scene, so acute became the tension as he brought the blind man nearer and nearer to the fatal edge, that suddenly Lord Chesterfield, who was sitting in the congregation, sprang up exclaiming, 'Good God! The man's gone.' 'No, my lord,' answered Whitefield, 'he is not quite gone; let us hope that he may yet be saved.' Then he went on to preach deliverance from the delusions of blind self-trust through faith in Jesus Christ.[6]

That is telling an illustration so vividly that the congregation actually sees it. Every preacher needs to strive for such mastery.

Sources of Illustrative Material

Where can a preacher go to get his illustrations? Let me suggest a few places. (1) The Bible itself has the most complete stockpile of illustrative material. Use both the Old and New Testaments. This is by far your best source. (2) Personal observation of the world around you yields illustrations. The great New York Yankee catcher Yogi Berra once said, "You observe a lot through observation." Keep your eyes open for illustrations. Watch for them and jot them down. (4) History is replete with examples and illustrations, especially the history of the great empires and their leaders. (5) Literature in all forms is a great source. Read and look to the classics, the Apocrypha, and modern writers for good illustrative material. (6) Science gives many examples of illustrative material. Experiments and properties are very interesting. Space and the universe abound with this type of illustration. (7) The arts, paintings, and music provide good material. (8) The world of industry and labor is also a source. (9) Law and government. See the Constitution and other historical documents for good material. (10)

[6]James S. Stewart, *Heralds of God* (New York: Charles Scribner's Sons, 1946), pp. 141–142.

Devotional booklets, such as *Our Daily Bread, The Secret Place, The Upper Room,* etc. (11) The world of sports provides many great stories. (12) Observation of children is a most useful enterprise, for everyone loves illustrations about children. (13) Biographies provide many personal illustrations of individuals. (14) The animal, mineral, and vegetable kingdoms were used by Jesus as illustrations. He spoke of sheep, goats, camels, birds, vines, vegetables, grain, corn, lilies, pearls, gold, salt, etc. (15) The newspapers, magazines, etc. give good illustration material that is thoroughly up-to-date. Read the newspaper every day to stay on top of current illustrative material.

From what has been said, it is obvious that a good supply of illustrations is needed. A preacher cannot, however, be expected to memorize all the possible illustrative material available to him. He also cannot repeat his illustrations too frequently. He may have to use a book of illustrations. Yet many wise preachers feel that this practice is not a good one. James Stewart says: "Ready-made collections of illustrations are a snare. Omnibus volumes of sermon anecdotes are the last refuge of bankrupt intelligence. The best illustrations are those which come to you as the harvest of your own reading and observation."[7] It is very difficult to appropriate an illustration from a book to a sermon. This does not mean that it cannot be done, only that one is far wiser to glean his illustrations for himself rather than relying on someone else. "Regardless of the theme in the mind of the preacher, he can by concentration call out of the past the choicest experiences of life. These do not smell of books and research, but of joy, sorrow, happiness—of life itself."[8]

It is practical for a speaker always to carry with him a small notebook to jot down sermon illustrations. After typing out the entire illustration he can then file it in two ways. First, illustrations can be filed in a textual file, that is, according to a pertinent text with which they may be used. Second, illustrations can be filed in a topical file which lists the illustration according to its topic. In such a file, among others, you ought to include such topics as: Archaeology, Bible, Christ, Christmas, Church History, Conversion, Cults, Death, Easter, Ethics, Evangelism, Evolution, Funerals, God, Heaven, Hell, Holy Spirit, Lord's Supper, Prayer, Prophecy, Redemption, Salvation, Sa-

---

[7]Ibid., p. 144.

[8]H. C. Brown, Jr., H. Gordon Clinard, Jesse J. Northcutt, *Steps to the Sermon* (Nashville: Broadman Press, 1963), p. 89.

tan, Sin, Tithing, Youth, and many, many more. After you have used an illustration, be sure to mark on the record where, when, and in what relation you used that particular illustration.

Remember, to illuminate don't hesitate to illustrate.

Application

After truth has been explained and the facts of that truth are argued, there remains the application of that truth. In his *Commentary on I Corinthians* (12:38), John Calvin correctly observes that it is necessary "to apply properly and adroitly the prophecies, threats, promises and all Scripture, according as the present necessity of the church requires it." This is true, but what is application? Consider these definitions.

"The application in a sermon is not merely an appendage to the discussion, or a subordinate part of it, but is the main thing to be done. Spurgeon says, 'Where the application begins, there the sermon begins.' We are not to speak before the people, but to them, and must earnestly strive to make them take to themselves what we say.'"[9]

"Application means to relate, to involve, to move to action. When the preacher uses application in a sermon, he speaks to the audience in such a way that they see how the sermon is appropriate, fitting, and suitable for them. Application means to show to the audience that they can use and put to a practical personal use the truth of the message."[10]

The application, then, is that part of the sermon which brings the truths of the Word to the listener on a personal basis. The application prevents the sermon from being what Michel Philibert calls "dull exegesis" or "irrelevant homilies about things that occurred long ago and far away.'"[11] It is the time when the congregation stops hearing the challenges confronting Moses, Daniel, Luke, or Paul and begins to see that these challenges face them as well. Reuel Howe observes that layman response to remote preaching without application is usually, "I'm sick and tired of being talked to as if I were a Corinthian."

---

[9] John A. Broadus, *On the Preparation and Delivery of Sermons* (Grand Rapids: Associated Publishers and Authors, Inc., 1971), p. 91.

[10] H. C. Brown, Jr., *A Quest for Reformation in Preaching* (Waco, TX: Word Books, 1968), p. 60.

[11] Michel Philibert, *Christ's Preaching—and Ours*, trans. David Lewis (Richmond, VA: John Knox Press, 1964)

Daniel Webster once remarked, "When a man preaches to me, I want him to make it a personal matter, a personal matter, a personal matter!" This is the purpose of the application—to make the sermon a personal matter with the listener.

Why is an application needed? Simply, the application is needed to make the personal connection between truth in the eternal and truth in present time. Most congregations do not have the spiritual ability, homiletical minds, mental skills, or hermeneutical acumen to acclimate the eternal truths of God's Word to their personal lives. Furthermore, most do not have the initiative to apply these truths to themselves. Thus, it is the preacher's task to accomplish this for them.

In his book, *The Preacher's Portrait,* John R. W. Stott advises: "Even when the text is understood, the preacher's work is only half done, for the elucidation of its meaning must be followed by its application to some realistic modern situation in the life of man today."[12]

When should the application be made? Traditionally, the application was made near the end of the sermon and was thus relegated to the conclusion. This should not be a hard, fast rule, however. There are some sermons where it would be better to make application at the close of each main division. By so doing you may repeat the application several times and deepen the impression made on your listener's mind that the truths which you speak apply to him. Expository sermons, which frequently are filled with exegesis, necessitate frequent application. To wait until the end to apply these truths would only confuse the listener. Too much material piled on his mind without sufficient application cannot be effectively "blanketed" with an application at the close.

Principles of Application

There are a number of basic principles to be remembered in making the application relevant to the needs of the congregation.

1. The truths must be applied to the basic needs of the listeners. It is your obligation as the pastor or speaker to acquaint yourself with the needs of your congregation. Get to know their life situations, their problems, their thinking, and thus you can not only introduce material which will instruct them, but you can apply that material in such a way as to make a lasting impression on their lives.

---

[12]John R. W. Stott, *The Preacher's Portrait* (Grand Rapids: Eerdmans Publishing Company, 1961), pp. 31-32.

2. Make sure the truths you preach, as well as the application of those truths, are relevant to the times and to your congregation. Take into consideration those prevalent sins and desires which may plague your listener. Speak to his day, not to the past. Although there will be a good deal of overlapping between the sins of Paul's day and those of today, speak to those that are most prevalent today.

3. The language of application will greatly affect the outcome. First person and second person pronouns make the application direct and more personal. Although it is a good idea to include yourself in the message ("All have sinned; each of us is tempted by Satan"), there must be a point in that message when you delete yourself and say, "What think ye of Christ?" Somewhere the sermon in application must be brought directly to the congregation. You cannot afford to speak in general terms. Avoid words like *person, someone, men, women, teenagers,* etc. Make these words personal, i.e. "What will *you* do about Jesus' commands?" Be tactful, courteous, and speak to everyone; but be straightforward, direct, and personal.

4. Make the application specific. This means make it specific to the individual and make it specific as to type. Don't be vague in what you are applying. An application that can apply to everyone, on every occasion, and for every purpose, will not apply to anyone on any occasion for any purpose. Application of salvation and service cannot be made at the same time and usually not too successfully in the same sermon. Pick a target and hit it.

The body of a sermon, then, contains the elements of explanation, argumentation, and application. In essence, the explanation answers the question *what*. What am I talking about? The argumentation answers the question *why*. Why should I believe what the preacher says? The application answers the question *what then*. What then should I do in light of what has been said?

Conclusion

The final functional element of the sermon is the conclusion. "If there are two places in the sermon," said the Archbishop of York, "which call for more care than others, they are the beginning and the ending." W. G. T. Shedd defines the conclusion as, "that part of the sermon which vigorously applies the truth which has been established in the proof, or developed in the treatment or discussion. As the introduction is conciliatory and explanatory, the conclusion is applicatory and hortatory.''[13] Simply, the conclusion is the climax of the sermon. In his book, *The Fine Art of Preaching,* Andrew W. Blackwood entitled his chapter on the conclusion, "The Most Vital Part of the Sermon.''[14] It is here that the preacher's aims are brought into focus and the goal is reached. Here the greatest impression is made. Here the unity of the sermon is on its greatest display.

Preaching is taking the congregation from where they are in their everyday world, bringing them to the Word of God, and returning them to the everyday world changed, strengthened, enriched, and better equipped to live the Christian life. The conclusion is that part of the sermon where you put the congregation back into their everyday world.

It is necessary that the preacher understand the importance of the conclusion before he can practice effective conclusions. Dale Carnegie says "Would you like to know in what parts of your speech you are most likely to reveal your inexperience or your expertness, your inaptitude or your finesse? I'll tell you: in the opening and the closing. There is an old saying in the theater, referring to actors: 'By their entrances and their exits shall ye know them.'

"The close is really the most strategic point in a speech; what one says last, the final words left ringing in the ears when one ceases— these are likely to be remembered longest. Beginners, however, seldom appreciate the importance of this coin of vantage. Their endings often leave much to be desired."[15]

It is accurate to say that the last five minutes of the sermon are the most important part of the entire sermon. Yet how little preparation the conclusion receives. Like the introduction, the conclusion usually receives the one word *conclusion* in the sermon outline. Thus, whatever the pastor conceives on the spur of the moment is what the conclusion becomes. Often the conclusion is just a series of aimless exhortations. The conclusion is far too important for that. The Greek orators thought of the conclusion as "the final struggle which decides the conflict." How many preachers feel the same way?

---

[13] W. G. T. Shedd, *Homiletics and Pastoral Theology* (London: Banner of Truth Trust, 1965), p. 171.
[14] Andrew W. Blackwood, *The Fine Art of Preaching* (Grand Rapids: Baker Book House, 1976), p. 123.
[15] Dale Carnegie, *Public Speaking and Influencing Men in Business* (New York: Association Press, 1953), p. 229.

Types of Conclusions

The types of conclusions are as varied as the types of introductions. Several of these types follow:

The Challenge

This method employs an emphatic appeal to take a particular course of action. You have placed Jesus Christ in the hands of the congregation and now you challenge them: "What will you do with Him?" The challenge is short, to the point, and compelling.

The Recapitulation

Cicero defines recapitulation as "recollection revived, not speech repeated." Recapitulation is more than repetition. It is a resumé or summary of that which you have said, using well-chosen words which will instill deeper meaning to what has been said.

The Restatement

Akin to recapitulation is restatement. Again, this does not mean that you simply repeat what you have said but that you say it again in another way. Perhaps this time you could embellish what has been said to heighten the impact.

The Quotation

A direct statement made by someone else, which has great bearing on your sermon, can be used with good effect. If, for instance, you are preaching about resting in God, you may close with the famous quotation of St. Augustine: "Thou madest us for Thyself, and our heart is restless, until it repose in Thee."[16]

The Illustration

A good way to close a sermon is with a story or illustration which enhances the truth which you have been presenting. Make sure, however, that the illustration actually illustrates your point. If it does not, it will weaken your closing.

The Surprise

The surprise method cannot be used too frequently, but it is still very effective. For example, I once preached a Christmas message from the

---

[16]St. Augustine, *Confessions*.

account of King Ahaz and his battle with Rezin, King of Syria (Isa. 7; II Kings 16). None of this account has anything to do with Christmas. It speaks of war and peace. But Isaiah tells Ahaz that the Lord God will give him a sign of everlasting peace in the midst of the storms of war. That sign to Ahaz is a sign to us of God's peace promise: "Therefore the Lord himself shall give you a sign; Behold a virgin shall conceive, and bear a son, and shall call his name Immanuel" (7:14). Suddenly and dramatically, the Christmas message is revealed and the sermon is ended.

Poetry

Another favorite form of conclusion is poetry. It may be a verse of a hymn or some other form of Christian poetry, but whatever it is, is should be short and well done. Poorly delivered poetry is worse than none at all. Poetry which takes more than a minute to deliver is too long and weakens the conclusion.

Personal Intention

This ending gives the intention of the speaker. If the speaker is particularly well respected, it will have a good effect on what the congregation will choose to do. Consider Patrick Henry's: "As for me, give me liberty or give me death!" Or consider Joshua's statement: ". . . choose ye this day whom ye will serve . . . but as for me and my house, we will serve the Lord" (Josh. 24:15).

Concluding Suggestions

Yielding a good conclusion is no easy task. Here are some suggestions to aid you in producing a good ending to your sermon.

1. Do not announce your conclusion. This is not needed. Avoid words like *finally* or *in conclusion*. Don't tell us what you are going to do, just do it. If, however, for some reason you do announce your conclusion, don't reannounce it five minutes later. Don't build the hopes of the congregation and then let them down by not finishing as promised.

2. Don't allow the conclusion to appear "tacked on" to the end of the sermon. It is an integral part and should be treated as such. Allow it to flow smoothly following the last main division of the sermon.

3. Don't resort to a clichéd conclusion or the same type of conclusion each time. People are tired of trite phrases. Stay away from them.

People also soon tire of the same conclusion to every message. Vary the conclusion as you would the body of the sermon.

4. The conclusion should be brief. Many preachers have a habit of dragging out that which should be short and concise. Make the conclusion no longer than the introduction and make it in proportion to the rest of the sermon. Generally, two or three minutes is more than ample time for a good conclusion.

5. The conclusion should be well-worded. This is no time to be fumbling for the right word. Plan what you will say ahead of time. Choose descriptive, hardhitting words which will get action, but be tactful and courteous.

6. The conclusion should be simple. This is not the place for a large amount of ornamentation. Simple, positive language is by far the best here. Make it understandable and clear to your congregation.

7. Prepare the conclusion. John Bright, perhaps the foremost political orator of the last century, said that however little preparation he may have made for the rest of the speech, he always carefully prepared the conclusion. Seeing that it is probably the most important part of the sermon, you should prepare the conclusion even more carefully than all other parts.

8. Having prepared it, memorize the conclusion. This is not a time to be concerned about whether or not you have said the right thing. Make sure. Memorize the conclusion so that you can deliver it with power and maximum eye contact.

9. Always end on a high note. Bring the congregation to a point of decision or action and make that the highest point of the sermon. This is the climax, the summit, the zenith, not the path which takes you there. Make your conclusion the "grand finale."

10. "Homiletical orthodoxy has always maintained that the conclusion is a recapitulation, restatement, exhortation, or invitation based on material already stated. If this is true, you should not introduce new material. If new material arises in the conclusion, it is an evidence of improper management of the sermon body. The conclusion should be a last word, a refocusing, a final look at what has preceded it—not a bearer of new information."[17]

---

[17]J. Daniel Baumann, *An Introduction to Contemporary Preaching* (Grand Rapids: Baker Book House, 1972), p. 145.

10

The "Practical" Approach to Homiletics

"From the word homilia *has come the English word 'homiletics,' which has reference to that science or art—or indeed both—which deals with the structure of Christian discourse, embracing all that pertains to the preparation and delivery of sermons and Bible addresses" —William Evans*

"Homiletics is the science which treats of the nature, the classification, the analysis, the construction, and the composition of a sermon. More concisely, it is the science of that of which preaching is the art, and sermon is the product" —Arthur S. Phelps

Although homiletics covers both content and delivery, in this chapter only the content of the sermon will be discussed. The form of delivery has already been discussed in the preceding chapters. In this section we concern ourselves with what you say, not how you say it.

One might ask why a course in homiletics should accompany a course in public speaking. Why should a text on preaching contain both? The answer is simple. Preaching involves both. Have you been to church lately? Did you receive anything from the message? If you cannot answer in the affirmative, you can readily see the need for the study of homiletics. Improper preparation and organization of sermon material cannot be made intelligible by even a great delivery. A good comedian cannot get laughs with poor material. It takes both good material and good delivery. The same is true of the preacher. He may be a great speaker and very charismatic, but if he has nothing to say, he will not be effective.

Why Study Homiletics?

Why study homiletics? Charles Koller suggests: "The last word has not been spoken or written in the field of homiletics. The need for fresh studies continues, and the interest never wanes. When Phillips Brooks had attained to fame as one of the world's greatest preachers, he continued to take lessons in homiletics. Many others, after years of successful pulpit experience, have added to their effectiveness by the discovery of structural principles which had previously eluded them."[1]

In his chapter on the nature of homiletics, W. G. T. Shedd devotes some time to the reasons for the cultivation of homiletics as a science.

1. The first reason is derived from the intrinsic dignity and importance of the sermon as a species of literature. For if we have regard to the subject-matter and the end in view, the sacred oration is the most grave and weighty of all intellectual productions. The eternal salvation of the human soul, through the presentation of divine truth, is the end of preaching.

2. A second reason for cultivating homiletics is derived from the intrinsic difficulty of producing an excellent sermon. In the first place, there is the difficulty which pertains to the department of rhetoric generally, arising from the fact that, in order to the production of eloquence, all the faculties of the mind must be in operation together, and concurring to an outward practical end. . . . In the second place, the production of the sermon is a difficult work, because of the nature and extent of the influence which it aims to exert. The sermon is designed to produce an effect upon human character. . . . The difficulty, in the third place, of constructing an excellent sermon is clearly apparent, when we consider the nature of the impression which is sought to be made. . . permanence of impression.

3. A third reason for cultivating homiletics is found in the increasingly higher demands made by the popular mind upon its public reli-

---

[1]Charles W. Koller, *Expository Preaching Without Notes* (Grand Rapids: Baker Book House, 1962), p. 9.

gious teachers. . . . The public mind is more distracted than it was. . . . It is addressed more frequently, and by a greater variety, both of subjects and of speakers. It is more critical and fastidious than formerly.[2]

Homiletics is a necessary study for any aspiring preacher of the Word. The Word of God is a logical book from cover to cover. It should not be presented to rational individuals in an irrational manner. Even though we depend on the Spirit of God to enlighten the minds of our hearers, we must do everything in our power to make our presentation logical. Homiletics does more than teach you how to make a sermon; it teaches you how to think logically. It is imperative that the message be presented in such a manner.

Definitions

When embarking on a practical study of classifying sermons it is important that the terminology used be understood. Unfortunately, homiletical terminology is anything but standard and this makes for confusion when different authors discuss homiletics. At this point, we should define certain terms with reference to their use in the classifications of sermons.

Subject. The subject is that broad category within which the theme is found. It is the specific thought which ultimately produces the sermon. Broadus indicates that subjects treated in the pulpit may be classified into four categories: doctrinal, moral, historical, and experimental. *Doctrinal* refers to such subjects as election, depravity, redemption, perfection, justification, etc. *Moral* refers to subjects which call for a devout and holy life, solemnity, service, practical morality, etc. *Historical* subjects are those which deal not only with the history in the Bible but narratives, biographies, and types as well. *Experimental* subjects include elements of doctrine, morality, and history but also deal with the actual experiences of men in receiving the Gospel, such as conversions, trials, journeys, and events.

Theme. The theme is the narrowing of the subject to a single thought. It is the particular aspect of the subject which the preacher plans to treat. For example, if the preacher selected "miracles" as his

---

[2]W. G. T. Shedd, *Homiletics & Pastoral Theology* (London: Banner of Truth Trust, 1965). See pages 37–46 for further detail concerning the cultivation of homiletics.

subject, he would find himself at a great disadvantage. There is simply too much that can be said about miracles. His sermon would not be concise or concrete. Thus the preacher must narrow his subject down to one phase or aspect. He may decide to preach on the miracles of Elijah. The result of this narrowing process is the theme.

Title. The title of the sermon is simply the theme stated in a manner which will enhance the theme or make it suitable for advertising. The title must be a true representation of the theme. It must be concise and attractive, without being gaudy or grandiose. Avoid sensational titles such as, "Hurdles to Hop on the Highway to Hell."[3] In most cases, titles should be biblical. When preaching on Naaman the leper, do not title your sermon "Seven Ducks in Muddy Water," for this is entirely misleading. "The title should be in keeping with the dignity of the pulpit."[4] At times, the theme itself will make a good title, such as, "The Miracles of Jesus."

Text. By studying the etymology of the word, we arrive at a definition of a text. The word is derived from the Latin *textus* which means "fabric" or "web." The verb is *texo,* meaning "to weave." Hence *textus* comes to mean the product or fabric of one's weaving. Thus, the text is that portion of Scripture which serves as the basic component of the sermon. In essence, the Word of God is woven into a sermon. The text is the raw material, so to speak, and the sermon is the product made from that material. The text, then, is a verse of Scripture woven into a sermon.

Method. The method is the particular avenue chosen by the preacher to accomplish the purpose of the sermon. There are essentially three methods of sermon delivery. They are:

1. The Teaching Method—primarily instructive and declarative.
2. The Proving Method—primarily persuasive and argumentative.
3. The Arousing Method—primarily actional and initiative.

Approach. The approach to a sermon has to do with the way the

---

[3]J. Daniel Baumann, in *An Introduction to Contemporary Preaching,* also criticizes sensationalism in sermon titles citing "Sex and the Single Girl" as an example of bad taste for a sermon on the virgin birth. It is difficult to justify, therefore, his stamp of approval on such winning titles as: "The Wages of Sin Is Aaaugh"; "A Pastor Ponders Vietnam"; "Morticians of the Mind"; and "How to Sin and Enjoy It" (p. . 129).

[4]James Braga, *How to Prepare Bible Messages* (Portland: Multnomah Press, 1969), p. 77.

preacher deals with the theme. He chooses an approach, a mechanical device which will best enable him to accomplish his purpose.

Purpose. The purpose is the immediate goal of the sermon. It is the end toward which you work. It is necessary to keep the purpose ever before you in sermon preparation. If you lose sight of your purpose, sermon construction will become a fiasco. It is the governing feature of sermon preparation and presentation.

Proposition. The proposition is a specific statement of what is to be accomplished in the main divisions of the sermon. The proposition consists of a statement of fact including the method to be used in the sermon, the approach used to develop the theme, and the theme of the sermon itself. This is the MATH construction (Method, Approach, THeme). It is the final statement before devising main divisions. If the proposition is frequently repeated in the mind of the preacher, the sermon will be more understandable and more enjoyable in the mind of the hearer.

Sermons generally fall into two broad categories: the *subject type* and the *text type*.

1. The **subject type** of sermon is formed largely upon the preacher's background of knowledge. By proper study of the Scriptures and general reading in the field of biblical and secular literature, the preacher forms a mental storehouse of truth. It is from this storehouse that he draws the material for the subject type of sermon. By mechanically applying the science of homiletics to the subject which he has chosen, the preacher proceeds to build one of three kinds of sermons. They are: (1) the *topical* sermon; (2) the *topical textual* sermon; and (3) the *topical expository* sermon. Note that each of these sermons is built on the word *topical,* for the discussion of the sermon is formed on the topic under consideration and not on a particular text.

2. The **text type** of sermon is based upon statements of Scripture. Although the pastor will utilize his general knowledge of the Bible, the sermon itself will be built only on the statements of the text. Here the difference between the *subject type* and the *text type* is readily seen. The main divisions of the *text type* must be derived from the Scripture under consideration and not simply "dreamed up" from the preacher's background of knowledge. The *text type* is evidenced in one of the following kinds of sermons: (1) the *textual* sermon; (2) the *expository*

sermon; or (3) the *textual expository* sermon. Here we discuss a passage or single verse, not a general biblical truth.

Subject Sermons

The Topical Sermon

In this sermon there is a single leading idea in which the main divisions are derived directly from a topic and are independent of a text. The main divisions are supplied by a mechanical method of homiletics and the subject matter has no analytical relation to any particular passage of Scripture. Please note that: (1) the sermon begins with a topic (theme) and that main divisions are drawn from the preacher's general knowledge of that theme; and (2) a text is not part of this type of sermon. This does not mean that the sermon will not be biblical, but merely that a text or passage of Scripture is not the source of the sermon.

By using the topical type of sermon, the preacher is faced with a vast array of topics upon which to preach. He must choose his topic wisely, picking one that will speak to his hearers and that is thoroughly biblical. To say that a preacher cannot discover sufficient themes of this nature is folly. W. G. T. Shedd says: "I can conceive of but two things which should cause the preacher any difficulty in regard to the abundance of subjects for his preaching. The first is the sterility of his own mind, the second is a stilted and unnatural idea of what the sermon he is going to write must be."[5] Let your mind be led by the Holy Spirit to the right theme for a particular service.

Teaching Method

The first method which we will apply to a topical sermon is the teaching method. Remember, the method is the avenue used to accomplish the purpose of the sermon. In the teaching method our purpose is instruction. If our goal is to produce better servants for the Lord, the method by which we hope to accomplish this is by teaching something about becoming a better servant of the Lord.

Listed below are several approaches to the topical sermon (as well as

---

[5]W. G. T. Shedd, *Homiletics*, p. 126.

other sermon types). Study these mechanical devices carefully and use them prayerfully in preaching topical sermons. The system of homiletics which employs these approaches was the brainchild of the late Dr. Gordon Davis, former President of the Practical Bible Training School (Binghamton, New York). Dr. Davis devised a mechanical system which would force the preacher to do his homework at home instead of in the pulpit. This system of homiletics was greatly revised both by Dr. John L. Benson and by the author. It will henceforth be known as the "Practical" system of homiletics.

THE "CHARACTERISTICS OF" APPROACH

This approach to the topical sermon is designed to indicate the properties, marks, features, qualities, or characteristics of the theme. In essence, this is a descriptive approach. It describes the theme by indicating what the characteristics of the theme are. It declares what a thing or person is, not what it or he does.

EXAMPLE: In the following sermon, notice the procedure used in describing the theme by telling what its characteristics are.

Subject:	Servants
Theme:	A Faithful Servant of the Lord
Type:	Topical
Method:	Teaching
Approach:	"Characteristics Of"
Purpose:	To help Christians recognize a faithful servant of the Lord.
Proposition:	Teaching the characteristics of a faithful servant of the Lord.

Main Divisions:

   I. One characteristic of a faithful servant of the Lord is that he is a *prepared* servant.

  II. Another characteristic of a faithful servant of the Lord is that he is a *prayerful* servant.

 III. A third characteristic of a faithful servant of the Lord is that he is a *productive* servant.

Notice in the example just given that there is no text or biblical passage which will yield these three characteristics of a faithful servant of the Lord. They are totally the invention of the preacher, based on his knowledge of the Word. Notice too that each main division consisted of the approach ("characteristics of"), the theme (A Faithful Servant of the Lord), and an adjective. The adjective is necessary and is standard in each main division. Since you are describing the noun *servant,* and since the only part of speech which can modify or describe a noun is an adjective (or participle—a verbal adjective), it is absolutely necessary that the adjective be present. A noun or verb simply will not do. Finally, notice that the finite verb is present in each main division. Some form of the verb "to be" (had been, has been, was, were, is, are, will be, shall be, etc.) is necessary for it brings about the predicate adjective. Without the finite verb there is no adjective, without the adjective there is no description of the noun and consequently no "characteristics of" approach.

   EXAMPLE: Let's look carefully at another example. To vary the form we shall consider the theme "Faithful Service to the Lord." Notice the changes.

Subject: Service
Theme: Faithful Service to the Lord
Type: Topical
Method: Teaching
Approach: "Characteristics Of"
Purpose: To help Christians recognize faithful service to the Lord.
Proposition: Teaching the characteristics of faithful service to the Lord.

Main Divisions:

   I.   One characteristic of faithful service to the Lord is that it is *reliable.*

   II. Another characteristic of faithful service to the Lord is that is is *reasonable.*

   III. A third characteristic of faithful service to the Lord is that it is *rewarding.*

   The first example indicated the use of the "characteristics of" approach with the personal servant. The second example used this approach with the inanimate service. Thus any noun, whether personal or impersonal, or any noun form like the gerund (Serving the Lord), can be described and hence can be used in the "characteristics of" approach. It is important to notice, however, that in both instances we talked about servants or service and not about the Lord. Thus, omniscience or omnipotence cannot be used as a characteristic.

Here are some examples of themes which can be submitted to the "characteristics of" approach. Bear in mind that these are themes, the narrowed subject. The broad category of the subject has been deleted to enable you to work directly with the theme. Devise main divisions from the following:

the Man of God	the Rapture of the Church
the Death of Christ	the Word of God
the Resurrection of Christ	the Peace of God
the Power of the Spirit	the Natural Man
the Early Church	the Inheritance of the Believer
the Apostle Paul	the Journeys of Paul
the Will of God	the Kingdom of God

The list is endless. Any biblical topic or theme which can be described, should be. There is no lack of material here.

THE "ADVANTAGES IN" APPROACH

This approach to the topical sermon demonstrates the benefits which may be derived from something or from being something. It tells of the advantage, reward, or profit which is received from the theme. It is designed to tell why the theme is desirable.

EXAMPLE: In the example below, notice the standard form that is used and how it differs from the previous approach.

Subject: Servants
Theme: A Faithful Servant of the Lord
Type: Topical
Method: Teaching
Approach: "Advantages In"
Purpose: To help people appreciate the faithful servant of the Lord.
Proposition: Teaching the advantages in being a faithful servant of the Lord.

Main Divisions
  I.   One advantage in being a faithful servant of the Lord is that the believer is blanketed by the protection of the Lord.

II.   Another advantage in being a faithful servant of the Lord is that
      the believer is blameless in his duty to the Lord.
III. A third advantage in being a faithful servant of the Lord is that
      the believer is blessed by the rewards of the Lord.

Now, as another example is given, watch carefully the presence of
the theme. A very similar theme will be used, but one that is non-
personal, i.e. "Faithful Service to the Lord."

Subject: Service
Theme: Faithful Service to the Lord
Type: Topical
Method: Teaching
Approach: "Advantages In"
Purpose: To help people (believers) appreciate faithful service to
                the Lord.
Proposition: Teaching the advantages in faithful service to the Lord.
Main Divisions:
  I.   One advantage in faithful service to the Lord is that sinners may
       receive salvation.
 II.   Another advantage in faithful service to the Lord is that saints
       may receive encouragement.
III.   A third advantage in faithful service to the Lord is that the
       Savior may receive glory.

In the first example, the advantages were restricted to those of the
believer, whereas in this example "Faithful Service to the Lord" was
seen to be advantageous to sinners, to other saints, and to the Savior
Himself. Consistency is one of the keys to good homiletics. It would
be unwise for you to have the first two main divisions pertain to the
believer and the final one to Satan. This would only tend to confuse
your congregation. Either speak of the advantages to one person in all
main divisions or to one person in each main division. Be consistent.
   Here are some themes which may be treated by the "advantages in"
approach. Study them carefully and then devise main divisions for
each one on your own.

Abiding in Christ   Union with Christ
Christian Fellowship   Memorizing the Word

Justification by Faith	the Peace of God
the New Covenant	the Resurrection of Christ
the Death of Christ	the Intercession of Jesus
the Presence of the Comforter	the Coming of Christ
the Assurance of Eternal Life	the Promises of God
the Ministry of Angels	

Again, the list could go on and on. We have now applied two approaches to the same themes and you have noted that the main divisions have not been the same. The marvel of the "Practical" system of homiletics is the fact that you can preach on the same theme for several months and never cover the same material twice.

THE "NECESSITIES FOR" APPROACH

This approach tells us what is absolutely necessary for the theme. It tells the purpose of or object in the theme. Here we answer the "why" of why a person needs to do something (theme) or needs to be something.

EXAMPLE: In this example of the "necessities for" approach to a topical sermon, be careful to note the conditional elements of the main divisions.

Subject: Servants
Theme: A Faithful Servant of the Lord
Type: Topical
Method: Teaching
Approach   "Necessities For"
Purpose: To help people know why being a faithful servant of the Lord is imperative.
Proposition: Teaching the necessity for being a faithful servant of the Lord.

Main Divisions:
  I.   One necessity for being a faithful servant of the Lord is to insure that Christ's commission may be fulfilled.
  II. A second necessity for being a faithful servant of the Lord is to insure that the local church may be filled.
  III. A third necessity for being a faithful servant of the Lord is to insure that Satan may be foiled.

You should observe in the preceding example that the main divisions are always stated in the passive voice. This is for two reasons: (1) Notice the "to insure" in each example. This is equivalent to the Greek ἵνα and requires the verb "may" in each case. (2) To distinguish this approach from the "advantages in" approach, the "necessities for" is always placed in the passive voice. "Advantages in" may be in the passive but "necessities for" must be in the passive.

You will notice that the "advantages in" and the "necessities for" approaches will sometimes lead in the same general direction and produce similar divisions. However, they do not lead to the same results. There will be some themes which are better treated by one approach and others better treated by the other. This you must decide when first approaching the theme.

In the second example that follows you will note that a change has been made. Thus far in the second example we have indicated how you would treat a non-personal theme which was very similar to the personal theme. We shall now depart from that procedure assuming that you have sufficient example to take account of the personal and non-personal themes. To give greater variety in viewing each approach we shall now take two different themes for each approach to the topical sermon.

Subject:	Proclamation
Theme:	Proclamation of the Word
Type:	Topical
Method:	Teaching
Approach:	"Necessities For"
Purpose:	To help people know why the Proclamation of the Word is imperative.
Proposition:	Teaching the necessity for the Proclamation of the Word.

Main Divisions:
 I.   One necessity for the proclamation of the Word is to insure that sinners may be convicted of their sins.
 II. Another necessity for the proclamation of the Word is to insure that sinners may be convinced of the truth of the Gospel.
 III. A third necessity for the proclamation of the Word is to insure that sinners may be converted from the error of their ways.

IV. Another necessity for the proclamation of the Word is to insure that saints may be comforted in discouragement.
 V. Another necessity for the proclamation of the Word is to insure that saints may be committed to the truth.
VI. A sixth necessity for the proclamation of the Word is to insure that saints may be confronted with their Christian responsibilities.
VII. A final necessity for the proclamation of the Word is to insure that saints may be commissioned unto discipleship.

In this example we have included seven main divisions, the first three of which deal with the sinner and the last four with the saint. This sermon could be split into two separate sermons of three main divisions and four main divisions respectively, but it is used here to indicate the antithetical type of preaching. Additional explanation of this type of preaching will be given later.

Below are themes which can be developed by the "Necessities For" approach. Try to form main divisions for a number of them.

the Promises of God
the Death of Christ
the Crucified Life
the Suffering of Saints
the Intercession of Christ
the Incarnation of Christ
the Return of Christ
the Upbuilding of the Saints
the Condemnation of the Wicked
the New Birth
the Creation of Woman
Faith in God
Controlling the Tongue
Repentance from Sin
God's Sovereignty

THE "REQUIREMENTS FOR" APPROACH

This approach provides for what is essential to the theme. In essence, the approach represents a "prerequisite" before the theme can be accomplished. This approach answers the question of what is absolutely required or indispensable to the theme.

EXAMPLE: Note carefully the visible lack of key wording or structure which was characteristic of the first three approaches.

Subject:	Servants
Theme:	A Faithful Servant of the Lord
Type:	Topical
Method:	Teaching
Approach:	"Requirements For"
Purpose:	To help people become a faithful servant of the Lord.
Proposition:	Teaching the requirements for becoming a faithful servant of the Lord.

Main Divisions:

I.   One requirement for becoming a faithful servant of the Lord is a salvation experience.

II. Another requirement for becoming a faithful servant of the Lord is a submission to Christ's lordship.

III. A third requirement for becoming a faithful servant of the Lord is a knowledge of the Word.

IV. A fourth requirement for becoming a faithful servant of the Lord is a sincere desire to serve the Savior.

V.   A final requirement for becoming a faithful servant of the Lord is a dedicated life.

In this approach we are speaking of the prerequisites or requirements for becoming something (theme). This means that all the main divisions should have to do with something that occurs prior to the actual fact of the theme. In the previous example, before a person could become a faithful servant of the Lord he had to fulfill the prerequisites of salvation, submission, knowledge, desire, and cleansing. These take place prior to service. The word *becoming* is the key here.

In the event that you are speaking of an impersonal theme, you cannot speak of *becoming* that theme. For example, in the theme, "Tears for the Lost," you cannot become tears. Thus, in the impersonal theme, the form must change. Note carefully that change in the second example.

Subject: Tears
Theme: Tears for the Lost
Type: Topical
Method: Teaching
Approach: "Requirements For"
Purpose: To help people attain tears for the lost.
Proposition: Teaching the requirements for tears for the lost.
Main Divisions:

I.   One requirement for tears for the lost is a love for their souls.
II. Another requirement for tears for the lost is a vision of the hell to which they are doomed.
III. A third requirement for tears for the lost is a sincere desire for service.

Here you do not become "tears for the lost" but you must yet fulfill the prerequisites or requirements for obtaining such tears. Without first having a love for the lost souls, a vision of Hell, and a sincere desire for service, you are not ready to shed tears.

Below are listed themes which may be treated under the "requirements for" approach. The themes on the left are to be treated as the first example; the impersonal themes treated as the second example are listed on the right.

Doers of the Word	Likeness to Christ
Ambassadors for Christ	Peace of God
Children of Light	Vision of God
Fishers of Men	Boldness in Christ
Enemies of God	Spiritual Growth
Giants of the Faith	Zeal for Christ
Vessels unto Honor	Crown of Life
Servants of Jesus Christ	Good Report
Examples of the Believer	Holiness of Life
Fighters of the Good Fight	Rest for the Weary

THE "ASPECTS OF" APPROACH

This approach provides the various parts or aspects of the theme. It tells what is integral to the theme. It speaks of the component parts of the theme, the different "sides" of the theme.

EXAMPLE: Here you will see the simplicity of this approach. There is little rigid form as there was in the first three approaches.

Subject: Servants
Theme: A Faithful Servant of the Lord
Type: Topical
Method: Teaching
Approach: "Aspects Of"
Purpose: To help people know about a faithful servant of the Lord.
Proposition: Teaching the aspects of a faithful servant of the Lord.
Main Divisions:

   I.   One aspect of being a faithful servant of the Lord is the person's qualifications.
   II. Another aspect of being a faithful servant of the Lord is the person's preparation.
   III. A third aspect of being a faithful servant of the Lord is the person's motivation.

In this approach, we are developing the theme by delineating its various aspects. Notice that each facet of the theme itself becomes a miniature theme. That is because we are breaking down the theme into all its parts so that we can view it as a whole. The "aspects of" can be a catchall approach, for themes which can hardly be treated under the other approaches can generally be fitted into the "aspects of" approach. Thus, many preachers use this approach even though they are unaware that they are doing so.

Let's consider another example.

Subject: Cross
Theme: The Cross of Jesus Christ
Type: Topical
Method: Teaching
Approach: "Aspects Of"
Purpose: To help people know about the cross of Jesus Christ.
Proposition: Teaching the aspects of the cross of Jesus Christ.
Main Divisions:

   I.   One aspect of the cross of Jesus Christ is its central place.
   II. Another aspect of the cross of Jesus Christ is its atoning purpose.
   III. A third aspect of the cross of Jesus Christ is its divine person.

Nearly all themes can be treated with the "aspects of" approach. A few are listed below.

the Coming of the Lord	the Wanderings of the
the Millennial Kingdom	Children of Israel
the Ministry of Angels	the Patience of Hope
the Judgment Seat of Christ	the Days of Noah
the Love of God	the Sickness of Society
the Culmination of the Age	the Depravity of Man
the Feeding of Sheep	the Disciplined Life
the Word of God	the Early Church

From our study of these five "Practical" approaches, we must make several observations. First, the wording of each sermon will seem extremely mechanical and difficult. However, do not fail to word the sermon exactly as it appears. Students who have tried to word the main divisions differently have, without exception, encountered difficulty in obtaining the desired end. Granted, when you get to the pulpit you will not repeat exactly what you have said here, nor will you carry to the pulpit the notes you have made in preparation of the sermon. Yet to arrive at the desired logical end, you must go through the mechanics of writing out the main divisions as has been suggested.

It is interesting to note that the preacher who goes through this laborious task in working out his sermon, will not have to go through it in delivering his sermon. The one who scantily prepares his sermon will be working it out as he delivers it. Don't be caught doing this. Get your homework done in the study, don't try to do it in the pulpit.

A second observation is that the preliminaries to the main divisions seem to be a chore. Are they actually needed? The answer is an emphatic *yes*. Again, your purpose is to achieve the desired end of the sermon. The reason why most preachers do not logically come to a conclusion is that they have not properly laid a solid foundation for that conclusion. Laying out your path step by step before you get to the main divisions will enable you to logically progress through the main divisions.

As you gain experience in preaching, you may tend to drop the preliminaries after you have formed a proper pattern and have become accustomed to the procedure. Even then this may not be a wise practice. It is the preliminary subject, theme, type, method, approach, purpose, and proposition which categorize your sermon. By checking this preliminary part you may see if you are too frequently preaching one type of sermon or on one particular theme or subject. Without these preliminaries you must go through the entire sermon to discover what type, etc. you have used.

A third observation is this. You have now seen the diversity which can be obtained by just one type of sermon and one method. You can triple the diversity by applying the other methods to this type of sermon (topical) and multiply many more times the sermon possibilities by switching to other types of sermons. With the "Practical" approach to homiletics mechanics becomes an aid, not a hindrance. It enables the preacher to see his goal and get there without taking side roads. It can be used to effectively prepare sermons, especially for the preacher whose congregation has been experiencing difficulty in understanding or following him.

Concerning the structure of a sermon, Phillips Brooks says: "The statement of the subject, the divisions into heads, the recapitulation at the end, all the scaffolding and anatomy of a sermon is out of favor, and there are many very good jests about it. I can only say that I have come to fear it less and less . . . I think that most congregations welcome, and are not offended by clear, precise statements of the course which a sermon is going to pursue, carefully marked divisions of its thoughts, and, above all, full recapitulation of its argument at the close."[6]

A final observation concerns the divisions of the sermon. You have probably noticed that the majority of the sermon examples have had three main divisions. It is by no means necessary to have three. As James Stewart says: "It is certainly not necessary that all sermons, like Gaul, should be divided into three parts. There is no intrinsic sanctity in the tripartite sermon division, nor is it (as some appear to hold) a prerequisite of a sound doctrine and essential to salvation."[7] However, three sermon divisions lend themselves to natural memory and symmetry. Three is probably the best number but it is by no means a limit. If the text or your mind calls for four, do not stop at three. Most

---

[6]Phillips Brooks, *Lectures on Preaching* (Grand Rapids: Baker Book House, 1969), pp. 177-178.

[7]James Stewart, *Heralds of God* (New York: Charles Scribner's Sons, 1946), p. 131.

homiliticians suggest that you have no fewer than two and no more than seven main divisions. Three to five are recommended.

It is important that the main divisions be equal in proportion. They should exhibit unity as well as progression. Equal time should be spent on each main division. To spend twelve minutes on each of the first two main divisions and only three minutes on the last one would indicate that the final division was of little importance and would thus weaken the final impact of your sermon.

Subdivisions should likewise be complete statements (none overly prominent), symmetrical, and formed much like the main divisions. To obtain subdivisions you may simply apply one of the above approaches to the main division. For example, if your main division is "A third aspect of the cross of Jesus Christ is the person on the Cross," then for the subdivision you would apply one of the approaches to the main thought of that division, i.e. *person* (not the cross of Jesus Christ). Your first subdivision may be "One characteristic of the person of Jesus Christ is that He is forgiving." With a variety of approaches, you always have a variety of angles from which to view the main thought of the division. At other times, you may decide to apply the questions *who, what, when, where,* or *why* to the main thought. Other methods which logically deal with that particular main division are available as well.

Remember, subdivisions are to explain and expand the main division, not to repeat it. "Although the subdivisions should appear in the preacher's outline, they should not be formally stated in the course of delivering the address."[8] In other words, the preacher should never say, "Now subdivision three is . . . ." Your listeners will have enough trouble remembering your main divisions. Don't confuse them by enumerating subdivisions.

Proving Method

Thus far we have considered the teaching method of preaching the topical sermon. We shall now consider the proving method. With a few minor alterations the methods are very similar. It will not be necessary to give as full an explanation of the proving sermon because it is built on the same homiletical devices as the teaching sermon. Once you have mastered the devices of each of the "Practical" approaches,

---

[8]James Braga, *Bible Messages*, p. 125.

you simply apply them to the proving sermons. There is, however, one approach to the proving sermon that was not given in the teaching method because it was not appropriate there.

THE "ACTUALITIES OF" APPROACH

This approach is designed to prove that the theme is true.

EXAMPLE: Note carefully the change of method in the sermon below.

Subject: Jesus Christ
Theme: The Resurrection of Jesus Christ
Type: Topical
Method: Proving
Approach: "Actualities Of"
Purpose: To bring men to believe in the fact of the resurrection of Jesus Christ.
Proposition: Proving the actuality of the resurrection of Jesus Christ.
Main Divisions:
 I.   One proof of the resurrection of Jesus Christ is the fact that the infallible Scriptures declare it.
 II. Another proof of the resurrection of Jesus Christ is the fact that reliable eyewitnesses testified to it.
 III. A third proof of the resurrection of Jesus Christ is the fact that the empty tomb witnessed to it.

In this method, we are not attempting to teach men something but to convince them of something. Thus, it is vitally important that words like *fact* and *proof* be used throughout. It is our purpose to convince men of the reality of the theme; in this case it is to convince them of the fact of the resurrection of Jesus Christ. It is also important to keep to the exact wording. Preachers frequently announce they are going to prove something, but they end up reeling off a string of statements, none of which prove anything. In the above example, the fact of the empty tomb, which was sealed and guarded, is ample proof of the resurrection. Eyewitnesses testified to this fact and the certain Word of God declares it. Each of these prove that the resurrection of Jesus Christ is actual. Nothing has been taught about the resurrection, but it has been proven to be true.

Note the emphasis on proving in the next example.

Subject: Demons
Theme: The Presence of Demons
Type: Topical
Method: Proving
Approach: "Actualities Of"
Purpose: To bring men to believe in the fact of the presence of demons.
Proposition: Proving the actuality of the presence of demons.

Main Divisions:

I.   One proof of the presence of demons is the fact that God promises the presence of demons.

II.   Another proof of the presence of demons is the fact that Jesus asserts the presence of demons.

III.   A third proof of the presence of demons is the fact that present experiences proves the presence of demons.

THE "CHARACTERISTICS OF" APPROACH

This approach does not lend itself well to the proving method of sermonizing, yet there are occasions when the preacher will want to use a "characteristic of" to prove something.

EXAMPLE: Note in the following example that there is but one characteristic used all the way through. Instead of indicating several characteristics of the theme, you are now listing reasons for believing that something is a characteristic of the theme.

Subject: Resurrection
Theme: Resurrection of Jesus Christ
Type: Topical
Method: Proving
Approach: "Characteristics Of"
Purpose: To bring men to believe in the fact that uniqueness is a characteristic of the resurrection of Jesus Christ.
Proposition: Proving the uniqueness of the resurrection of Jesus Christ.

Main Divisions:

I.   One proof that uniqueness is a characteristic of the resurrection of Jesus Christ is the fact that history attests to it.

II.   Another proof that uniqueness is a characteristic of the resurrec-
      tion of Jesus Christ is the fact that the Bible asserts it.
III. A final proof that uniqueness is a characteristic of the resurrec-
      tion of Jesus Christ is the fact that Christ's intercessory work
      demands it.

There are several important things to recognize here. First, you will
remember in the teaching method of the "characteristics of" approach
it was necessary that an adjective be present. This is not so here. You
are not proving an adjective but the fact of a noun, i.e. uniqueness.
Second, notice that your theme has become somewhat amended by the
insertion of the word *uniqueness*. You are not proving the fact of the
resurrection but the fact that uniqueness is a characteristic of that
resurrection. Thus, even though the word *uniqueness* does not appear
in the theme, it does appear in the proposition.

　　Look for these facts in the following example.
Subject:　　　Creations
Theme:　　　The Human Race
Method:　　　Proving
Purpose:　　To bring men to believe in the fact that sinfulness is a
　　　　　　　characteristic of the human race.
Proposition:　Proving that sinfulness is a characteristic of the human
　　　　　　　race.
Main Divisions:
　I.　One proof that sinfulness is a characteristic of the human race is
　　　the fact that history attests to it.
　II.　Another proof that sinfulness is a characteristic of the human race
　　　is the fact that the Garden of Eden event proves it.
　III.　A third proof that sinfulness is a characteristic of the human race
　　　is the fact that our own hearts testify to it.

　Again, see the fundamental differences between "characteristics
of" in the teaching method and the proving method. In the teaching
method an adjective was needed. In this method it is a noun. Again,
sinfulness is listed as a characteristic in each main division in this
method, not just in one main division as in the teaching method.

THE "ADVANTAGES IN" APPROACH

This approach sets out the proof for the profitability of something (theme). It indicates those facts which show the advantages in the theme. Note the following examples.

EXAMPLE:

Subject:	Resurrection
Theme:	Resurrection of Jesus Christ
Type:	Topical
Method:	Proving
Approach:	"Advantages In"
Purpose:	To bring men to favor the resurrection of Jesus Christ.
Proposition:	Proving the advantages in the resurrection of Jesus Christ.

Main Divisions:

I.   One proof that the resurrection of Jesus Christ is beneficial is the fact that the resurrected Lord is now providing for our own resurrection.

II. Another proof that the resurrection of Jesus Christ is beneficial is the fact that the resurrected Lord is now preparing a place for us.

III. A third proof that the resurrection of Jesus Christ is beneficial is the fact that the resurrected Lord is now interceding in our behalf.

In this example, note that it is advantageous for us that Jesus Christ be risen from the dead because: (1) His conquering of death made our conquering death possible; (2) without His resurrection from the dead He could not prepare the home in Heaven we all await; and (3) we would have no intercessor between God and us. The resurrection of Jesus accomplished all of this and thus is extremely profitable to us.

Note the following example on a different theme.

Subject:	Christ
Theme:	The Coming of Christ
Type:	Topical
Method:	Proving
Approach:	"Advantages In"
Purpose:	To bring me to favor the coming of Christ.
Propositions:	Proving the advantages in the coming of Christ.

Main Divisions:

I.   One proof that the coming of Christ is advantageous is the fact that Old Testament prophecies predict it to be so.

II. Another proof that the coming of Christ is advantageous is the fact that the New Testament apostles assert it to be so.

III. A third proof that the coming of Christ is advantageous is the fact that Jesus Himself declares it to be so.

THE "NECESSITIES FOR" APPROACH

This approach enumerates the reasons for believing something (theme) is needed. Using the given facts, the theme is proven necessary. Note the following examples.

EXAMPLE:

Subject: Resurrection
Theme: The Resurrection of Jesus Christ
Type: Topical
Method: Proving
Approach: "Necessities For"
Purpose: To bring men to believe that the resurrection of Jesus Christ is imperative.
Proposition: Proving the necessity for the resurrection of Jesus Christ.

Main Divisions:

I.   One proof that the resurrection of Jesus Christ is necessary is the fact that God's program of salvation demands it.

II. Another proof that the resurrection of Jesus Christ is necessary is the fact that Christ's deity demands it.

III. A third proof that the resurrection of Jesus Christ is necessary is the fact that our eternal future demands it.

Notice the emphasis on giving reasons for believing the resurrection is necessary. We are not saying only what the necessities are but also asserting that these necessities prove that Christ's resurrection was imperative in order to bring about the fulfillment of God's program of salvation, a clear understanding of Christ's deity, and our own eternal future.

Subject: Birth
Theme: The Birth of Christ

Type: Topical
Method: Proving
Approach: "Necessities For"
Purpose: To bring men to believe that the birth of Christ is imperative.
Proposition: Proving the necessity for the birth of Christ.
Main Divisions:

I. One proof that the birth of Christ is necessary is the fact that God's love demanded it.

II. Another proof that the birth of Christ is necessary is the fact that fulfillment of prophecy demanded it.

III. A third proof that the birth of Christ is necessary is the fact that the provision for a Messiah demanded it.

THE "REQUIREMENTS FOR" APPROACH

This approach examines the reasons why something is a requirement for the theme. Note that unlike the "requirements for" approach in the teaching method, in the proving method you simply pick one requirement and give different reasons for believing that this is a requirement. In this respect, it is similar to the change noted in the "characteristics of" approach of the proving method. Each of the main divisions presents a reason for believing that the requirement given is a prerequisite to the theme. More understanding will come from studying the following example.

EXAMPLE: This example proves why Christ's deity is a requirement for the resurrection.

Subject: Resurrection
Theme: Resurrection of Jesus Christ
Type: Topical
Method: Proving
Approach: "Requirements For"
Purpose: To bring men to believe that Christ's deity is a requirement for the resurrection of Jesus Christ.
Proposition: Proving that Christ's deity is a requirement for the resurrection of Jesus Christ.
Main Divisions:

I. One proof that Christ's deity is a requirement for His resurrection is the fact that without being divine He could not have raised Himself from the dead.

II.   Another proof that Christ's deity is a requirement for His resurrection is the fact that if He were not divine there would have been no purpose in raising Him from the dead.

III. A third proof that Christ's deity is a requirement for His resurrection is the fact that the biblical concept of a perfect sacrifice in death to sin and resurrection to life requires Christ's deity.

It is important to wade through this cumbersome form of speech to get to the kernel of truth underneath. We are trying to logically arrive at reasons for the fact that Christ's deity is a requisite to His resurrection. This form is necessary to assure that the end is faithfully obtained.

Subject:	Faith
Theme:	Salvation Faith
Type:	Topical
Method:	Proving
Approach:	"Requirements For"
Purpose:	To bring men to believe that faith is a requirement for salvation.
Proposition:	Proving that faith is a requirement for salvation.

Main Divisions:

I.   One reason for believing that faith is a requirement for salvation is the fact that the New Testament writers declare it.

II.   Another reason for believing that faith is a requirement for salvation is the fact that the testimony of man asserts it.

III. A third reason for believing that faith is a requirement for salvation is the fact that personal experience confirms it.

By now you have become bogged down in the mechanics of the "practical" approaches to homiletics. Do not let this discourage you. In fact, that is exactly what this system of homiletics is designed to do. The purpose of these various approaches is to counteract preaching which is muddled and has no general aim. Since much preaching today is clouded and incomprehensible it is necessary to approach the preparation of a sermon in a logical manner. If you spend a great deal of time working out in your mind and on paper the logic of your sermon, you will have little difficulty in making your hearers understand you. The problem has been that preachers have not been willing to go through the agony of working out their sermons mechanically and logically in the study and it has borne witness in the pulpit. Sometime in the course of the sermon your mind must work out these mechanics. Too often they have been worked out in the actual presentation of the sermon. No wonder preaching has been muddled. By getting this out of the way in preparation, you will have little problem in presentation.

Please note that you will not carry this paper work into the pulpit. For example, in the preceding sermon you would not say when delivering this sermon that your main division one is, "One reason for believing that faith is a requirement for salvation is the fact that the New Testament writers declare it." If you do, you will soon be looking for a new job. Your skeletal outline certainly will not have all this on it as well. For point one, your outline may simply read "N.T. writers declare faith is required for salvation" or even less. Although you do not say it word for word in your presentation, yet in the back of your mind it is always there. There should not be one question in your mind about what you are driving at and, if your presentation is satisfactory, the congregation will know as well what you are driving at.[9]

"When will I use a proving sermon?" This may be a legitimate question for you to ask. The answer is "not too frequently." Hopefully your flock will not need convincing as much as they will need teaching. Yet there are occasions when you will want to use the proving method. If, for instance, you are pastoring in a college town and many students are in your congregation, you may occasionally want to preach a proving sermon on some of the cardinal points of the faith. Or, if a question of doctrine should arise in your church and it is necessary for you to prove why something is true or something else is false, the proving sermon will be exactly what you need. Granted, it is a more difficult concept to grasp and prepare than the teaching method; nevertheless it is important. Do not be caught by someone pointing out flaws in your reasoning. Prove logically. Ask the Spirit of God for guidance and wisdom in preparing and presenting this method of preaching and He will guide you into all truth.

---

[9]The "Aspects Of" approach is deleted from the proving method in that nothing is accomplished by proving that something is an aspect of your theme.

Arousing Method

The purpose of the arousing method of sermonizing is to excite Christians or to stir them to action. It is by this method that you appeal for a response or decision. Although some sort of a decision may be called for in any sermon, this method leads to a decision from the word *go*. You are inspiring Christians to receive, gain, choose, do, accomplish, perform, or become the theme.

This method is quite general and very easily adapted to any theme. By following some general principles listed below you may easily prepare an arousing sermon. There is only one approach to the arousing method, for you are not teaching "characteristics of" or proving "advantages" but simply arousing your congregation to do something about your theme. Look at the examples given below.

EXAMPLE: The main divisions of this first example are taken directly from Dr. Gordon Davis who devised the "Practical" approaches to topical sermons.

THE "ADVISABILITY OF" APPROACH

Subject:	Power
Theme:	Spiritual Power
Type:	Topical
Method:	Arousing
Approach:	"Advisability Of"
Purpose:	To urge men to decide that spiritual power should be considered.
Proposition:	Arousing to a consideration of the advisability of spiritual power.

Main Divisions:
  I.   One consideration for the advisability of spiritual power is that great Bible characters were men of spiritual power.
 II.   Another consideration for the advisability of spiritual power is that a powerless Christian is a menace to the work of the Master.
III.   A third consideration for the advisability of spiritual power is that many beneficial results are brought about by spiritual power.

You will note that this method is not nearly as complicated as the proving method in that you do not have to jealously guard your logic.

The proving method is lengthy and complicated in order to protect you from producing weak and inadequate reasons for what you are proving. The arousing method simply attempts to inspire you to consider the advisability of the theme. Consider another example.

Subject:	Love
Theme:	Loving Your Neighbor
Type:	Topical
Method:	Arousing
Approach:	"Advisability Of"
Purpose:	To urge men to decide that loving your neighbor should be considered.
Proposition:	Arousing to a consideration of the advisability of loving your neighbor.

Main Divisions:

I. One consideration for the advisability of loving your neighbor is that by doing so you fulfill the second to the greatest commandment.

II. Another consideration for the advisability of loving your neighbor is that by doing so you are an example of a present day good Samaritan.

III. Another consideration for the advisability of loving your neighbor is that by doing so you have exhibited the greatest of spiritual gifts.

IV. A final consideration for the advisability of loving your neighbor is that by doing so you have fulfilled the law of Christ.

Let's go back to our original example in the teaching method for a theme and apply it to the arousing method.

Subject:	Servants
Theme:	A Faithful Servant of the Lord
Type:	Topical
Method:	Arousing
Approach:	"Advisability Of"
Purpose:	To urge men to decide that being a faithful servant of the Lord should be considered.
Proposition:	Arousing to a consideration of the advisability of being a faithful servant of the Lord.

Main Divisions:

   I. One consideration for the advisability of being a faithful servant
       of the Lord is that Jesus may be glorified.
  II. Another consideration for the advisability of being a faithful
       servant of the Lord is that the lost may be saved.
 III. A third consideration for the advisability of being a faithful ser-
       vant of the Lord is that the kingdom of God may be enlarged.
  IV. A fourth consideration for the advisability of being a faithful
       servant of the Lord is that you may be blessed.

It can be safely said that anything which can be advised can be the
theme to which the "advisability of" approach may be applied. Thus,
the themes are innumerable. Press for a decision. This can be best
accomplished by using the arousing method.

Thus far we have considered several approaches and three methods
of sermonizing. However, each of these have been applied only to the
topical sermon. You should have noticed that nowhere in our discussion has a text been used. This is because all sermon examples to this
point have been of the topical type. They are derived from the fertile
garden of the well-read preacher's mind.

Having considered the topical sermon in which a text is not at all
used in arriving at main divisions, let us now proceed to another
sermon type which has a marked difference from the first. This type is
the topical textual sermon.

The Topical Textual Sermon

This sermon is one in which the main divisions are suggested by the
text. Those truths that are authorized or implied by the text are used as
the basic "stuff" from which the sermon is constructed. By deducing
truths from the text you have a list of ideas which will lead you to main
divisions. The basic difference between the topical textual sermon and
the topical sermon is that in the topical textual sermon your ideas are
taken from the list of truths derived from a text, whereas in the topical
sermon ideas are taken from your head.

The method of preparation for the topical textual sermon is a simple
one. There are three steps. Formulate a list of truths which are implied,
inferred, or suggested by the text. From the listed ideas group the

statements so that parallel ideas in the list are discerned. Develop a theme which will unify the ideas implied from the text and those ideas taken directly from the text.

By far the best way to see how this process works is by example. Therefore, notice in the following example the deductions taken from the text. Our text will be II Corinthians 5:18: "And all things are of God, who hath reconciled us to himself by Jesus Christ, and hath given to us the ministry of reconciliation."

EXAMPLE: Deductions from the text:
1. God is the cohesive force of the universe.
2. God is the sovereign of the universe.
3. Reconciliation is solely an act of God.
4. Reconciliation to God is accomplished through Jesus Christ.
5. Reconciliation is absolutely necessary.
6. Not only is reconciliation from God, but it is also made to God.
7. God is the author of the process of reconciliation.
8. Jesus Christ is the agent of the process of reconciliation.
9. The Christian is one who has already been reconciled to God.
10. We have been committed to a ministry because we have been reconciled.
11. Rights always bring responsibilities.
12. Our ministry comes directly from God the reconciler.
13. The ministry of the Christian is that of reconciliation.
14. Although God reconciles us unto Himself, we have no active part in our own reconciliation.
15. Reconciliation with God cannot be preached unless Jesus Christ is preached.

Now from these deductions we find a theme which is prevalent and which will unify the deductions. One possible theme is:

Theme: The Wonderful Acts of God.
I.   One act of God is the act of creation.
II. Another act of God is the act of reconciliation.
III. A third act of God is the act of commission.

In this example, it can be readily seen that the act of creation is implied from the statement, "all things are of God." The act of reconciliation is deduced from the statement, "God, who hath reconciled us.'' The act of commission is implied from, ''and hath given to us the ministry.'' Hence, by looking at our list of ideas from the text, we have topically applied ourselves to a text. This is then a topical textual sermon.

Let's look at another example, using the same list of ideas, and another possible theme.

Theme: The Characteristics of Reconciliation.
I.   One characteristic of reconciliation is that it is divinely originated (all things are of God).
II.   Another characteristic of reconciliation is that it is divinely enacted (who hath reconciled us to Himself).
III. A third characteristic of reconciliation is that it is divinely accomplished (reconciled us . . . by Christ Jesus).

Again, these main divisions have come from the list of ideas drawn from the text.

Looking at another text, we can deduce other ideas. Our text is I Corinthians 15:51–52: "Behold, I show you a mystery; We shall not all sleep, but we shall all be changed, in a moment, in the twinkling of an eye, at the last trump; for the trumpet shall sound, and the dead shall be raised incorruptible, and we shall be changed.''

EXAMPLE: Deductions from the text:
1. A mystery is revealed to the believer.
2. The Lord's return is not fully comprehensible.
3. Death is not unconquerable.
4. Not all who live will die.
5. All who live will someday be changed.
6. The Lord's return takes but a moment of time.
7. The Lord's return will happen before a man can blink his eye.
8. The Lord's return marks the last trumpet call.
9. The Lord's return is the end of God's free call to salvation.
10. The Lord's return is accompanied by the sounding of a trumpet.
11. The trumpet calls the dead forth from the grave.
12. The Lord's return is accompanied by a bodily resurrection.
13. The dead in Christ are raised incorruptible from the grave.
14. Bodily change accompanies resurrection.
15. Those who are alive at the Lord's return will be made immortal.

16. Eternal bodies are not at all like temporal bodies.
17. Living and dead alike are affected by the Lord's return.

From this list we shall now choose a theme and devise some main divisions.

Theme: Characteristics of the Lord's Return
   I.   One characteristic of the Lord's return is that it is mysterious.
  II.   Another characteristic of the Lord's return is that it is sudden.
 III.   A third characteristic of the Lord's return is that it is audible.
 IV.   A final characteristic of the Lord's return is that it is quickening.

Notice in these characteristics the ideas from which they were drawn. Main division one was taken from ideas (1) and (2). Main division two was taken from ideas (6) and (7). Main division three was taken from ideas (8) and (10). Main division four was taken from ideas (11) and (12). Thus, since these ideas were derived from a text, this is not just the "characteristics of" approach to the topical sermon but is the use of that approach to the topical textual sermon. The preacher did not pull these characteristics from the back of his homiletical mind, but from the text itself and from the topical deductions from that text.

Another example is taken from the text Proverbs 3:5-7: "Trust in the Lord with all thine heart, and lean not unto thine own understanding. In all thy ways acknowledge him, and he shall direct thy paths. Be not wise in thine own eyes; fear the Lord, and depart from evil."

EXAMPLE: Deductions from the text:
1. The Lord is to be the object of our trust.
2. Trust is to be wholehearted.
3. Trust in the Lord requires a change of heart.
4. The Lord is the end of wisdom.
5. Self wisdom is not as good as knowledge from the Lord.
6. Relying on one's own wisdom excludes trust in the Lord.
7. If the Lord is only partially trusted then we are relying on our own understanding for the rest.
8. The Lord is to be acknowledged as God.
9. The Lord is to be constantly praised.
10. The Lord is the object of our praise.
11. We are always to recognize the Lord as supreme.
12. Our path is directed by the Lord.
13. Acknowledgment of the Lord brings results.

14. The wisdom of the world is foolishness with the Lord.
15. Self-esteem is but foolishness.
16. Wisdom comes from the Lord.
17. Evil is to be shunned always.
18. The Lord is to be feared.
19. One cannot fear the Lord and accompany evil.
20. Each phase of our life should show forth the Lord.

Theme: What the Lord Should Receive from Us.
  I.   The Lord is the object of our trust. (1–2)
 II.   The Lord is the object of our praise. (8–11)
III.   The Lord is the object of our reverence. (18)

Theme: Purgings from Our Life.
  I. One thing that should be purged from our life is self-reliance. (6)
 II. Another thing that should be purged from our life is self-esteem. (15)
III. A third thing that should be purged from our life is self-indulgence. (17)

Theme: Requirements for Direction from the Lord.
  I. One requirement for direction from the Lord is to forsake yourself. (4–5)
 II. Another requirement for direction from the Lord is to flee to the Lord. (8–11)
III. A third requirement for direction from the Lord is to follow after the Lord. (17–20)

Theme: Contrasts in Wisdom.

Earthly Wisdom Says . . .	Heavenly Wisdom Says . . .
I. Trust yourself. (1–3)	I. Trust the Lord.
II. Acknowledge yourself as wise. (5–7)	II. Acknowledge the Lord as wise.
III. Reverence wisdom. (14–15 18–19)	III. Reverence the Lord.

Yet another example of a text which may be treated in a topical textual manner is John 3:36: ''He that believeth on the Son hath everlasting life; and he that believeth not the Son shall not see life, but the wrath of God abideth on him.''

EXAMPLE: Deductions from the text:
1. Everlasting life is to be desired.
2. Everlasting life comes from belief in the Son.
3. Everlasting life is a present reality to the believer.
4. Unbelief results in not seeing everlasting life.
5. God's wrath is upon the unbeliever.
6. God's wrath is not upon the believer.
7. God's wrath remains on the unbeliever forever.
8. There are but two ends—life or wrath.
9. Belief in the Son makes the difference in the two ends.
10. God's wrath is not to be desired.
11. Unbelievers shall not see life let alone enjoy it.
12. God blesses believers, curses unbelievers.
13. Everlasting life is guaranteed for the believer.
14. The unbeliever is guaranteed wrath.
15. Everlasting life can be had for it is available.
16. The unbeliever does not possess the Son.
17. The believer possesses the Son.

Theme: Possessions of the Believer.
I.   One possession of the believer is everlasting life. (9)
II.   Another possession of the believer is assurance of everlasting life. (13)
III. A third possession of the believer is the present reality of everlasting life. (3)

Theme: Characteristics of Belief in the Son.
I.   One characteristic of belief in the Son is that it is to be desired. (1)
II.   Another characteristic of belief in the Son is that it is effectual. (2, 9, 12)
III. A third characteristic of belief in the Son is that it is essential. (4, 6)

Theme: What the Unbeliever Does Not Have.
I.   The unbeliever does not have the Son. (16)
II.   The unbeliever does not have everlasting life. (2, 4, 11)
III. The unbeliever does not have an escape from the wrath of God. (5, 14)

Theme: Characteristics of the Wrath of God.

I.   One characteristic of the wrath of God is that it is exclusive. (5, 6)

II. Another characteristic of the wrath of God is that it is ever-present. (7)

III. A third characteristic of the wrath of God is that it is escapable. (6, 12, 15)

Each of the above examples have come from the single list of ideas drawn from our text, John 3:36. You can see how the topical textual method can provide many sermons from one text. Thus far, however, just the main divisions have been given. Let's take the last example and add subdivisions to it.

Theme: Characteristics of the Wrath of God.

I.   One characteristic of the wrath of God is that it is exclusive.
     1. Exclusive to the enemies of God. Nahum 1:2
     2. Exclusive to the sons of darkness. Colossians 3:6
     3. Exclusive to the unsaved. Romans 1:18

II. Another characteristic of the wrath of God is that it is ever-present.
     1. Present in the past. II Kings 22:13, et al.
     2. Present in the present. Psalm 90:9
     3. Present in the future. Revelation 6:17, et al.

III. A third characteristic of the wrath of God is that it is escapable.
     1. Escapable by God's mercy. Ephesians 2:3–6
     2. Escapable by God's justification. Romans 5:9
     3. Escapable by God's salvation. I Thessalonians 5:9–10

Sufficient examples should have been given by now to enable the reader to understand the procedure in preparing a topical textual sermon. Two points must be made to aid in this type of preparation. First, one of the key words here is "implied." We are concerned with what the text says, but we are more concerned with the truths that the text implies. We are not picking the exact words out of the text to preach on them but are picking the themes out of the text. This is why it is necessary to formulate a list of ideas from the text and parallel these ideas. This is done so that the topics of the text may be clearly seen and a unifying theme may be formulated. You cannot preach a topical textual sermon from main divisions which are not directly suggested or implied by the text. For example, from the text Luke 18:10: "Two men went up into the temple to pray; the one a Pharisee and the other a publican." You cannot preach on the reasons why these men went to the temple to pray. These reasons are neither stated by the text nor implied in it.

Secondly, the text you choose has a great deal to do with your success in preaching the topical textual sermon. You must choose a text with enough "meat" in it to warrant preaching. It would be difficult to preach a topical textual sermon on John 11:35: "Jesus wept," or Nehemiah 12:4: "Iddo, Ginnetho, Abijah," or even Acts 27:14: "But not long after there arose against it a tempestuous wind, called Euroclydon." There is simply not enough meaningful material in these verses to work with. You do not know why Jesus wept from this verse alone. You need the statements of the rest of the passage. You can't draw a biographical sketch of the three men in Nehemiah 12:4, because nothing is said about them. Even Acts 27:14 doesn't have enough substance to warrant preaching on it alone. Generally, the longer the verse the more easily it lends itself to the topical textual type of sermon. Also, look for multiples of ideas in the text. This will aid you in producing a sufficient list of ideas.

The topical textual sermon can be used to good advantage in speaking about a particular subject using Scripture as a base. Thus, you can not only speak to a special subject which needs attention but also firmly ground what you say in the authority of the Word of God. Unfortunately, this type of sermon is frequently misused. It degenerates into a springboard affair where a man reads his text and then totally departs from it to say "what he wanted to say in the first place." This should never be allowed to happen.

Having seen the development of the topical sermon and the variant form of this sermon known as the topical textual sermon, let us continue with a study of the topical expository sermon.

The Topical Expository Sermon

This type of sermon is one in which the theme and main divisions are taken from the applications made from a passage of Scripture. Similar to the topical textual sermon, this type involves listing the main ideas or statements of the passage of Scripture. The topical expository sermon is, however, not just a long topical textual sermon. Nor is it a running commentary on a passage of Scripture. Notice the difference in the instructions for preparing a topical expository and those with which you are now familiar from the topical textual sermon.

In order to prepare a topical expository sermon you must:
(1) Formulate a list of statements made directly in the passage.
(2) Formulate a list of practical applications to the statements.
(3) Decide which of these applications is parallel to each other.
(4) Formulate a theme which will unify these parallel applications.
(5) Draw main divisions from the theme and parallel applications.

EXAMPLE: Let's look at an example and learn by observation. Our passage is Exodus 4:1-5. This example is again taken directly from Dr. Gordon Davis.

Statements of the passage:
1. God called Moses to lead His people from Egypt.
2. Moses objected by saying that the people would not believe him.
3. God commanded that Moses tell what was in his hand.
4. Moses answered that it was a rod.
5. God commanded Moses to throw the rod upon the ground.
6. God performed a miracle with that rod.
7. God promised that this miracle would help to establish the faith of the people in Moses.
8. God commanded Moses to use this miracle in the accomplishing of His work in Egypt.

Application of the statements of the passage:
1. As God called Moses to lead His people from Egypt, so He calls us to be Christian leaders.
2. As Moses objected by saying that the people would not believe him, so we often object to our calling.
3. As God commanded that Moses tell what was in his hand, so He asks us to take account of our talents.
4. As Moses answered that it was a rod, so God asks us to reply to His question concerning our talents.
5. As God commanded Moses to throw the rod upon the ground, so He commands us to obey Him in regard to our talents.

6. As God performed a miracle with that rod, so He performs miracles with our talents.
7. As God promised that this miracle would help to establish the people's faith in Moses, so He promised us that He will astound the world with what He will do with our talents.
8. As God commanded Moses to use this miracle in accomplishing His work, so He commands us to use our talents for His glory.

Theme: What God Asks Us to Do Regarding our Talents.
  I. One element in the things that God asks us to do regarding our talents is that, as God commanded that Moses tell what was in his hand, so He asks us to take account of our talents.
 II. Another element in the things that God asks us to do regarding our talents is that, as God commanded Moses to throw the rod upon the ground, so He commands us to obey Him.
III. A third element in the things that God asks us to do regarding our talents is that, as God commanded Moses to use this miracle in accomplishing His work in Egypt, so He commands us to use our talents for His glory.

EXAMPLE: Another example of the topical expository sermon is seen in the treatment of Luke 19:1–10.

Statements of the passage:
 1. Zacchaeus sought to see Jesus.
 2. Zacchaeus did not let obstacles stand in his way of seeing Jesus.
 3. Zacchaeus made sure that Jesus saw him by making himself obvious.
 4. Zacchaeus learned he would not be satisfied until he saw Jesus.
 5. Zacchaeus immediately obeyed the command of Jesus.
 6. Zacchaeus was joyful at the call of Jesus.
 7. Zacchaeus was called by name.
 8. Zacchaeus's coming to Jesus made the world around him unhappy.
 9. Zacchaeus began to be convicted about his past life.
10. Zacchaeus began a program of sharing with the poor.
11. Zacchaeus made restitution for the deeds of his past life.
12. Zacchaeus received assurance of his salvation directly from Jesus.

13. Zacchaeus's assurance of salvation came immediately upon his encounter with Jesus.
14. Zacchaeus received instruction immediately from Jesus.

Application of the statements of the passage:
1. As Zacchaeus sought to see Jesus, so must the sinner seek Jesus as Savior.
2. As Zacchaeus did not let obstacles stand in his way of coming to Jesus, so the sinner must not let anything stand in his way of coming to Jesus.
3. As Zacchaeus made sure that Jesus saw him, so the sinner must lay bare his life before the Lord.
4. As Zacchaeus learned he would not be satisfied until he saw Jesus, so the sinner must learn that he cannot be satisfied without Jesus.
5. As Zacchaeus immediately obeyed the command of Jesus, so the sinner must heed the call of the Savior.
6. As Zacchaeus was joyful at the call of Jesus, so the sinner must be joyful when he is called by Jesus.
7. As Zacchaeus was called by name, so the sinner must recognize that Jesus is calling him specifically by name.
8. As Zacchaeus's coming to Jesus made the world around him unhappy, so the sinner's coming to Jesus will make the world unhappy to lose his company.
9. As Zacchaeus began to be convicted about his past life, so must the sinner be convicted by the Spirit of God.
10. As Zacchaeus began a program of sharing with the poor, so the converted sinner must begin to share in word and deed.
11. As Zacchaeus made restitution for the deeds of his past life, so the converted sinner must make restitution for the deeds of his past life.
12. As Zacchaeus received assurance of his salvation directly from Jesus, so the converted sinner will receive assurance of salvation from Jesus.
13. As Zacchaeus's assurance of salvation came immediately upon his encounter with Jesus, so the converted sinner's assurance of salvation will come immediately upon meeting the Master.
14. As Zacchaeus received instruction immediately from Jesus, so the sinner will receive light on his salvation immediately.

Theme: The Sinner's Steps to Salvation.
I.   One of the sinner's steps to salvation is to seek the help of the Savior. Jeremiah 29:13
II.   Another of the sinner's steps to salvation is to expose himself to the Savior. Romans 10:9–10
III. A third of the sinner's steps to salvation is to obey the command of the Savior. Matthew 11:28

Theme: Results of Obedience to the Savior.
I.   One result of obedience to the Savior is joy for the believer. (vs. 6)
II.   Another result of obedience to the Savior is an unhappiness with the world. (vs. 7)
III. A third result of obedience to the Savior is benevolence toward the poor. (vs. 8)
IV.   A fourth result of obedience to the Savior is restitution to the wronged. (vs. 8)
V.   A fifth result of obedience to the Savior is assurance of salvation. (vs. 9)
VI.   A final result of obedience to the Savior is instruction by the Lord. (vs. 9)

Theme: What Jesus Does on Our Behalf.
I.   Jesus seeks the sinner on our behalf. (vs. 10)
II.   Jesus calls the sinner on our behalf. (vs. 5)
III. Jesus convicts the sinner on our behalf. (vs. 8)
IV.   Jesus saves the sinner on our behalf. (vs. 9)

EXAMPLE: An Old Testament example of the topical expository sermon is seen in Daniel 1.

Statements of the passage:
1. The people of God fell under the submission of the ruler of wickedness.
2. The ruler of wickedness robbed the people of God of their youth.
3. The youth taken by the ruler of wickedness were the most able and skillful.
4. The wicked ruler provided apparent luxury and enticement for the youth.

5. The wicked ruler attempted to change the life styles of the youths.
6. One youth, Daniel, decided to stand up for what he believed.
7. Daniel remained true to his religious convictions.
8. The wicked ruler submitted the youths to a test for their faith.
9. After the test, the youths who held to their convictions were enriched physically.
10. After the test, the youths who held to their convictions were enriched mentally.
11. After the test, the youths who held to their convictions were enriched spiritually.
12. After the test, the youths who held to their convictions were enriched socially.

Application of the statements of the passage:
1. As the people of God fell under the submission of the ruler of wickedness, so we can occasionally expect to fall under the submission of present rulers of wickedness.
2. As the ruler of wickedness robbed the people of God of their youth, so we can expect that our youth will be robbed by the rulers of wickedness.
3. As the youth taken by the ruler of wickedness were the most able and skillful, so we can expect that the ruler of wickedness will take the most able and skillful of our youth today.
4. As the wicked ruler provided apparent luxury and enticement for the youth, so we receive apparent luxury and enticement from the ruler of wickedness today.
5. As the wicked ruler attempted to change the life styles of the youths, so the ruler of wickedness will attempt to change our life styles.
6. As one of the youths decided to stand up for what he believed, so we ought to stand up for what we believe.
7. As Daniel remained true to his religious convictions, so we ought to remain true to our religious convictions.
8. As the wicked ruler submitted the youths to a test for their faith, so will we be submitted to tests for our faith.
9. As after the test the youths who held to their convictions were enriched physically, so also will we be enriched physically if we remain true to our convictions.

10. As after the test the youths who held to their convictions were enriched mentally, so also will we be enriched mentally if we remain true to our convictions.
11. As after the test the youths who held to their convictions were enriched spiritually, so also will we be enriched spiritually if we remain true to our convictions.
12. As after the test the youths who held to their convictions were enriched socially, so also will we be enriched socially if we remain true to our convictions.

Theme: Steps in Undermining a Nation.
  I.   One step in undermining a nation is to engage the most skillful youths to join the company of wickedness.
  II. Another step in undermining a nation is to provide apparent luxury and enticements for the youths.
  III. A third step in undermining a nation is to offer a new society to the youths, taking them from the old one.
  IV. A fourth step in undermining a nation is to change the life style of good youths.
  V.   A final step in undermining a nation is to void the religious beliefs of the youths.

Theme: Blessings Brought By Obedience.
  I.   One blessing brought by obedience to God is physical blessing.
  II. Another blessing brought by obedience to God is mental blessing.
  III. A third blessing brought by obedience to God is spiritual blessing.
  IV. A final blessing brought by obedience to God is social blessing.

Observations

It can be readily seen that this method of preparing sermons is similar to the topical textual except for the fact that you are not dealing with implied ideas but rather with applied ideas of an extended passage. This type of sermon can be best used to liken our present day experience with biblical narratives and draw parallels. The application is the thing. Show how biblical truth is in action in our lives now.

You have now had opportunity to view the three kinds of sermons which are classified under the Subject type. Remember, this type of sermon relies heavily upon one's general, over-all knowledge of the truths of the Scripture. The subject type of sermon comes primarily from out of the mind by application of the "Practical" mechanical method of homiletics.

Text Sermons

The Textual Sermon

The custom of founding religious discourse upon a text, has prevailed ever since there has been a body of inspiration from which to take a text. In the patriarchal age, religious teachers spoke as they were moved by the Holy Ghost, without a passage from the Canon of inspiration, because the Canon was not yet formed. Noah was a 'preacher of righteousness,' and probably reasoned of righteousness, temperance, and judgment to come, much as Paul did before Felix, without any formal proposition derived from a body of Holy Writ. As early as the time of Ezra, however, we find the Sacred Canon, which during the Captivity had fallen into neglect, made the basis of religious instruction. Ezra, accompanied by the Levites, in a public congregation, 'read in the law of God distinctly, and gave the sense, and caused them to understand the reading.' Our Saviour, as his custom was, (conforming, undoubtedly, to the general Jewish custom), went into the synagogue on the Sabbath day, and 'stood up for to read' the Old Testament. He selected the first and part of the second verse of the sixty-first chapter of Isaiah for his text, and preached a sermon upon it, which fastened the eyes of every man in the synagogue upon Him in the very beginning, and which, notwithstanding its gracious words, finally developed their latent malignity, and filled them with wrath, so that they led Him to the brow of the precipice on which their city was built, that they might cast Him down headlong. The apostles also frequently discoursed from passages of Scripture. Peter, soon after the return of the disciples from the Mount of Ascension, preached a discourse from Psalm 109:8, the object of which was to induce the Church to choose an apostle in the place of Judas. And again, on the day of Pentecost, this same apostle preached a discourse, founded upon Joel 2:28-32, which was instrumental in the conversion of three thousand souls.[10]

Church history gives evidence of the use of a text in preaching as well. Origen was the first to base a formal and orderly address on a

---

[10]W. G. T. Shedd, *Homiletics,* pp. 140-141.

select portion of Scripture. The writings of Justin Martyr indicate that in the church services of the second century, an apostle would read the Scriptures, or another lector, and an address would follow to instruct the people to appropriate what they had heard. Using a text is a custom with a long and illustrious history.

Choosing a Text

Shedd says that there are two things requisite to the production of a good textual sermon—viz. a significant text, and a talent to discover its significance. The preacher must then ask himself, How shall I choose a text? Much problem can be avoided by choosing the right text. The following are some guidelines for choosing a text of Scripture.

1. DO choose texts that attract the mind.
2. DO preserve the dignity of Scripture by selecting texts with serious meaning. Foolish jestings and ridiculous texts are a bane to the seriousness of preaching.
3. DO remember the variety of people in your congregation. In every service there may be the unsaved, the discouraged, the bereaved, and the joyful. Pick texts which have something to say to more than one group.
4. DO remember the cycle of truth when you are preaching. Make sure that you are not always preaching on the same thing, the same doctrine, the same book.
5. DO remember your own ability when selecting a text. Avoid choosing texts which you do not understand or have not as yet acquired the ability to interpret.
6. DO choose texts which meet the needs of your congregation. In other words, scratch where it itches. Not all texts are for your people.
7. DO choose texts which are complete within themselves and not run-on texts to others.
8. DO select texts which tend to naturally fall into divisions. Look for parallel expressions and words when selecting a text. They provide potential divisions.
9. DON'T choose obscure texts. Elucidating an obscure text for the sake of elucidation is pure foolishness. Preach with meaning and with proper motives.
10. DON'T choose fragmentary texts. Use the entire sentence of a text

not simply a phrase. Make sure it fits into a context. "And Jesus said," is not a good text.

11. DON'T select texts characterized by oddity or eccentricity. Your purpose is not to be "cute" but to "preach the Word."

12. DON'T choose mutilated texts or texts which represent half truths. Such texts would be, "All men are liars . . ." or "There is no God . . .", etc.

13. DON'T select trivial texts. Acts 9:37 is Scripture but your time is more valuable than to spend it preaching on trivia. Look for the meat of the Word.

14. DON'T choose a text that is too broad or general to be adequately covered. The beginning preacher often encounters sermon difficulty because he chooses a text that is too broad.

15. DON'T choose unfulfillable texts. Don't preach on the "glories of heaven" or a text producing the theme "streets paved with gold," for you will build the expectations of the congregation and not be able to fulfill them.

16. DON'T choose spurious texts. Such texts as I John 5:7, which is generally considered spurious, do not make a good sermon text.

17. DON'T choose texts from the sayings of uninspired men. Remember, the Bible records history and in doing so has within it the statements of men. Although the inclusion of the statements is inspired, the content of the statements may not be wholesome. Avoid such statements.

18. DON'T choose a text which is opposite to the occasion for preaching. For example, it is ridiculous to preach a church funeral from Psalm 122:1: "I was glad when they said unto me, Let us go into the house of the Lord."

19. DON'T avoid familiar texts just because they are familiar. Many times new light can be shed on a familiar text just by taking a new approach.

20. DON'T avoid any section of Scripture. I once was associated with a pastor who told me that he never preached from the Old Testament. All Scripture is given by inspiration of God and is beneficial. We want to hear from it.

Rightly Handling the Text

Since it is the eternal, inspired Word of God the preacher is handling, it is imperative that the text be handled correctly. Several things should be kept in mind in handling the text.

1. Be faithful to the text. In reading a text, the preacher is in essence promising to preach from that text. The pulpit is not the place to let the congregation down or renege on your promise. Once you have read the text you are committed to preach it. Stick to it, don't wander off to something else.

2. Interpret the text. Never draw a meaning from the text that isn't there. See that your interpretation of the verse is what the writer intended. Compare three examples:

a. Hebrews 7:25: "Wherefore he is able to save them to the uttermost that come to God by Him," is not saying that Christ is able to save all men, even the worst sinners. The word *uttermost* means "completely" or "to the fullest extent." Even though Christ is able to save the vilest of sinners, this verse says that He is able to save completely and thoroughly.

b. I Thessalonians 5:22: "Abstain from all appearance of evil" is a favorite verse used to tell us that we should not let people see us with a brown soft drink bottle in our hand for fear that people will think it is not a soft drink. However, the meaning is clear in the original, "Abstain from every kind of evil." The word translated *appearance* is more correctly understood as *kind* or *form*.

c. II Timothy 2:15: "Study to show thyself approved unto God" is frequently used as an admonition to "hit the books," especially the Bible. While this is admirable, this verse literally says "Give diligence to show thyself approved unto God."

See that your interpretation of the text is the proper one, one which was intended by the writer of Holy Writ.

3. Exhaust the text. Do not allow the text to be superficially treated. Make sure that when you have finished a text you have gotten out of it what was put into it. This does not mean emptying a text. This is never possible. But it does mean leaving out nothing of real importance in the text that should be gained from the sermon.

4. Adapt the text. The needs of the congregation must be met. To do this the preacher must not only understand the *then* of the text but the *now* as well. The text must never become just a commentary on a past civilization. It must be adapted to the present situation. Such adaptation can never be forced; to adapt you must never alter. The adaptation should be smooth and obvious to those who hear the text.

The textual sermon may be defined as a sermon in which the main divisions are taken directly from a limited passage of Scripture. Although the divisions do not need to be stated in the exact words of the text, they must express the exact idea found in that verse or verses.

Developing the Text

The textual sermon is developed in the following manner:

1. Choose a text (one or several related, consecutive verses) which has potential divisons. Such a verse will be determined when parallel ideas or parallel words occur in the verse.

2. Having chosen the text, next decide upon the main thought or central idea of that text. The central idea gives the kernel of truth in the text or the key to understanding the text. It sums up the text. For example, in the text Titus 3:5: "Not by works of righteousness which we have done, but according to his mercy he saved us, by the washing of regeneration, and renewing of the Holy Ghost," we learn that the central idea is "the agents of Salvation."

3. From the central idea then select a theme. This can be done by devising a theme or by simply using the central idea as the theme.

4. Finally, approach the theme the same way you would a topical sermon by using one of the "approaches." Try "characteristics of," "advantages in," "requirements for," etc. The "aspects of" approach is especially good for the textual sermon. Remember, however, these "approaches" are not the only means of tackling the text. They are only suggestive. You may find "reasons," "steps," "categories," "purposes," "types," "cautions," or any one of a hundred other nouns that fit the particular verse. Or you may simply list the items found in the verse without the use of a noun common to each main division.

EXAMPLES:

The first group of examples shows the method of picking out the verbs of the text and using them for the main divisions. This is done successfully when the verbs in the text are vivid action verbs. Nondescriptive verbs will kill this approach to the sermon.

(1). Mark 10:21: "Then Jesus, beholding him, loved him, and said unto him, One thing thou lackest; go thy way, sell whatever thou hast, and give to the poor, and thou shalt have treasure in heaven; and come, take up the cross, and follow me."

Central Idea: What an Obedient Servant Should Do

I.   The obedient servant is commanded to *go* in a direction that he would not normally choose.

II. The obedient servant is commanded to *sell* what he has in order to break ties with his former life.
III. The obedient servant is commanded to *give* to the poor in order to undertake a program of charity.
IV. The obedient servant is commanded to *come* to Jesus in order to be cleansed from his sin.
V.   The obedient servant is commanded to *take up* the cross in order to be marked as a Christian.
VI. The obedient servant is commanded to *follow* Jesus in order to become a disciple of the Master.

(2). Luke 15:20: "And he arose, and came to his father, But when he was yet a great way off, his father saw him, and had compassion and ran and fell on his neck, and kissed him."

Central Idea: The Father's Steps in Reconciliation

I.   The first step in reconciliation was that the father *saw* the deplorable condition of the prodigal son.
II. The second step in reconciliation was that the father *had compassion* on the poor lost son.
III. The third step in reconciliation was that the father *ran* to meet the son while the son was yet outside of the house.
IV. The fourth step in reconciliation was that the father *embraced* the son, showing his forgiveness.
V.   The fifth step in reconciliation was that the father *kissed* the son, sealing his welcome back into the family.

(3). Genesis 3:6: "And when the woman saw that the tree was good for food, and that it was pleasant to the eyes, and a tree to be desired to make one wise, she took of the fruit thereof, and did eat, and gave also unto her husband with her; and he did eat."

Central Idea: The Path that Leads to Sin

I.   The first step on the path to sin was when the woman *saw* the object which led to her sin.
II. The second step on the path to sin was when the woman *desired* the object which led to her sin.
III. The third step on the path to sin was when the woman *took* the object which led to her sin.
IV. The fourth step on the path to sin was when the woman *ate* the object which led to her sin.

V.   The final step on the path to sin was when the woman *gave* to her husband and involved him in the object which led to her sin.

The next group of examples shows the method of picking out the nouns or the ideas which those nouns represent in the text and using them as the main divisions.

(4). Revelation 21:4: "And God shall wipe away all tears from their eyes; and there shall be no more death, neither sorrow, nor crying, neither shall there be any more pain; for the former things are passed away."

Central Idea: Things Absent in Heaven

I.   One thing absent in heaven is *tears*.
II. A second thing absent in heaven is *death*.
III. A third thing absent in heaven is *sorrow*.
IV. A fourth thing absent in heaven is *crying*.
V.   A fifth thing absent in heaven is *pain*.

(5). I Timothy 2:22: "Flee also youthful lusts, but follow righteousness, faith, charity, peace, with them that call on the Lord out of a pure heart."

Central Idea: Virtues that Ought to Be Followed

I.   Follow righteousness.
II. Follow faith.
III. Follow love.
IV. Follow peace.

(6). I Peter 2:9: "But ye are a chosen generation, a royal priesthood, a holy nation, a peculiar people, that ye should show forth the praises of him who hath called you out of darkness into his marvelous light."

Central Idea: The Believer's Standing Before the Lord

I.   The Believer is a member of the chosen generation.
II. The Believer is a member of the royal priesthood.
III. The Believer is a member of the holy nation.
IV. The Believer is a member of the peculiar people.

(7). I Thessalonians 1:3: "Remembering without ceasing your work of faith, and labor of love, and patience of hope in our Lord Jesus Christ, in the sight of God and our Father."

Central Idea: Paul's Remembrance of the Thessalonians

I.   The first remembrance Paul had of the Thessalonians was their work of faith.

II. The second remembrance Paul had of the Thessalonians was their labor of love.

III. The third remembrance Paul had of the Thessalonians was their patience of hope.

(8). Philippians 3:10: "That I may know him, and the power of his resurrection, and the fellowship of his suffering, being made conformable unto his death."

Central Idea: That Which Paul Desires to Know

I.   Paul desires to know *Him,* the Lord Jesus Christ.

II. Paul desires to know the *power of His resurrection.*

III. Paul desires to know the *fellowship of His sufferings.*

(9). James 3:6: "And the tongue is a fire, a world of iniquity; so is the tongue among our members that it defileth the whole body, and setteth on fire the course of nature, and it is set on fire of hell."

Here, as is frequently the case, there are two central ideas; what the tongue *does,* and what the tongue *is.* You must never deal with a split idea. Deal only with one of them. We shall deal with what the tongue is.

Central Idea: What the Tongue Is

I.   The tongue is a *fire.*

II. The tongue is a *world of iniquity.*

III. The tongue is a *defiler.*

(10). Titus 3:5: "Not by works of righteousness which we have done, but according to his mercy he saved us, by the washing of regeneration, and renewing of the Holy Ghost."

Central Idea: The Aspects of Our Salvation

I.   One aspect of our salvation is *God's mercy.*

II. A second aspect of our salvation is the *washing of regeneration.*

III. A third aspect of our salvation is the *renewing of the Holy Ghost.*

In the next examples you will see the use of the adverb or adjective in drawing the central idea from the text.

(11).   Titus 2:12: "Teaching us that denying ungodliness and worldly lusts, we should live soberly, righteously, and godly, in this present world."

Central Idea: How We are Presently to Live

I.   One way we are presently to live is *soberly*.
II.   Another way we are presently to live is *righteously*.
III. A third way we are presently to live is *godly*.

You notice that this example is telling us how to live. It does not describe life, it is not the use of the noun or the verb, but it is the use of the adverb.

(12).   I Corinthians 15:58: "Therefore, my beloved brethren, be ye steadfast, unmovable, always abounding in the work of the Lord, forasmuch as ye know that your labor is not in vain in the Lord."

Central Idea: The Character of our Witness

I.   Our witness is to be *steadfast*.
II.   Our witness is to be *unmovable*.
III. Our witness is to be always *abounding*.

This verse describes the witness to the Lord. Thus, adjectives, in one form or another, are used as the main divisions.

(13).   Colossians 1:12-14: "Giving thanks unto the Father, who hath made us meet to be partakers of the inheritance of the saints in light; Who hath delivered us from the power of darkness, and hath translated us into the kingdom of his dear son; In whom we have redemption through his blood, even the forgiveness of sins."

In this example you will note that more than one verse is used. A text can be more than one verse but generally should not be more than two or three if the central idea continues into the second and third verse. Also, you will notice that the words used are not necessarily those found directly in the text but do represent the express ideas found in the text.

Central Idea: What the Father has Done for Us

I.   The Father has *fitted* us to partake in heavenly inheritance.
II.   The Father has *delivered* us from the power of darkness.
III. The Father had *translated* us into the kingdom.
IV.   The Father has *redeemed* us through the Son's blood.
V.   The Father has *pardoned* us from the guilt of our sin.

Each of the above examples illustrates the method of taking a text, extracting from it the central or key idea, and from it elucidating the main divisions. Now let's take a closer look at one of these outlines and provide subdivisions for it.

Notice carefully that the main divisions are taken directly from the words or expressed ideas of the text. The subdivisions are drawn from parallel incidents in the Scriptures. The approach to the subdivisions does not in any way lessen the fact that the sermon (main divisions) is a textual one.

Text: Genesis 3:6: "And when the woman saw that the tree was good for food, and that it was pleasant to the eyes, and a tree to be desired to make one wise, she took of the fruit thereof, and did eat, and gave also unto her husband with her; and he did eat."

I.   The first subjugating step to sin was when the woman *spied* the object of sin.
    1.   Sin begins with sight.
    ·   Examples: Noah—Ham saw his naked father. Genesis 9:22.
              Achan—saw the spoils of war. Joshua 7:21.
              David—saw the beautiful Bathsheba. II Samuel 11:2.
    2.   Sin should be avoided by avoiding the sight of sin.
       I Thessalonians 5:22; II Timothy 2:22.
II. The second subjugating step to sin was when the woman *desired* the object of sin.
    1.   Although sin begins with sight, the sight of sin itself is no crime. Deuteronomy 5:21; Matthew 5:28.
    2.   Desire of sin takes the sinner beyond mere sight.
       Examples: Achan. Joshua 7:21.
               David. II Samuel 11:3-4.
III. The third subjugating step to sin was when the woman *indulged* in the object of sin.
    1.   To see and covet sin is bad, but to take deepens one's sin.
       Example: Achan. Joshua 7:21
    2.   Indulgence in sin necessitates an active pursuit of the object of sin.
     Example: David. II Samuel 11:4.
IV. The fourth subjugating step to sin was when the woman *involved* her husband in the object of sin.
    1.   The tragedy of sin is that it always involves others before it is brought to completion.
       Example: Achan. Joshua 7:4-9.

2. Those involved in sin are damaged as much or more than those who first indulged in the sin.
Example: David. II Samuel 11:15, 24.

The textual sermon is an appropriate avenue for teaching the Word of God. As this example shows, with proper introduction, conclusion, and application, the hearer is not only taught about the steps to sin but is shown the possibility of these steps being actuated in his own life. Thus he may beware that he does not follow the same downward path that the examples above followed. Textual preaching gives great credence to what you wish the congregation to know, for your main divisions are taken directly from the Word of God. Do not fail to use this powerful tool—the textual sermon—for men need to hear, "thus saith the Lord."

The Textual Expository Sermon

Sometimes referred to as the Bible reading, this type of sermon is one in which the theme is taken from one passage of Scripture but the main divisions are drawn from parallel passages. It is possible that one main division may come from the verse containing the theme, but the other divisions must be drawn from some other passage or verse in the Bible.

How does one go about preparing this type of sermon? The directions are quite basic.

1. This type of sermon makes good use of a concordance. Take a good Bible concordance (*Strong's, Young's, or Cruden's*) and locate a particular word or phrase which you feel will make good preaching. This may have been suggested to you by a verse, passage, or whatever. For an example, we shall use the word "abide."

2. Next, list a number of verses which contain the word "abide" or even better, write out these verses so you may compare them. If you have several Bibles or versions you may lay them side by side to view these verses. Here are some examples of verses containing the word "abide."

I John 2:27-28	Philippians 1:24
Romans 11:23	John 15:10
John 15:4, 6-7	Psalm 91:1
Psalm 61:4	I Samuel 19:2
Job 39:28	Proverbs 15:31
I John 2:10	II John 1:9

3. After you have carefully studied the content of these verses, you will readily notice that many of them are parallel. From these parallel verses you will then select a central thought or main idea. This central idea must be present in each parallel verse you select. Occasionally, although not frequently, you may find a central idea which will qualify for all the verses that you have listed.

"Abide"—Central Idea: Recommended Places to Abide

I. In Christ. John 15:1–7
II. In Christ's Love. John 15:10
III. In God's Tabernacle. Psalm 61:4
IV. In the Secret Place. Psalm 91:1; I Samuel 19:2
V. In the Light. I John 2:10
VI. In The Doctrine of Christ. II John 1:9

Those verses listed above which do not fit into this central idea may be used in preparing subdivisions for these six main divisions or simply discarded for the time being. When presenting main divisions, make sure the truths that you have selected are all from parallel verses and that they all relate to the same central idea. Notice the following examples:

EXAMPLES:

Central Idea: Things to Thirst After

I. Thirst after God. Psalm 42:2
II. Thirst after righteousness. Matthew 5:6
III. Thirst after living water. John 4:14–15

Central Idea: Types of Biblical Armor

I. The armor of light. Romans 13:12
II. The armor of righteousness. II Corinthians 6:7
III. The armor of God. Ephesians 6:13

Central Idea: The Truth in John's Gospel

I. The agent of truth. 1:17
II. The power of truth. 8:32
III. The person of truth. 14:6

Central Idea: The Three-way Street of Love in I John

I. God loves us. 3:1, 16; 4:8–10, 16
II. We love God. 4:19; 20; 5:2
III. We love one another. 3:14, 18; 4:7, 11, 20

Central Idea: Those We Are to Honor

I. Honor Father and Mother. Exodus 20:12; Ephesians 6:2

II.   Honor the Lord. Proverbs 3:9; John 5:23
III.   Honor true widows. I Timothy 5:3
IV.   Honor all men. I Peter 2:17
V.   Honor the King. I Peter 2:17

Central Idea: Biblical Judgments

I.   The judgment of Christians. II Corinthians 5:10; Colossians 3:24
II.   The judgment of angels. Jude 6; Revelation 20:10; Matthew 25:41
III.   The judgment of Satan. Isaiah 14:12; John 12:31; Revelation 20:2ff
IV.   The judgment of Gentiles. Matthew 25:31
V.   The judgment of Israel. Malachi 3:2; 4:1; Psalm 50
VI.   The judgment of sin. John 5:24; Romans 5:9; 8:1; Galatians 3:13

Central Idea: Biblical Crowns

I.   The crown of life. James 1:12; Revelation 2:10
II.   The crown of righteousness. II Timothy 4:8
III.   The crown of glory. I Peter 5:4
IV.   The crown of incorruptibility. I Corinthians 9:25
V.   The crown of rejoicing. I Thessalonians 2:19

Central Idea: False Persons of the New Testament

I.   The false prophets. Mark 13:22
II.   The false witnesses. I Corinthians 15:15
III.   The false apostles. II Corinthians 11:13
IV.   The false brethren. II Corinthians 11:26
V.   The false accusers. II Timothy 3:3; Titus 2:3

Central Idea: Things to Be Avoided

I.   The path of the wicked. Proverbs 4:15
II.   Those who cause divisions in doctrine. Romans 16:17
III.   Foolish and unlearned questions. II Timothy 2:23
IV.   Strivings about the Law. Titus 3:9
V.   Fornication. I Corinthians 7:2
VI.   Genealogies. Titus 3:9
VII.   Contentions. Titus 3:9

Central Idea: Conditions Found in I John 1

I.   If we say that we have fellowship with Him.
II.   If we walk in the light.
III.   If we say that we have no sin.
IV.   If we confess our sins.
V.   If we say that we have not sinned.

Central Idea: Jesus Christ the Finisher
I.   Jesus Christ is the finisher of creation. Genesis 2:1
II.   Jesus Christ is the finisher of redemption. John 19:30
III. Jesus Christ is the finisher of our faith. Hebrews 12:2

Central Idea: Persons to Consider in Hebrews
I.   Consider the apostle and High Priest. 3:1
II.   Consider the great Melchizedek. 7:4
III. Consider one another. 10:24
IV.   Consider those who rule over you. 13:7

Central Idea: That in Which We Are to Continue
I.   Continue in prayer. Romans 12:12; Colossians 4:2
II.   Continue in the Word. John 8:31
III. Continue in love. John 15:9
IV.   Continue in unity. Acts 1:14; 2:26
V.   Continue in grace. Acts 13:43
VI.   Continue in faith. Acts 14:22; I Timothy 2:15; Colossians 1:23
VII. Continue in goodness. Romans 11:22

Central Idea: Three Biblical Days
I.   The day of Christ. I Corinthians 1:8
II.   The day of the Lord. Joel 1:15; Revelation 19:19
III. The day of destruction. Revelation 20:11

Central Idea: Seven Bible Fools
I.   The fool who denies God. Psalm 14:1; 53:1
II.   The fool who despises instruction. Proverbs 1:7; 15:5
III. The fool who mocks sin. Proverbs 14:9
IV.   The fool who walks in darkness. Ecclesiastes 2:14
V.   The fool who is full of words. Ecclesiastes 10:14
VI.   The fool who uttereth all his mind. Proverbs 29:11
VII. The fool who trusteth his own heart. Proverbs 28:26

Central Idea: Those Chosen of God
I.   He hath chosen Christ. Luke 23:35; I Peter 2:4
II.   He hath chosen foolish things. I Corinthians 1:27
III. He hath chosen weak things. I Corinthians 1:27
IV.   He hath chosen despised things. I Corinthians 1:28
V.   He hath chosen the poor. James 2:5
VI.   He hath chosen the believer. John 15:16, 19; I Peter 2:9

Central Idea: Nine Liars in the Bible
I.   Devil. Genesis 3:4

    II.   Cain. Genesis 4:9
   III.   Sarah. Genesis 18:15
   IV.   Jacob. Genesis 27:19
    V.   Samson. Judges 16:10
   VI.   Saul. I Samuel 15:13
  VII.   David. I Samuel 21:2
 VIII.   Peter. Matthew 26:72
   IX.   Ananias. Acts 5:4

Central Idea: What We Ought to Be Ready to Do

    I.   We ought to be ready to declare our faith. I Peter 3:15
   II.   We ought to be ready to preach. Romans 1:15
  III.   We ought to be ready to be offered. II Timothy 4:6
   IV.   We ought to be ready to die for Jesus. Acts 21:13
    V.   We ought to be ready to fly with Jesus. Matthew 24:44

Central Idea: Things Unsuccessfully Hidden

    I.   Adam and Eve unsuccessfully hid themselves. Genesis 3:8
   II.   Moses unsuccessfully hid the slain Egyptian. Exodus 2:12
  III.   Achan unsuccessfully hid the gold and silver. Joshua 7:21,22
   IV.   A Man unsuccessfully hides his sin. Psalm 69:5; Mark 4:22

Central Idea: Seven Happy People

    I.   He who suffers for righteousness. I Peter 3:14; 4:14; James 5:11
   II.   He who prevents another's stumbling. Romans 14:22
  III.   He who trusts in the Lord. Proverbs 16:20
   IV.   He who findeth wisdom. Proverbs 3:13,18
    V.   He who hath God for help. Psalm 144:15; 146:5
   VI.   He who walks in the way of the Lord. Psalm 128:1,2
  VII.   He whom God correcteth. Job 5:17

Central Idea: Things Which Ought to Be Pure

    I.   Things thought upon. Philippians 4:8
   II.   Consciences. I Timothy 3:9; II Timothy 1:3
  III.   Religion. James 1:27
   IV.   Thyself. I Timothy 5:22.
    V.   Wisdom from above. James 3:17
   VI.   Heart. I Peter 1:22
  VII.   Minds. II Peter 3:1

Central Idea: Benefits Accompanying Christ's Shed Blood

    I.   Shed blood brings justification. Romans 5:9
   II.   Shed blood brings redemption. Ephesians 1:7; Colossians 1:14

III. Shed blood brings remission. Hebrews 9:22
IV. Shed blood brings salvation. Revelation 1:5
V. Shed blood brings communion. I Corinthians 10:16
       Central Idea: What the Bible Teaches About Witchcraft
  I. Witchcraft is proclaimed as sin. I Samuel 15:23
 II. Witchcraft is strictly forbidden. Leviticus 19:26, 31; Deuteron-
       omy 18:10
III. Witchcraft is a deceiver of all nations. Revelation 18:23
IV. Witchcraft is a producer of death. Revelation 21:8; 22:15
 V. Witchcraft is doomed by God. Micah 5:12

Once you have arrived at these main divisions, it is a simple task to take each main division and devise a theme which pertains to that division. For instance, in the sermon "Benefits Accompanying Christ's Shed Blood," you may take the first main division and speak of the "method of redemption," the "characteristics of communion," the "necessities for justification," or any other method of devising subdivisions from main divisions. The important thing is that you have arrived at your main divisions by listing texts which have a common word or phrase, paralleling some of those words and excluding others, carefully scrutinizing these verses to discover a common central theme, and then individually expounding these texts so as to produce one main division per verse. By doing thus you have prepared a textual expository sermon.

The Expository Sermon

The final type of sermon to be studied at length is the expository sermon. It is safe to say that this is the most important type of sermon. Let us consider what an exposition is.

W. G. T. Shedd indicates: "The expository sermon, as its name indicates, is an explanatory discourse. The purpose of it is to unfold the meaning of a connected paragraph, or section of Scripture, in a more detailed manner than is consistent with the structure of either the topical or the textual sermon."[11]

The expository sermon is longer than a textual sermon but it is a gross error to say that the exposition is just a long textual sermon. It is

---

[11]W. G. T. Shedd, *Homiletics*, pp. 133–134.

much more. The greatest distinction between the expository and textual sermons is in manner of treatment and not in length. An expository sermon is one in which the main divisions, the subdivisions, and the subpoints are all taken directly from a single passage of Scripture. The exact statements of the passage, or the expositor's own words, provided they give exact expression to the intended meaning of the passage, are used as divisions. While the textual sermon is confined to one or more verses, the expository sermon involves a longer passage, sometimes even an entire book. Also, while the textual sermon requires that the main divisions be taken directly from the text, the subdivisions and subpoints may be taken from parallel portions of Scripture. The expository sermon demands that all divisions and points be taken from the passage under consideration.

Before examples of expository sermons are given, let's consider some of the advantages and possible disadvantages to the expository method of preaching.

Advantages

1. One obvious advantage in expository preaching is that it produces biblical preachers and hearers. The preacher will find it difficult to stray into error or false doctrine when his divisions are taken directly from the text. Also, men cannot sit long under the teaching of the Holy Word through the Holy Spirit and not be biblical in their Christian beliefs.

2. Another advantage in expository preaching is that it gives the pastor much greater authority when preaching. What he says is corroborated by Scripture and said in the words of the Holy Spirit Himself. What more authority or power can the preacher of the Word ask?

3. A third advantage is that expository preaching speaks to the needs of the people. The most fundamental need of the human being is the forgiveness of his sin and the removal of his alienation from God. Faithful and consistent preaching of the Word, in a systematic, expository fashion, deals with this need and all other needs which arise in association with it.

4. Fourth, expository preaching provides a bank of sermonic material that cannot be matched by any other method. There is never any dearth of preachable material for the preacher who is constantly cultivating the Word of God and expounding its truths. One sermon will

ultimately suggest another because of the related truths discovered in expounding a passage.

5. Expository preaching provides opportunity to treat a wide variety of topics by treating usually untreated passages. One cannot very well skip over a passage if he is treating a chapter or a book. The truths contained in that passage may never be touched topically or textually, but with the expository method they must be treated.

Although there exists many secondary advantages to the expository method, let us turn our attention to possible disadvantages.

Disadvantages

1. One possible disadvantage is that the expository method of preaching may become monotonous to the congregation. If you preach too many successive Sundays from one passage or one book, the congregation will tire of the study. "Twenty years in Romans" is a boast of some pastors, but not a very wise one.

2. Another possible disadvantage in expository preaching is that it may engender a lazy pastor. It is easy to allow an expository sermon to degenerate into a group of random rambling remarks. If the pastor is pressed for time during the week, he may resort to such tactics on Sunday. Great truth needs to be treated in a better manner. The preacher cannot afford to "persecute one passage and flee to the next."

3. It is sometimes objected that expository preaching presents a disadvantage in that it deals with such a long passage that the congregation cannot remember what the entire passage is about.

Remember, these are but surface disadvantages. Proper budgeting of time and interesting presentation will allow the pastor to successfully use this method. Expository preaching can be considered as a preventative medicine. By consistently exposing the congregation to the exposition of the Word the preacher can build up some immunity to the temptation to sin that plagues every believer. Why "problem preach" after a difficulty arises when you could avert the problem by a systematic exposition of the Word of God?

Suggestions for Preparing Expository Sermons

1. Begin with a passage that is long enough to allow sufficient exposition but do not begin with an entire book.

2. Pick a well-known passage or chapter which lends itself to easy exposition. Shy away, however, from the Psalms (in the beginning) for many of them lack the unity that is so necessary for expository sermons.

3. Before listing main divisions that you have elucidated from the passage, allow yourself to become thoroughly familiar with the passage and its context. Once you have discerned the general train of thought, the passage will fall open much more easily.

4. See that you treat every part of the passage. Sometimes a main division will just leap from the page at you and other times you will read several verses which seem to have nothing to say to your theme. Read them carefully; chances are you are missing something.

5. When hunting main divisions in a passage here are a few key things to look for: parallel words, parallel phrases, outstanding series of nouns, strong or noticeable verbs, position of words in each sentence (such as first or second word), frequently appearing words, the same frequently appearing parts of speech (such as frequent adverbs, adjectives, etc.). Half of sermonizing is looking for the right things.

6. Make sure your main divisions are mutually exclusive. Each main division should be an entity in itself and not overlap into the next. It may lead into the next main division, but it must not be the same as the next.

7. Every main division must be integrally related to the theme and parallel to the other main divisions. Do not allow one division to be the sermon and the others to "come along for the ride" simply because you need more than one division.

8. See that each division of the outline represents one single thought. Don't lump ideas together in the main divisions.

9. Use alliteration whenever possible to aid memory, but be careful. To some preachers alliteration is a useful tool, to others it is a bane. Do not allow alliteration to govern your outline. Don't trump up a word so that you can get all "P's" or something else. The Word, not alliteration, should master your outline.

10. Finally, the outline should not master you. Don't make it so strict that it becomes a straitjacket. Make it flexible but governed by the words of the text.

For further hints refer to the section of this book on outlining and divisions. Also, see the following example.

Aspects of Deliverance
Psalm 91
Introduction.
  I.   Importance of the Psalm. Literary, Comfort, Blessing.
 II.   Imagery of the Psalm. A pageant of words.
III.   Author of the Psalm. Probably Moses.
 IV.   Antiphony of the Psalm. Liturgical use.
  V.   Relevance of the Psalm. Bridging the 'Security Gap.'

  I.   The Abode of Deliverance. vv. 1–2
       1. The *Duration* of the abode. (1)
       2. The *Originator* of the abode. (1,2)
       3. The *Identification* of the abode.
 II.   The Assurance of Deliverance. vv. 3–10
       1. The *Promise* of deliverance. (3)
       2. The *Picture* of deliverance. (4)
       3. The *Persistence* of deliverance. (5–6)
       4. The *Protection* of deliverance. (7–8)
       5. The *Promise* of deliverance repeated. (9–10)
III.   The Agents of Deliverance. vv. 11–13
       1. The *Charge* to deliverance. (11)
       2. The *Conditions* of deliverance. (11)
       3. The *Care* of deliverance. (12)
       4. The *Confirmation* of deliverance. (13)
 IV.   The Author of Deliverance. vv. 14–16
       1. The *Reason* for promises. (14)
       2. The *Revelation* of promises. (15–16)
          1. Deliverance   4. Presence
          2. Honor   5. Long Life
          3. Answer   6. Salvation

Conclusion.
  I.   The Abode.
 II.   The Assurance.
III.   The Agents.
 IV.   The Author.
  V.   The Appeal.

Principles of Exposition

There are several principles evident in this exposition which should always be present in an expository sermon. Note what those principles are.

1. Each main division contains a noun which is the "meat" of the division. There is not a mixture of nouns, verbs, run-on sentences, etc. There is, however, consistency in presentation. Because main division one says "The Abode of Deliverance," main division two does not say "Deliverance Is Assured." This would not be consistent when it is possible to state the division as above.

2. Alliteration was used whenever possible. However, when the text does not lend itself to alliteration such as the subdivisions under main division one, it is not used.

3. Each subdivision pertains to the main division and to it only. The subdivisions are all expansions of the main divisions.

4. Each main division, as well as each subdivision, comes directly from the text of Psalm 91. These are not gleaned from the mind of the preacher or from parallel passages, but directly from the text and only from the text.

5. The entire passage is dealt with as announced. Since Psalm 91 was chosen, all of Psalm 91 is expounded. It would be improper to announce Psalm 91 as your Scripture passage and then deal only with verse one. Even though it is not necessary, this particular exposition also dealt with every verse in the Psalm.

I Corinthians 13. QUALITIES OF LOVE.

(Introduction and conclusion will be omitted in the following examples as we are presently only concerned with main divisions and subdivisions).

I.   The Preeminence of Love. vv. 1–3
    1. Without love I give out nothing. (1).
    2. Without love I am nothing. (3).
    3. Without love I gain nothing. (3).

II. The Performance of Love. vv. 4–7
    1. Love performs humbly. (4–5).
    2. Love performs truthfully. (6).
    3. Love performs universally. (7).

III. The Permanence of Love. vv. 8–13
    1. The passing of gifts. (8).
    2. The progression of life. (9–11).
    3. The perfection of understanding. (12).
    4. The possession of love. (13).

There are several ways in which this chapter may be divided; this is just one of them. By carefully studying the passage you will arrive at other main divisions which are equally as good.

Philippians 4. POSSESSIONS IN CHRIST.

I. Steadfastness in Christ. vv. 1–4.
    1. Remain in Christ. (1).
    2. Remain in unity. (2).
    3. Remain in assistance. (3).
    4. Remain in rejoicing. (4).

II. Supplication in Christ. vv. 5–6.
    1. The realm of supplication. (6).
    2. The realization of supplication. (6).
    3. The request of supplication. (6).

III. Security in Christ. v. 7.
    1. The promise of security. (7).
    2. The place of security. (7).
    3. The person of security. (7).

IV. Satisfaction in Christ. vv. 10–12.
    1. Paul was cared for. (10).
    2. Paul was content. (11).
    3. Paul was complete. (12).

V. Strength in Christ. v. 13.
    1. The possession of strength. (13).
    2. The portion of strength. (13).
    3. The provider of strength. (13).

VI. Supply in Christ. v. 19.
    1. The resource of supply. (19).
    2. The riches of supply. (19).
    3. The route of supply. (19).

Daniel 3. ASPECTS OF A MIRACLE

I.   The Image of Gold. vv. 1–7.
   1. The call to worship. (1–3).
   2. The command to worship. (4–6).
   3. The commitment of worship. (7).

II. The Invincible Jews. vv. 8–18.
   1. The refusal to the King. (12).
   2. The audience with the King. (13–15).
   3. The witness to the King. (16–18).

III. The Infuriated King. vv. 19–23.
   1. The King's wrath. (19).
   2. The King's command. (20).
   3. The King's court. (21–23).

IV. The Invisible God. vv. 24–30.
   1. God astonished the King. (23–24).
   2. God convinced the King. (25–27).
   3. God changed the King. (28–30).

Isaiah 6. ISAIAH'S TRANSFORMING VISIONS

I.   Vision of God's Sovereignty. vv. 1–2.
     1. He saw God on the throne. (1).
     2. He saw God exalted. (1).
     3. He saw God accompanied by seraphim. (2).

II. Vision of God's Holiness. v. 3.
     1. The testimony of the seraphim. (3).
     2. The triple repetition of holy. (3).
     3. The totality of God's Holiness. (3).

III. Vision of God's Power. v. 4.
     1. The building shook. (4).
     2. The building filled with smoke. (4).

IV. Vision of Himself. v. 5.
     1. Pronouncement of woe. (5).
     2. Confession of sin. (5).
     3. Recognition of sinful surroundings. (5).

V.   Vision of His Cleansing. vv. 6–7.
     1. The agent of cleansing. (6).
     2. The act of cleansing. (7).
     3. The announcement of cleansing. (7).

VI. Vision of the Need. v. 8a
     1. God directed the vision. (8).
     2. God delivered the invitation. (8).
     3. God inspired the response. (8).

VII. Vision of His Calling. v. 8b–13.
     1. Object of His calling. (9).
     2. Message of His calling. (10).
     3. Duration of His calling. (11–13).

Mark 4:35-41. REMAINING CALM IN THE STORM

I. The Master Retreats. vv. 35-36.
   1. The late hour. (35).
   2. The weary master. (35-36).
   3. The pressing crowd. (36).

II. The Master Rests. vv. 37-38.
   1. The present danger. (37).
   2. The sleeping master. (38).
   3. The watchful God. (38).

III. The Master Rebuffed. v. 38.
   1. The excited disciples. (38).
   2. The sarcastic inquiry. (38).
   3. The incongruous statement. (38).

IV. The Master Rebukes. vv. 39-41.
   1. He rebukes the wind. (39).
   2. He rebukes the sea. (39).
   3. He rebukes the disciples. (40).

We have now traveled the long road of homiletics. As a pilgrim, you have viewed the topical sermon with its several "approaches" and its system of gleaning main divisions from the homiletical garden of the preacher's mind. You have also ascended the hill of the topical textual sermon to view the list of truths which were suggested or inferred by the text. Then, by paralleling the ideas, you have developed a theme and its main divisions. Sliding down the other side of the hill you passed by the topical expository sermon. Here, you not only listed ideas or statements found in the text but you drew applications from these statements and, after paralleling them, elicited a theme and main divisions from the applications.

With little difficulty you climbed to the plateau of the textual sermon in which one or more verses were chosen. In the text, you identified the central idea and founded the theme on that central idea. Then you climbed even higher to the textual expository sermon and found the use of a concordance very helpful. By listing a thought, word, or phrase you were able to compare these verses and draw out a central idea. The theme and main divisions then came naturally. Finally, you ascended to the heights of the expository sermon. You could now familiarize yourself with a passage of Scripture and then zero in on the meaning expressed in the passage. You received great satisfaction in not only drawing the main divisions but the subdivisions as well directly from this passage. You have now expounded the Word of God, a Word which will never return to you empty.

Additional Sermonizing Methods. There are several other types of sermon methods which will be mentioned in passing. They are not dealt with at length in *Prescription for Preaching* as it is the purpose here to record the "Practical" approach to homiletics. Yet each of these additional methods provides a unique change of pace in sermonizing. None of them should become a steady diet, however.

1. Hegelian Preaching. This form of preaching receives its name from the philosopher George William Friedrich Hegel (1770–1831). Hegel's system of *thesis—antithesis—synthesis* is employed. Here we see action, reaction, resolvement: "boy meets girl," "boy likes girl," "boy marries girl." In the spiritual realm, one might say: "man rebels against God," "God dies for man," "man is reconciled to God."

2. Exegetical Preaching. Exegesis literally means "to lead out" or "to guide out." Exegetical preaching is done in order to bring out the

nuances of meaning which generally escape the average reader of the Scriptures. Exegetical preaching is primarily philological (indicating the etymology of a word), grammatical (indicating the usage of a word), or historical (indicating the background of a word).

3. Antithetical Preaching. This is preaching by contrast. Here you would say: "On the one hand . . . on the other hand." In this form of preaching you show the difference between light and darkness, life and death, love and hate, believers and disciples, heaven and hell, the believer and the unbeliever, the path of the righteous and the path of the wicked. A fine example of this type of preaching can be seen in sermons on Psalm 1. The preacher sets up an antithesis between the godly man and the ungodly man.

4. Narrative Preaching. Best done in the expository type of sermon, the narrative takes the congregation on a journey conducted by the pastor. By using the *multiple approach*, i.e. placing yourself in the position of different characters at different times during the sermon, the preacher can successfully get the congregation to visualize the story and learn from it. This type of preaching may be either historical or biographical.

5. First Person Preaching. Similar to the narrative, first person preaching is done when the preacher assumes the identity of a Bible character and dramatizes the actions of this character in a chapter or book. Good characters with which to use this approach are disciples like Peter and Andrew, Paul, the repentant thief, Pilate, Judas, Abraham and Lot, Lazarus and Dives, etc.

6. Homily Preaching. An ancient and honorable form of preaching, the homily had its origin in the days of Ezra who "read in the book in the law of God distinctly, and gave the sense, and caused them to understand the reading" (Neh. 8:80). It is based on explanation, not homiletics. It is not expository preaching (although many preachers confuse their homilies with what they call expository preaching). The preacher simply gives a running commentary causing the congregation to understand the verses and then draws a conclusion at the end. This is an effective form but should not become a pattern for preaching.

7. Life Situation Preaching. This method of preaching is the taking to task of a problem or situation which needs to be dealt with in the church. It is definitely useful when a problem does arise or when people are known to have special burdens. Therapeutic preaching must

never become the consistent bill of fare, however. It is only for medicinal purposes.[12]

8. Analogical Preaching. Although highly spiritual, this approach may at times be useful. In analogical preaching, a biblical proposition is given and an analogy is given showing the results gained from the proposition. The gist of the sermon is in the analogy. This is not to be frequently used in that it is not preaching from the Bible but preaching rather on an analogy of the Bible.

9. Analytical Preaching. Also an approach not frequently used, the analytical approach consists of preaching on the analysis of a concept or event in Scripture. For instance, you may preach on the concept of love as seen in I Corinthians 13. The key is the concept of love and the analysis of the concept.

10. Proposition of Correction Preaching. This approach is designed to show that the Bible has the answer to man's problems. In effect, the procedure used is: (1) analysis of the problem; (2) discussion of the extra-biblical or unbiblical views; (3) the biblical solution. Again this may be useful as a change, but it is not to be used exclusively.

Conclusion

As you have undoubtedly noticed, there is much more to preaching than meets the eye. Many have said that they don't want to be "corrupted" by homiletics or public speaking. They feel that a close analysis of the nuts and bolts of preaching will cool their fervor for the Lord. They just want to "get out there and preach." It is admirable that they want to preach, but a "Mickey Mush Mouth" with no rhyme nor reason to his sermon may be more detrimental to the gospel than if he had just remained silent and served the Lord in another capacity.

When the young lad told his lumberjack father that he too wanted to become a lumberjack, the father was pleased. The lad was eager to try his hand at felling some of those giant wood wonders of God. But the first day on the job his father did not allow the lad to accompany him to the depths of the forest. Instead, the lumberjack instructed the boy to

---

[12]The classic treatment of this form of sermonizing is Charles F. Kemp, *Life Situation Preaching* (St. Louis: The Bethany Press, 1956).

remain at the lumbering shack and sharpen his axe. The next day the boy was again eager, but the story was the same. "Stay at the shack and sharpen your axe. It is important to have a sharp axe in lumbering," the father said.

This went on for about a week. Finally, filled with pent-up desire to be a lumberjack like his father, the boy complained, "Dad, when am I going to have the opportunity to cut down some trees?" "Soon," the father replied, "but I wanted you to learn the most valuable lesson a good lumberjack can learn. I wanted you to learn that you will ultimately cut down more trees with a sharp axe than with a dull one."

What is true for the lumberjack is certainly true for the preacher of the Gospel. Young preachers are usually anxious to get to the pulpit and preach. But, like the young lad, they must learn that they will ultimately be of more value to God if they first sharpen their axe. Many a young preacher has anxiously but prematurely been thrust into the preaching ministry only to bludgeon his parishoners on his way to becoming a used car salesman. Learn to sharpen your axe. Remember the prescription of the old country preacher. Before he "let himself go," he "read himself full, thought himself clear, and prayed himself hot." He sharpened his axe.

The manner of preaching is very important because as a preacher you are involved in the highest calling in communications, the communication of the Word of God. It should be done with the professionalism of a network newscaster. After all, aren't you broadcasting the Good News?

The mechanics of preaching are equally important, for the mind operates in a logical manner and is "turned off" by that which is illogical. Granted, you cannot change an unregenerated mind without the aid of the Holy Spirit, but you must realize that it is your responsibility as a preacher to make the truth of the gospel as intelligible as possible. A preacher who doesn't get along with homiletics soon shows it in the non-understandability of his sermon, the ignorance of his congregation concerning the Bible, and the emptiness of his church.

Excellence is a vanishing virtue today. The pursuit of excellence in sermonizing is a high goal indeed. After all, that which is done for the Master is to be our very best. Anything less is sin. To halfheartedly prepare or present a sermon is not only a disappointment to the Savior, it is a disgrace to the highest of professions as well. The Lord Jesus demands our best. We must make sure He gets it, especially in our preaching.

My three-point homiletical outline for happiness and success in preaching is:

I.   *Present* your bodies (Rom. 12:1)

II. *Press* toward the mark (Phil. 3:14)

III. *Preach* the Word (II Tim. 4:2)

But above all, prepare thoroughly, pray intensely, and preach heartily for the glory of God.

A Bibliography
of One Hundred Years
# of Great Preaching

1. Adams, Jay E. *Pulpit Speech*. Philadelphia: Presbyterian & Reformed Publishing Company, 1974.
2. _____. *Studies in Preaching*, 2 vols. Philadelphia: Presbyterian & Reformed Publishing Company, 1976.
3. Allen, Arthur. *The Art of Preaching*. New York: Philosophical Library, 1943.
4. Atkins, Gaius Glenn, ed. *Master Sermons of the Nineteenth Century*. New York: Harper & Brothers, 1940.
5. _____. *Preaching and the Mind of Today*. New York: Round Table Press, Inc., 1934.
6. Baab, Otto J. *Prophetic Preaching*. Nashville: Abingdon Press, 1956.
7. Baird, John E. *Preparing for Platform and Pulpit*. Nashville: Abingdon Press, 1968.
8. Barth, Karl. *Prayer and Preaching*. Naperville, IL: SCM Book Club, 1964.
9. Bartlett, Gene E. *The Audacity of Preaching*. New York: Harper & Brothers, 1962.
10. Baumann, J. Daniel. *An Introduction to Contemporary Preaching*. Grand Rapids: Baker Book House, 1972.
11. Baxter, Batsell Barrett. *The Heart of the Yale Lectures*. New York: The Macmillan Company, 1947.

12. _____. *Speaking for the Master*. New York: The Macmillan Company, 1954.

13. Bedsole, Adolph. *The Pastor in Profile*. Grand Rapids: Baker Book House, 1967.

14. Behrends, A. J. F. *The Philosophy of Preaching*. New York: Charles Scribner's Sons, 1890.

15. Black, James. *The Mystery of Preaching*. New York: Fleming H. Revell Company, 1924.

16. Blackwood, Andrew W. *Biographical Preaching for Today*. New York: Abingdon Press, 1954.

17. _____. *Doctrinal Preaching for Today*. New York: Abingdon Press, 1956.

18. _____. *Expository Preaching for Today*. New York: Abingdon-Cokesbury Press, 1953.

19. _____. *The Fine Art of Preaching*. New York: The Macmillan Company, 1937.

20._____. *Preaching from the Bible*. New York: Abingdon-Cokesbury Press, 1946.

21. _____. *The Preparation of Sermons*. New York: Abingdon-Cokesbury Press, 1948.

22. _____. *The Protestant Pulpit*. New York: Abingdon Press, 1947.

23. Booth, John Nicolls. *The Quest for Preaching Power*. New York: The Macmillan Company, 1943.

24. Bowie, Walter Russell. *Preaching*. Nashville: Abingdon Press, 1954.

25. Braga, James. *How to Prepare Bible Messages*. Portland, OR: Multnomah Press, 1969.

26. Brastow, Lewis O. *The Modern Pulpit*. Cincinnati: Jennings & Graham, 1906.

27. _____. *Representative Modern Preachers*. London: Hodder & Stoughton, 1904.

28. _____. *The Work of the Preacher: A Study of Homiletic Principles and Methods*. New York: Pilgrim Press, 1914.

29. Breed, David R. *Preparing to Preach*. New York: George H. Doran Co., 1911.

30. Broadus, John A. *Lectures on the History of Preaching*. New York: Sheldon & Company, 1876.

31. _____. *On the Preparation and Delivery of Sermons*. New York: Harper & Brothers, 1944.

32. Bromiley, G. W. *Christian Ministry*. Grand Rapids: Wm. B. Eerdmans Publishing Company, 1959.

33. Brooks, Phillips. *Lectures on Preaching*. Grand Rapids: Baker Book House, reprint 1969.

34. Brown, Charles Reynolds. *The Art of Preaching*. New York: The Macmillan Company, 1926.

35. Brown, H. C., Jr. H. Gordon Clinard, and Jesse J. Northcutt. *Steps to the Sermon*. Nashville: Broadman Press, 1963.

36. Brown, H. C., Jr. *A Quest for Reformation in Preaching*. Waco, TX: Word Books, 1968.

37. Bryan, Dawson C. *The Art of Illustrating Sermons*. Nashville: Cokesbury, 1938.

38. Bull, Paul B. *Preaching: The Sermon Construction*. New York: The Macmillan Company, 1922.

39. Burrell, David James. *The Sermon—Its Construction and Delivery*. New York: Fleming H. Revell Company, 1913.

40. Buttrick, George. *Jesus Came Preaching*. New York: Charles Scribner's Sons, 1931.

41. Byington, Edwin Hallock. *Open Air Preaching*. Hartford, CT: Hartford Theological Seminary, 1892.

42. Cadman, Samuel Parkes. *Ambassadors of God*. New York: The Macmillan Company, 1920.

43. Caemmerer, Richard R. *Preaching for the Church*. St. Louis: Concordia Publishing House, 1959.

44. Cairns, Frank. *The Prophet of the Heart*. New York: Harper and Brothers, 1935.

45. Calkins, Harold. *Master Preachers, Their Study and Devotional Habits*. Washington, D.C.: Review and Herald Publishing Association, 1960.

46. Calkin, Raymond. *The Romance of the Ministry*. Boston: Pilgrim Press, 1944.

47. Carpenter, William Boyd. *Lectures on Preaching*. London: Macmillan and Company, 1895.

48. _____. *Prophets of Christendom*. London: Hodder & Stoughton, 1876.

49. Chappell, Clovis Gellham. *Anointed to Preach*. New York: Abingdon-Cokesbury Press, 1951.

50. Christlieb, Theodor. *Homiletic: Lectures on Preaching*. New Edinburgh: T & T Clark, 1897.

51. Clarke, James W. *Dynamic Preaching*. Westwood, NJ: Fleming H. Revell Company, 1960.

52. Cleland, James T. *Preaching to be Understood*. New York: Abingdon Press, 1965.

53. _____. *The True and Lively Word*. New York: Charles Scribner's Sons, 1954.

54. Clowney, Edmund. *Preaching and Biblical Theology*. Grand Rapids: Wm. B. Eerdmans Publishing Company, 1961.

55. Coffin, Henry Sloane. *Communion Through Preaching*. New York: Charles Scribner's Sons, 1952.

56. Cooke, J. B. D. *The Carpenter's Method of Preaching*. Philadelphia: Seaboard Press, 1953.

57. Craig, Archibald Campbell. *Preaching in a Scientific Age*. London: SCM Press, Ltd., 1954.

58. Craig, William C. *The Preacher's Voice*. Columbus: The Wartburg Press, 1943.

59. Dabney, Robert L. *Sacred Rhetoric: Lectures on Preaching*. New York: Anson D. P. Randolph and Company, 1870.

60. Dale, R. W. *Nine Lectures on Preaching*. London: Hodder & Stoughton, 1898.

61. Davis, H. Grady. *Design for Preaching*. Philadelphia: Fortress Press, 1958.

62. Davis, Ozora S. *Preaching by Laymen*. New York: Fleming H. Revell Company, 1923.

63. _____. *Principles of Preaching*. Chicago: University of Chicago Press, 1924.

64. _____. *Using the Bible in Public Address*. New York: Association Press, 1916.

65. Dawson, David Miles, Jr. *More Power to the Preacher*. Grand Rapids: Zondervan Publishing House, 1957.

66. Demaray, Donald. *An Introduction to Homiletics*. Grand Rapids: Baker Book House, 1974.

67. De Welt, Don. *If You Want to Preach*. Grand Rapids: Baker Book House, 1957.

68. Dodd, C. H. *The Apostolic Preaching*. New York: Harper and Brothers, 1950.

69. Duggy, William R. *Preaching Well*. Milwaukee: Bruce Publishing Company, 1950.

70. Ellicott, Charles John. *Homiletical and Pastoral Lectures*. New York: A. C. Armstrong & Son, 1880.

71. Etter, John W. *The Preacher and His Sermon*. Dayton, OH: United Brethren Publishing House, 1891.

72. Evans, William. *How to Prepare Sermons and Gospel Addresses*. Chicago: The Bible Institute Colportage Association, 1913.

73. Farmer, Herbert H. *The Servant of the Word*. New York: Charles Scribner's Sons, 1912.

74. Faw, Chalmer. *A Guide to Biblical Preaching*. Nashville: Broadman Press, 1962.

75. Ferris, Theodore Parker. *Go Tell The People*. New York: Charles Scribner's Sons, 1951.

76. Fisher, William. *Evangelistic Moods, Methods, and Messages*. Kansas City, MO: The Beacon Hill Press of Kansas City, 1967.

77. Fisk, F. W. *Manual of Preaching*. New York: A. C. Armstrong & Sons, 1896.

78. Ford, Leighton. *The Christian Persuader*. New York: Harper & Row, 1966.

79. Forsyth, P. T. *Positive Preaching and the Modern Mind*. Naperville, IL: Allenson, 1957.

80. Foxwell, W. J. *Sermon and Preacher, Essays on Preaching*. New York: E. P. Dutton & Company, 1904.

81. Fritz, John H. C. *Essentials of Preaching: A Refresher Course in Homiletics for Pastors*. St. Louis: Concordia Publishing Company, 1948.

82. Fry, Jacob. *Elementary Homiletics: or, Rules and Principles in the Preparation and Preaching of Sermons*. Reading, PA: Henry H. Bieber, Printer, 1893.

83. Garrison, Webb B. *Creative Imagination in Preaching*. Nashville: Abingdon Press, 1960.

84. _____. *The Preacher and His Audience*. Westwood, NJ: Fleming H. Revell Company, 1954.

85. Garvie, Alfred Ernest. *The Christian Preacher*. New York: Charles Scribner's Sons, 1921.

86. _____. *A Guide to Preaching*. London: Hodder and Stoughton, 1907.

87. Gibbs, Alfred P. *The Preacher and His Preaching*. Fort Dodge, Iowa: Walterick Publishing Company, 1951.

88. _____. *A Primer on Preaching*. Fort Dodge, Iowa: Walterick Publishing Company, nd.

89. Gibson, George Miles. *Planned Preaching*. Philadelphia: The Westminster Press, 1954.

90. Gossip, Arthur J. *In Christ's Stead*. Grand Rapids: Baker Book House, reprint 1968.

91. Gowan, Joseph. *Homiletics or the Theory of Preaching*. London: E. Stock, 1922.

92. Graves, Henry Clinton. *Lectures on Homiletics*. Philadelphia: American Baptist Publication Society, 1906.

93. Greer, David H. *The Preacher and His Place*. New York: Charles Scribner's Sons, 1895.

94. Guffin, Gilbert L. *Called of God: The Work of the Ministry*. Westwood, NJ: Fleming H. Revell Company, 1951.

95. Hall, Thor. *The Future Shape of Preaching*. Philadelphia: Fortress Press, 1971.

96. Handy, Francis Joshua. *Jesus the Preacher*. New York: Abingdon-Cokesbury Press, 1949.

97. Haselden, Kyle. *The Urgency of Preaching*. New York: Harper & Row, Publishers, 1963.

98. Hervey, George Winfred. *A System of Christian Rhetoric for the Use of Preachers and Other Speakers*. New York: Harper & Brothers, 1873.

99. Hiltner, Seward. *Ferment in the Ministry*. Nashville: Abingdon, 1969.

100. Hogue, Wilson T. *Homiletics and Pastoral Theology*. Winona Lake, IN: Free Methodist Publishing House, 1949.

101. Hoppin, James M. *Homiletics*. New York: Dodd, Mead and Company, 1881.

102. Howe, Reuel L. *Partners in Preaching*. New York: The Seabury Press, 1967.

103. Hoyt, Arthur S. *The Preacher—His Person, Message, and Method*. New York: The Macmillan Company, 1909.

104. _____. *Vital Elements of Preaching*. New York: The Macmillan Company, 1914.

105. _____. *The Work of Preaching*. New York: The Macmillan Company, 1917.

106. Jackson, Edgar N. *How to Preach to People's Needs*. New York: Abingdon Press, 1956.

107. _____. *A Psychology for Preaching*. Great Neck, NY: Channel Press, 1961.

108. _____. *The Preacher: His Person, Message, and Method*. New York: The Macmillan Company, 1909.

109. Jackson, J. Dodd. *The Message and the Man*. London: Primitive Methodist Publishing House, 1912.

110. Jefferson, Charles Edward. *The Minister As Prophet*. New York: Thomas Y. Crowell & Company, 1905.

111. Jeffs, Harry. *The Art of Exposition*. Boston: Pilgrim Press, 1910.

112. Jordan, G. Ray. *You Can Preach*. New York: Fleming H. Revell, 1951.

113. Jones, Edgar DeWitt. *American Preachers of Today*. Indianapolis: Bobbs-Merrill, 1933.

114. _____. *The Royalty of the Pulpit*. New York: Harper & Brothers Publishing Company, 1951.

115. Jones, Illion T. *The Pastor: The Man and His Ministry*. Philadelphia: The Westminster Press, 1961.

116. _____. *Principles and Practice of Preaching*. New York: Abingdon Press, 1966.

117. Jordan, Gerald Ray. *You Can Preach*. New York: Fleming H. Revell, 1951.

118. Jowett, John Henry. *The Preacher—His Life and Work*. New York: George H. Doran Company, 1912.

119. Kemp, Charles E. *Life Situation Preaching*. St. Louis: Bethany Press, 1956.

120. _____. *Pastoral Preaching*. St. Louis: Bethany Press, 1963.

121. Kennedy, Gerald. *For Preachers and Other Sinners*. New York: Harper and Row, Publishers, 1964.

122. _____. *God's Good News*. New York: Harper & Brothers, Publishers, 1955.

123. _____. *His Word Through Preaching*. New York: Harper & Brothers, Publishers, 1947.

124. Kern, John Adam. *The Ministry to the Congregation: Lectures on Homiletics*. New York: Jennings and Graham, 1897.

125. _____. *Lectures on the History of Preaching*. London: Hodder and Stoughton, 1888.

126. Kidder, Daniel F. *A Treatise on Homiletics*. New York: Carlton and Lanahan, 1866.

127. Killinger, John. *The Centrality of Preaching in the Total Task of the Ministry*. Waco, TX: Word Books, 1969.

128. Kirkpatrick, Robert White. *The Creative Delivery of Sermons*. New York: The Macmillan Company, 1944.

129. Knott, Harold E. *How to Prepare an Expository Sermon*. Cincinnati: Standard Publishing Company, 1931.

130. Knox, John. *The Integrity of Preaching*. New York: Abingdon Press, 1957.

131. Koller, Charles W. *Expository Preaching Without Notes*. Grand Rapids: Baker Book House, 1962.

132. Lantz, John E. *Speaking in the Church*. New York: The Macmillan Company, 1954.

133. Leavell, Roland Q. *Prophetic Preaching Then and Now*. Grand Rapids: Baker Book House, 1963.

134. Lenski, T.C.H. *The Sermon, Its Homiletical Construction*. Columbus: The Lutheran Book Concern, 1927.

135. Liske, Thomas V. *Effective Preaching*. revised edition New York: The Macmillan Company, 1962.

136. Littorin, Frank T. *How to Preach the Word with Variety*. Grand Rapids: Baker Book House, 1953.

137. Lloyd-Jones, D. Martyn, *Preaching & Preachers*. Grand Rapids: Zondervan, 1971.

138. Luccock, Halford E. *Communicating the Gospel*. New York: Harper & Brothers, 1954.

139. Macartney, Clarence Edward. *Preaching Without Notes*. New York: Abingdon-Cokesbury Press, 1946.

140. MacColl, Alexander. *The Sheer Folly of Preaching*. New York: George H. Doran Company, 1923.

141. Macgregor, W.M. *The Making of a Preacher*. Philadelphia: The Westminster Press, 1946.

142. MacLennan, David Alexander. *Entrusted with the Gospel*. Philadelphia: The Westminster Press, 1956.

143. _____. *Pastoral Preaching*. Philadelphia: The Westminster Press, 1955.

144. _____. *Preaching Week by Week*. Westwood, NJ: Fleming H. Revell, 1963.

145. MacLeod, Donald. *Here Is My Method*. Westwood, NJ: Fleming H. Revell, 1952.

146. MacPherson, Ian. *The Burden of the Lord*. New York: Abingdon Press, 1955.

147. Maguire, Clyde Merrill. *Magnify Your Office*. Nashville: Broadman Press, 1956.

148. Marcel, Pierre Ch. *The Relevance of Preaching*. Grand Rapids: Baker Book House, 1963.

149. Mark, Harry C. *Patterns for Preaching*. Grand Rapids: Zondervan Publishing House, 1959.

150. McComb, Samuel. *Preacher in Theory and Practice*. New York: Oxford University Press, 1926.

151. McCracken, Robert J. *The Making of the Sermon*. New York: Harper and Brothers, 1956.

152. McLaughlin, Raymond W. *Communication for the Church*. Grand Rapids: Zondervan Publishing House, 1968.

153. McNeil, Jesse Jai. *The Preacher-Prophet in Mass Society*. Grand Rapids: Wm. B. Eerdmans Publishing Company, 1961.

154. Meyer, Frederick B. *Expository Preaching—Plans and Methods*. New York: George H. Doran Company, 1912.

155. Miller, Donald G. *Fire in Thy Mouth*. New York: Fleming H. Revell, 1939.

156. Mills, Glen E. *Message Preparation: Analyses and Structure*. Indianapolis: The Bobbs-Merrill Company, Inc., 1966.

157. Montgomery, Richard A. *Preparing Preachers to Preach*. Grand Rapids: Zondervan Publishing House, 1939.

158. Morgan, G. Campbell, *The Ministry of the Word*. Grand Rapids: Baker Book House, reprint 1970.

159. _____. *Preaching*. New York: Fleming H. Revell Company, 1937.

160. Mounce, Robert. *The Essential Nature of New Testament Preaching*. Grand Rapids: Wm. B. Eerdmans Publishing Company, 1960.

161. Neill, Stephen C. *Fulfill Thy Ministry*. New York: Harper & Brothers, 1952.

162. Nicoll, Sir W. Robertson. *Princes of the Church*. London: Hodder & Stoughton, 1921.

163. Niles, D. T. *The Preacher's Calling to be Servant*. New York: Harper & Brothers, 1959.

164. Noyes, Morgan Phelps. *Preaching the Word of God*. New York: Charles Scribner's Sons, 1943.

165. Oates, Wayne E. *The Christian Pastor*. Philadelphia: The Westminster Press, 1951.

166. Oxnam, G. Bromley, ed. *Creative Preaching*. New York: Abingdon Press, 1930.

167. Parker, T. H. L. *The Oracles of God*. London: Lutterworth Press, 1947.

168. Pattison, R. Harwood. *The Making of the Sermon*. Philadelphia: The American Baptist Publication Society, 1941.

169. Patton, Carl Safford. *The Use of the Bible in Preaching. A Plea for Modern Biblical Knowledge in the Pulpit*. New York: Willett, Clark & Company, 1936.

170. ———. *The Preparation and Delivery of Sermons*. New York: Willett, Clark & Company, 1936.

171. Pearson, Roy. *The Ministry of Preaching*. New York: Harper and Brothers, 1959.

172. Perry, Lloyd M. *Biblical Sermon Guide*. Grand Rapids: Baker Book House, 1970.

173. ———. *Manual for Biblical Preaching*. Grand Rapids: Baker Book House, 1965.

174. ——— and Faris D. Whitesell. *Variety in Your Preaching*. Westwood, NJ: Fleming H. Revell Company, 1954.

175. Phelps, Austin. *The Theory of Preaching: Lectures on Homiletics*. New York: Charles Scribner's Sons, 1894.

176. Philibert, Michel. *Christ's Preaching—and Ours*. trans. David Lewis. Richmond: John Knox Press, 1964.

177. Phillips, Harold Cooke. *Bearing Witness to the Truth*. New York: Abingdon-Cokesbury Press, 1949.

178. Pickell, Charles N. *Preaching to Meet Men's Needs*. New York: Exposition Press, 1958.

179. Pierson, Arthur T. *The Divine Art of Preaching*. New York: Baker & Taylor Company, 1892.

180. ———. *The Making of a Sermon*. New York: Gospel Publishing House, 1907.

181. Potter, Thomas Joseph. *Sacred Eloquence or the Theory and Practice of Preaching*. New York: Fr. Pustet, 1891.

182. Prichard, Harold Adye. *The Minister, The Method, and The Message: Suggestions on Preaching*. New York: Charles Scribner's Sons, 1932.

183. Purkiser, W. T. *The New Testament Image of the Ministry*. Grand Rapids: Baker Book House, reprint 1970.

184. Ray, Jefferson Davis. *Expository Preaching*. Grand Rapids: Zondervan Publishing House, 1940.

185. Read, David Haxton Carswell. *The Communication of the Gospel*. London: SCM Press, 1952.

186. Reu, Michael. *Homiletics, A Manual of the Theory and Practice of Preaching*. Minneapolis: Augsburg Publishing House, 1950.

187. Rhoades, Ezra. *Case Work in Preaching*. New York: Fleming H. Revell Company, 1942.

188. Rhodes, Walter. *Homiletics and Preaching*. Baltimore: Peters Publishing & Printing Company, 1906.

189. Riley, William B. *The Preacher and His Preaching*. Wheaton, IL: Sword of the Lord Publishers, 1948.

190. Roach, Corwin Carlyle. *Preaching Values in the Bible*. Louisville: Cloister Press, 1946.

191. Robbins, Howard C. *Preaching the Gospel*. New York: Harper & Brothers, 1939.

192. Roberts, Richard. *The Preacher as a Man of Letters*. Nashville: Abingdon Press, 1931.

193. Robertson, A. T. *The Glory of the Ministry*. Grand Rapids: Baker Book House, reprint 1967.

194. Roddy, Clarence S. *We Prepare and Preach*. Chicago: Moody Press, 1959.

195. Rudin, John J. *The Effective Ministry of Preaching and Public Worship*. Durham, NC: Duke University Press, 1951.

196. Sangster, William Edwin. *The Approach to Preaching*. Philadelphia: The Westminster Press, 1952.

197. _____. *The Craft of Sermon Construction*. Grand Rapids: Baker Book House, reprint 1972.

198. _____. *Doctrinal Preaching: Its Neglect and Recovery*. Birmingham, England: Berean Press, 1953.

199. _____. *Power in Preaching*. Nashville: Abingdon Press, 1958.

200. Scherer, Paul. *For We Have This Treasure*. New York: Harper and Row, 1965.

201. Schroeder, Frederick W. *Preaching the Word with Authority*. Philadelphia: The Westminster Press, 1954.

202. Shedd, William G. T. *Homiletics and Pastoral Theology*. New York: Charles Scribner's Sons. 1895.

203. Short, Roy Hunter. *Evangelistic Preaching*. Nashville: Tidings, 1946.

204. Sizoo, Joseph Richard. *Preaching Unashamed*. New York: Abingdon-Cokesbury Press, 1949.

205. Skinner, Craig. *The Teaching Ministry of the Pulpit: Its History, Theology, Psychology, and Practice for Today*. Grand Rapids: Baker Book House, 1973.

206. Sleeth, Ronald E. *Persuasive Preaching*. New York: Harper & Brothers, 1956.

207. Smithson, Robert J., ed. *My Way of Preaching*. London: Pickering and Inglis, 1956.

208. Smyth, Charles. *The Art of Preaching*. New York: The Macmillan Company, 1940.

209. Smyth, John Paterson. *The Preacher and His Sermon*. New York: George H. Doran Company, 1922.

210. Spurgeon, Charles Haddon. *Lectures to My Students*. Grand Rapids: Zondervan Publishing House, reprint 1965.

211. Stalker, James. *The Preacher and His Models*. Grand Rapids: Baker Book House, reprint 1967.

212. Stamm, Frederick Keller. *So You Want to Preach*. Nashville: Abingdon Press, 1958.

213. Stanfield, Vernon L. *Effective Evangelistic Preaching*. Grand Rapids: Baker Book House, 1965.

214. Stevenson, Dwight E. *In the Biblical Preacher's Workshop*. Nashville: Abingdon Press, 1967.

215. _____ and Charles F. Diehl. *Reaching People from the Pulpit*. New York: Harper and Row, Publishers, 1958.

216. Stewart, James S. *Exposition and Encounter: Preaching in the Context of Worship*. Birmingham, England: Berean Press, 1956.

217. _____. *A Faith to Proclaim*. New York: Charles Scribner's Sons, 1953.

218. _____. *Heralds of God*. Grand Rapids: Baker Book House, 1972.

219. _____. *Preaching*. London: The English Universities Press, Ltd., 1955.

220. Stibbs, Alan M. *Expounding God's Word*. Grand Rapids: Wm. B. Eerdmans Publishing Company, 1961.

221. _____. *Word of Faith Which We Preach*. London: Westminster Chapel, 1957.

222. Stidger, William L. *Building Sermons with Symphonic Themes*. New York: George Doran Company, 1926.

223. _____. *Preaching Out of the Overflow*. Nashville: Cokesbury Press, 1929.

224. Storrs, Richard S. *Preaching Without Notes*. Cincinnati: Jennings and Graham, 1875.

225. Stott, John R. W. *The Preacher's Portrait*. Grand Rapids: Wm. B. Eerdmans Publishing Company, 1961.

226. Thielicke, Helmut. *The Trouble with the Church*. trans. by John W. Doberstein. New York: Harper and Row, 1965.

227. Thomas, W. H. Griffith. *The Work of the Ministry*. New York: Hodder & Stoughton, nd.

228. Thompson, William D. and Gordon C. Bennett. *Dialogue Preaching*. Valley Forge, PA: The Judson Press, 1969.

229. _____. *A Listener's Guide to Preaching*. Nashville: Abingdon Press, 1966.

230. Tittle, Ernest Fremont. *The Foolishness of Preaching*. New York: Henry Holt & Company, 1930.

231. Tizard, Leslie J. *Preaching—The Art of Communication*. New York: Oxford University Press, 1959.

232. Turnbull, Ralph G. *The Preacher's Heritage, Task and Resources*. Grand Rapids: Baker Book House, 1968.

233. Unger, Merrill F. *Principles of Expository Preaching*. Grand Rapids: Zondervan Publishing House, 1955.

234. Valentine, Ferdinand. *The Art of Preaching*. London: Burns, Dates & Washbourne, 1951.

235. Vance, James I. *Being a Preacher*. New York: Fleming H. Revell Company, 1923.

236. Volbeda, Samuel. *The Pastoral Genius of Preaching*. Grand Rapids: Zondervan Publishing House, 1960.

237. Wagner, Don M. *The Expository Method of G. Campbell Morgan*. Westwood, NJ: Fleming H. Revell Company, 1957.

238. Weatherspoon, Jesse B. *Sent Forth to Preach*. New York: Harper and Brothers, 1954.

239. Webber, Frederick R. *A History of Preaching in Britain and America*. 3 vols. Milwaukee: Northwestern Publishing House, 1957.

240. White, Douglas M. *He Expounded*. Chicago: Moody Press, 1952.

241. Whitesell, Faris D. *The Art of Biblical Preaching*. Grand Rapids: Zondervan Publishing House, 1950.

242. _____. *Evangelistic Preaching and the Old Testament*. Chicago: Moody Press, 1947.

243. _____. *Power in Expository Preaching*. Westwood, NJ: Fleming H. Revell Company, 1963.

244. _____. *Preaching on Bible Characters*. Grand Rapids: Baker Book House, 1955.

245. Williams, Jerome Oscar. *The Gospel Preacher and His Preaching*. Nashville: Broadman Press, 1949.

246. Wood, A. Skevington. *The Art of Preaching*. Grand Rapids: Zondervan Publishing House, 1964.

247. Wood, John. *The Preacher's Workshop: Preparation for Expository Preaching*. Chicago: Inter-Varsity Press, 1965.
248. Worley, Robert C. *Preaching and Teaching in the Earliest Church*. Philadelphia: The Westminster Press, 1967.
249. Yates, Kyle M. *Preaching from the Prophets*. New York: Harper & Brothers, Publishers, 1942.
250. Yohn, David Waite. *The Contemporary Preacher and His Task*. Grand Rapids: Wm. B. Eerdmans Publishing Company, 1969.

Index of Subjects

Abraham, 162, 253

Achan, 235, 240

Ackley, Alfred H., 132

Action step, use of in sermon, 152

Acts, 6

Adams, Jay E., 14, 64, 111

Adams, John Quincy, 26

Age of Scientific Realism, religion in, 5– 9

Allegory, use of, 66

Alliteration:
use of, in expository sermons, 244, 246
use of, in memorization, 124

Aly, Brown, 161 fn.

Analogical preaching, 254

Analogy:
use of, for clarification, 60
use of, for illustration, 170
use of, in argumentation, 168– 169

Analytical preaching, 254

Anecdotes, use of, in introduction, 163

Antithetical preaching, 253

Apology, 77

Application:
meaning of, 176
need of, 177
place of, in the sermon, 177
principles of, 177– 178

Argumentation, use of, in presentation, 167– 169

Aristotle, 62, 159

Armstrong, Neil, 7

Arousing method:
"advisability of" approach to the, 210
examples of, 210– 212
purpose of, 210

Arrangement, 154– 155

Articulation, definition of, 46– 48

Attention step, use of, in sermon, 152

Audience:
adjusting to, 112– 113
disturbances of, 108– 110
maintaining the attention of, 104– 105
types of, 113

Audience analysis, 111– 112, 129
post, 43– 44
present, 43